THE BOOK OF JOSHUA

Expository Lectures

on

The Book of Joshua

William Garden Blaikie

Solid Ground Christian Books
Birmingham, Alabama USA

Solid Ground Christian Books
2090 Columbiana Rd, Suite 2000
Birmingham, AL 35216
205-443-0311
sgcb@charter.net
http://solid-ground-books.com

Expository Lectures on the Book of Joshua

William Garden Blaikie (1820-1899)

First published in 1893

Solid Ground Classic Reprints

First printing of new edition November 2005

Cover work by Borgo Design, Tuscaloosa, AL
Contact them at nelbrown@comcast.net

Cover image is Joshua Commands the Sun to Stand Still, in Joshua 10:12-14, done by Gustave Dore (1832-1883).

ISBN: 1-59925-025-X

CONTENTS.

CHAPTER I.
	PAGE
INTRODUCTORY:—THE BOOK OF JOSHUA	1

CHAPTER II.
JOSHUA'S ANTECEDENTS 22

CHAPTER III.
A SUCCESSOR TO MOSES 37

CHAPTER IV.
JOSHUA'S CALL 48

CHAPTER V.
JOSHUA'S ENCOURAGEMENT 60

CHAPTER VI.
JOSHUA'S CHARGE TO THE PEOPLE 70

CHAPTER VII.
THE SPIES IN JERICHO 82

CHAPTER VIII.
JORDAN REACHED 95

CHAPTER IX.

JORDAN DIVIDED 106

CHAPTER X.

CIRCUMCISION AND PASSOVER—MANNA AND CORN . 117

CHAPTER XI.

THE CAPTAIN OF THE LORD'S HOST 128

CHAPTER XII.

THE FATE OF JERICHO 140

CHAPTER XIII.

RAHAB SAVED 153

CHAPTER XIV.

ACHAN'S TRESPASS 165

CHAPTER XV.

ACHAN'S PUNISHMENT 177

CHAPTER XVI.

THE CAPTURE OF AI 189

CHAPTER XVII.

EBAL AND GERIZIM 201

CHAPTER XVIII.

THE STRATAGEM OF THE GIBEONITES 211

CHAPTER XIX.
THE BATTLE OF BETHHORON 223

CHAPTER XX.
THE BATTLE OF MEROM 236

CHAPTER XXI.
JOSHUA'S OLD AGE—DIVISION FOR THE EASTERN TRIBES 249

CHAPTER XXII.
THE INHERITANCE OF CALEB 262

CHAPTER XXIII.
THE DISTRIBUTION OF THE LAND 275

CHAPTER XXIV.
THE INHERITANCE OF JUDAH 287

CHAPTER XXV.
THE INHERITANCE OF JOSEPH 300

CHAPTER XXVI.
THE DISTRIBUTION COMPLETED 312

CHAPTER XXVII.
THE CITIES OF REFUGE 326

CHAPTER XXVIII.
THE INHERITANCE OF THE LEVITES 340

CHAPTER XXIX.
NO FAILURE OF GOD'S PROMISE 353

CHAPTER XXX.
THE ALTAR ED 365

CHAPTER XXXI.
JEHOVAH THE CHAMPION OF ISRAEL 376

CHAPTER XXXII.
JOSHUA'S LAST APPEAL 388

CHAPTER XXXIII.
JOSHUA'S WORK FOR ISRAEL 402

CHAPTER I.

INTRODUCTORY: THE BOOK OF JOSHUA.

WITH a purely historical book like Joshua before us, it is of importance to keep in view two ways of regarding Old Testament history, in accordance with one or other of which any exposition of such a book must be framed.

According to one of these views, the historical books of Scripture, being given by inspiration of God, have for their *main* object not to tell the story or dwell on the fortunes of the Hebrew nation, but to unfold God's progressive revelation of Himself made to the seed of Abraham, and to record the way in which that revelation was received, and the effects which it produced. The story of the Hebrew nation is but the frame in which this Divine revelation is set. It was God's pleasure to reveal Himself not through a formal treatise, but in connection with the history of a nation, through announcements and institutions and practical dealings bearing in the first instance on them. The historical books of the Hebrews therefore, while they give us an excellent view of the progress of the nation, must be studied in connection with God's main purpose, and the supernatural interpositions by which from time to time it was carried out.

The other view regards the historical books of the Hebrews in much the same light as we look on those of other nations. Whatever may have been their origin, they are, as we find them, like other books, and our purpose in dealing with them should be the same as in dealing with books of similar contents. We are to deal with them, in the first instance at least, from a natural point of view. We are to regard them as recording the history and development of an ancient nation—a very remarkable nation, no doubt, but a nation whose progress may be referred to ascertainable causes. If we find natural causes sufficient to account for that progress, we are not to call in supernatural. It is an acknowledged law, at least as old as Lord Bacon, that no more causes are to be assigned for phenomena than are true and sufficient to account for them. This law, and the investigations which have taken place under it, have expunged much that used to be regarded as supernatural from the history of other nations; and it will only be according to analogy if the same result is reached in connection with the history of Israel.

In this spirit we have recently had several treatises dealing with that history from a purely natural standpoint. Very earnest endeavours have been made to clear the atmosphere, to expiscate facts, to apply the laws of history, to weigh statements in the balances of probability, to reduce the Hebrew history to the principles of science. The general effect of this method has been to bring out results very different from those previously accepted. In particular, there has been a thorough elimination of the supernatural from Hebrew history. Natural causes have been judged sufficient to explain all that occurred. The introduction of the supernatural in the narrative was due to those obvious causes that have operated in the case of other nations and other religions :—love of the mythical, a patriotic desire to glorify the nation, the exaggerating tendency of tradition, and readiness to translate symbolical pictures into statements of literal occurrences. Hebrew historians were not exempted from the tendencies and weaknesses of other historians, and were ready enough to colour and apply their narratives according to their own views. It is when we subject the Hebrew books to such principles as these (such writers tell us) that we get at the real history of the nation, deprived no doubt of much of the glory with which it has usually been invested, but now for the first time reliable history, on which the most scientific may depend. And as to its moral purpose, it is just the moral purpose that runs through the scheme of the world, to show that, amid much conflict and confusion, the true, the good, the just, and the merciful become victorious in the end over the false and the evil.

The difference between the two methods, as an able writer remarks, is substantially this, that "the one regards the Hebrew books as an unfolding of God's nature, and the other as an unfolding of the nature of man."

The naturalistic method claims emphatically to be scientific. It reduces all events to historical law, and finds for them a natural explanation. But what if the natural explanation is no explanation ? What becomes of the claim to be scientific if the causes assigned are not sufficient to account for the phenomena? If science will not tolerate unnatural causes, no more should it tolerate unnatural effects. A truly scientific method must show a fit proportion between cause and effect. Our contention is that, in this respect, the naturalistic method is a failure. In many instances its causes are wholly inadequate to the effects. We are compelled to fall back on the supernatural, otherwise we are confronted with a long series of occurrences for which no reasonable explanation can be found.

We are reminded of an incident which a popular writer, under the *nom de plume* of Edna Lyall, has introduced in a novel, bearing the title "We Two." Erica, the daughter of an atheist, assists her father in conducting a journal. She gets from him for review a Life of David Livingstone, with instructions to leave his religion entirely out. As she proceeds with the work, she becomes convinced that the condition is impossible. To describe Livingstone without his religion would be like playing *Hamlet* without the part of Hamlet. Not only does she find her task impossible, but when she comes to an incident where Livingstone, in most imminent danger of his life, gets entire composure of mind from an act of devotion, she becomes convinced that this could not have happened had there not been an objective reality corresponding to his belief; and she is an atheist no more. Erica now believes in God. *Se non e vero e bene trovato.*

In like manner, we believe that to delineate Old Testament history without reference to the supernatural is as impossible as to describe Livingstone apart from his religion. You are baffled in trying to explain actual events. Long ago, Edward Gibbon tried to account for the rapid progress and brilliant success of Christianity in the early centuries by what he called secondary causes. It was really an attempt to eliminate the supernatural from early Christian history. But the five causes which he specified were really not causes, but effects,—effects of that supernatural action which had its source in the supernatural person of Jesus

Christ. These "secondary causes" never could have existed had not Jesus Christ already commended Himself to all sorts of men as a Divine Saviour, sent by God to bless the world. In like manner we maintain that behind the causes by which our naturalistic historians attempt to explain the remarkable history of the Jewish people, there lay a supernatural force, but for which the Hebrews would not have been essentially different from the Edomites, the Ammonites, the Moabites, or any other Semitic tribe in their neighbourhood. It was the supernatural element underlying Hebrew history that made it the marvellous development it was; and that element began at the beginning, and continued more or less actively till Jesus Christ came in the flesh.

Let us try to make good this position. Let us select a few of the more remarkable occurrences of early Hebrew history, and, in the language of Gibbon, make "a candid and reasonable inquiry" whether or not they can be accounted for, on the ordinary principles or human nature, without a supernatural cause.

1. It is certain that from the earliest times, and during at least the first four centuries of their history, the Hebrew people had an immovable conviction that the land of Canaan was divinely destined to be theirs. Of the singular hold which this conviction took of the minds of the patriarchs, we have innumerable proofs. Abraham leaves the rich plains of Chaldæa to dwell in Canaan, and spends a hundred years in it, a stranger and a pilgrim, without having a single acre of his own. When he sends to Padan Aram for a wife to Isaac he conjures his servant on no account to listen to any proposal that Isaac should settle there; the damsel must at all hazards come to Canaan.

When Jacob determines to part from Laban, he sets his face resolutely towards his native land across the Jordan, although his injured brother is there, thirsting as he knows for his blood. When Joseph sends for his father to go down to Egypt, Jacob must get Divine permission at Beersheba before he can comfortably go. Joseph, for his services to Egypt, might reasonably have looked for a magnificent tomb in that country to cover his remains and perpetuate his memory; but, strange to say, he prefers to remain unburied for an indefinite time, and leaves a solemn charge to his people to bury him in Canaan, carrying his bones with them when they leave Egypt. In the bitterness of their oppression by Pharaoh it would have been much more feasible for their champions, Moses and Aaron, to try to obtain a relaxation of their burdens; but their demand was a singular one—liberty to go into the wilderness, with the hardly concealed purpose of escaping to the land of their affections. Goshen was a goodly land, but Canaan had a dearer name—it was the land of their fathers, and of their brightest hopes. The uniform tradition was, that the God whom Abraham worshipped had promised to give the land to his posterity, and along with the land other blessings of mysterious but glorious import. With this promise was connected that Messianic hope which like a golden thread ran through all Hebrew history and literature, brightening it more and more as the ages advanced.

It is vain to account for this extraordinary faith in the land as theirs, and this remarkable assurance that it would be the scene of unwonted blessing, apart from a supernatural communication from God. To suppose that it originated in some whim or fancy of Abraham's or in the saga of some old bard like Thomas the Rhymer, and continued unimpaired century after century, is to suppose what was never realized in the history of any people. In vain do we look among natural causes for any that could have so impressed itself on a whole nation, and swayed their whole being for successive ages with irresistible force. That "God spake to Abraham to give him the land" was the indefeasible conviction of his descendants; nor could any consideration less powerful have sustained their hopes, or nerved them to the efforts and perils needful to realize it.

2. No more can the leaving of Egypt, with all that followed, be accounted for without supernatural agency. It is the contention of the naturalistic historian that the Israelites were very much fewer in number than the Scripture narrative alleges. But if so, how could an empire, with such immense resources as the monuments show Egypt to have had, have been unable to retain them? Wellhausen affirms that at the time Egypt was weakened by a pestilence. We know not his authority for the statement; but if the Egyptians were weakened, the Israelites (unless supernaturally protected) must have been weakened too. Make what we may of the contest between Moses and Pharaoh, it is beyond dispute that Pharaoh's pride was thoroughly roused, and that his firm determination was not to let the children of Israel go. And if we grant that his six hundred chariots were lost by some mishap in the Red Sea, what were these to the immense forces at his disposal, and what was there to hinder him from mustering a new force, and attacking the fugitives in the wilderness of Sinai? Pharaoh himself does not seem to have entered the sea with his soldiers, and was therefore free to take other steps. How, then, are we to account for the sudden abandonment of the campaign?

3. And as to the residence in the wilderness, even if we suppose that the Israelites were much fewer in number than is stated, they were far too great a multitude to be supported from the scanty resources of the desert. The wilderness already had its inhabitants, as Moses knew right well from his experience as a shepherd; it had its Midianites and Amalekites and other pastoral tribes, by whom the best of its pastures were eagerly appropriated for the maintenance of their flocks. How, in addition to these, were the hosts of Israel to obtain support?

4. And how are we to explain the extraordinary route which they took? Why did they not advance towards Canaan by the ordinary way—the wilderness of Shur, Beersheba, and Hebron? Why cross the Red Sea at all, or have anything to do with Mount Sinai and its awful cliffs, which a glance at the map will show was entirely out of their way? And when they did take that route, what would have been easier than for Pharaoh, if he had chosen to follow them with a new force, to hem them in among these tremendous mountains, and massacre or starve them at his pleasure? If the Israelites had no supernatural power to fall back on, their whole course was simply madness. We may talk of good fortune extricating men from difficulties, but what fortune that can be conceived could have availed a people, professing to be bound for the land of Canaan, that, without food or drink or stores of any kind, had wandered into the heart of a vast labyrinth, for no reasonable purpose under the sun?

5. Nor can the career of Moses be made intelligible without a supernatural backing. The contention is, that the desire of the people in Egypt for deliverance having become very strong, especially in the tribe of

Levi, they sent Aaron to find Moses, remembering his former attempt on their behalf; and that, under the able leadership of Moses, their deliverance was secured by natural means. But does this explain the actual campaign in Sinai? Who ever heard of a leader that, after he had roused the enthusiasm of his people by a brilliant deliverance, arrested their further progress in order to preach to them for a twelvemonth, and give them a system of law? Did Moses not possess that instinct of a general that must have urged him to push on the moment the Egyptians were drowned, and amid the enthusiasm of his own troops and the consternation of the Canaanites, fling his army upon the seven nations, and seize their land by a *coup de main*? Abraham before him and Joshua after him found the value of such prompt, sudden movements. Never had a leader a more splendid opportunity. What could have induced Moses to throw away his chance, bury his people among the mountains, and remain inactive for months upon months? Is there any conceivable explanation but that he acted by supernatural direction? The Divine plan was entirely different from any that human wisdom would have contrived. It is as clear as day that, had there been no Divine power controlling the movement, the course taken by Moses would have been simply insane.

6. Nor could the law of Moses, first given in such circumstances, have acquired the glory which surrounded it ever after, had there been no manifestation of the Divine presence at Sinai. The people were greatly dissatisfied, especially at their delays. The only course that would have quieted them was to push on towards Canaan, so that their minds might be animated by the enthusiasm of hope. Under their detentions

they greedily seized every occasion that presented itself for growling against Moses. How little they were in sympathy with his ideas of religion and worship was apparent from the affair of the golden calf. The history of the time is an almost unbroken record of murmuring, complaining, and rebellion. Yet the law which originated with Moses in these circumstances became the very idol of the people, and, according to the naturalistic historians, was the means of creating the nation, and welding the tribes into a living unity! We can quite easily understand how, in spite of all their growlings, the law as given at Sinai should have taken the firmest hold of their imagination and kindled their utmost enthusiasm in the end, if it was accompanied by those tokens of the Divine presence which the whole literature of the Hebrews assumes. And if Moses was closely identified with the Divine Being, the surpassing glory of the occasion must have been reflected on him. But to suppose that a discontented people should have had their enthusiasm roused for the law simply because this Moses commanded them to observe it, and that they should ever after have counted it the holiest, the most Divine law that men had ever known, is again to postulate an effect without a cause, and to suppose a whole people acting in disregard of the strongest propensities of human nature.

7. Then, as to the generalship of Moses. How are we to explain the further detention of the people in the wilderness for nearly forty years? If this was not the result of a supernatural Divine decree, it must have proceeded from the inability of Moses to lead the people to victory. No people who had struggled out of bondage in order to enter a land flowing with milk and honey, would of their own accord have spent forty

years in the wilderness. At Hormah, they were willing to fight, but Moses would not lead them, and they were beaten. Either the wandering of the forty years was a Divine punishment, or the generalship of Moses was at fault. He abandoned himself to inaction for an unprecedented period. There was no shadow of benefit to be gained by this delay; nothing could come of it (apart from the Divine purpose) but wearing out the patience of the people, and killing them with the sickness of hope deferred. And if it should be said that the forty years' wandering was a myth, and that probably the wilderness sojourn did not exceed a year or two at most, is it conceivable that any people in its senses would invent such a legend?—a legend that covered them with shame, and that was felt to be so disgraceful that the whole region was shunned by them; insomuch that with the exception of Elijah, we do not read of any member of the nation ever making a pilgrimage to the spot which otherwise must have had overwhelming attractions.

8. At last Moses suddenly awakes to activity and courage. And the next difficulty is to account for his success at the eleventh hour of his life, if he had no supernatural help. No phrase occurs more frequently in naturalistic explanations than "it is likely." Likelihood is the touchstone to which all extraordinary statements are brought, although, as Lord Beaconsfield used to tell us, "it is the unexpected that happens." Borrowing the touchstone for the nonce, we may ask, Is it likely that, after a sleep of eight-and-thirty years, Moses of his own accord, without any apparent change of circumstances, sprang suddenly to his feet, and urged the people to attempt the invasion of the land? Is it likely that all the inertia and fears of the people vanished in

a moment, as if at the touch of a magician's wand? And when it came to actual fighting, is it likely that these shepherds of the desert were able of themselves not only to stand before a trained and successful warrior like Sihon King of the Amorites, who had so lately overrun the country, but to defeat him utterly and take possession of his whole territory? Is it likely that Sihon's neighbour, Og King of Bashan, though warned by the fate of Sihon, and therefore sure to make a more careful defence, shared the fate of the other king? Or if Og was a mere myth, as Wellhausen strangely maintains, is it likely that the Israelites got possession of the powerful cities and well-defended kingdom of Bashan without striking a blow? Is it likely that, after this brilliant victory, Moses, who was still in full vigour, detained them again for weeks to preach old sermons, and sing them songs, and make pathetic speeches, instead of dashing at once at the petrified people on the other side, and acquiring the great prize—Western Palestine? Strange mortal this Moses must have been!—wise enough to give the people an unexampled constitution and system of laws, and yet blind to the most obvious laws of military science, and the most elementary perceptions of common sense.

And now we come to Joshua, and to the book that records his achievements.

Joshua was no prophet; he made no claim to the prophetic character; he succeeded Moses only as military leader. Consequently the Book of Joshua contains little matter that would fall under the term "revelation." But both the work of Joshua and the book of Joshua served an important purpose in the plan of Divine manifestation, inasmuch as they showed

God fulfilling His old promises, vindicating His faithfulness, and laying anew a foundation for the trust of His people. In this point of view, both the work and the book have an importance that cannot be exaggerated. The naturalistic historian regards the book as merely setting forth, with sundry traditional embellishments, the manner in which one people ousted another from their country, much as those who were then evicted had dispossessed the previous inhabitants. But whoever believes that, centuries before, God made a solemn promise to Abraham to give that land to his seed, must see in the story of the settlement the unfolding of a Divine purpose, and a solemn pledge of blessings to come. "The Ancient of days," who "declares the end from the beginning," is seen to be faithful to His promises; and if He has been thus faithful in the past, he may surely be trusted to be faithful in the future.

If, then, Joshua's work was a continuation of the work of Moses, and his book of the books of Moses, both must be regarded from the same point of view. You cannot explain either of them reasonably in a merely rationalistic sense. Joshua could no more have settled the people in Canaan by merely natural means than Moses could have delivered them from Pharaoh and maintained them for years in the wilderness. In the history of both you see a Divine arm, and in the books of both you find a chapter of Divine revelation. It is this that gives full credibility to the miracles which they record. What happened under Joshua formed a most important chapter of the process of revelation by which God made Himself known to Israel. In such circumstances, miracles were not out of place. But if the Book of Joshua is nothing more than the record of a raid by one nation on another, miracles were uncalled for, and must be given up.

Rationalists may count us wrong in believing that the Hebrew historical books are more than Hebrew annals—are the records of a Divine manifestation. But they cannot hold us unreasonable or inconsistent if, believing this, we believe in the miracles which the books record. Miracles assume a very different character when they are connected into a sublime purpose in the economy of God; when they signalize a great epoch in the history of revelation—the completion of a great era of promise, the fulfilment of hopes delayed for centuries. The Book of Joshua has thus a far more dignified place in the history of revelation than a superficial observer would suppose. And those historians who bring it down to the level of a mere record of an invasion, and who leave out of account its bearing on Divine transactions so far back as the days of Abraham, spoil it of its chief glory and value for the Church in every age. There is nothing of more importance, whether for the individual believer or for the Church collectively, than a firm conviction, such as the Book of Joshua emphatically supplies, that long delays on God's part involve no forgetfulness of His promises, but that whenever the destined moment comes " no good thing will fail of all that He hath spoken."

The Book of Joshua consists mainly of two parts; one historical, the other geographical. It was the old belief that it was the work of a single writer, with such slight revision at an after time as a writing might receive without essential interference with its substance. The author was sometimes supposed to be Joshua himself, but more commonly one of the priests or elders who outlived Joshua, and who might therefore fitly record his death. It has been remarked that there are several traces in the book of contemporary origin, like the remark on Rahab—" She dwelleth in Israel even unto this day" (vi. 25). It must be allowed, we think, that there is not much in this book to suggest to the ordinary reader either the idea of a late origin or of the use of late materials.

But recent critics have taken a different view. Ewald maintained that, besides the Jehovist and Elohist writers of whose separate contributions in Genesis the evidence seems incontrovertible, there were three other authors of Joshua, with one or more redactors or revisers. The view of Kuenen and Wellhausen is similar, but with this difference, that the Book of Joshua shows so much affinity, both in object and style, to the preceding five books, that it must be classed with them, as setting forth the origin of the Jewish nation, which would not have been complete without a narrative of their settlement in their land. The composition of Joshua is therefore to be brought down to a late date; we owe it to the documents, writers, and editors concerned in the composition of the Pentateuch; and instead of following the Jews in classing the first five books by themselves, we ought to include Joshua along with them, and in place of the Pentateuch speak of the Hexateuch. Canon Driver substantially accepts this view; in his judgment, the first part of the book rests mainly on the JE (Jehovist-Elohist) document, with slight additions from P (the priestly code) and D^2 (the second Deuteronomist). The second half of the book is derived mainly from the priestly code. But Canon Driver has the candour to say that it is much more difficult to distinguish the writers in Joshua than in the earlier books; and so little is he sure of his ground that even such important documents as J and E have to be designated by new letters, *a* and *b*. But, all the same, he goes right on with his scheme, furnishing us with tables all through, in which he shows that the Book of Joshua consists of ninety different pieces, no two consecutive pieces being by the same author. Most of it he refers to three earlier writings, but some of these were composite, and it is hard to say how many hands were engaged in putting together this simple story.

One is tempted to say of this complicated but confidently maintained scheme, that it is just too complete, too wonderfully finished, too clever by half. Allowing most cordially the remarkable ability and ingenuity of its authors, we can hardly be expected to concede to them the power of taking to pieces a book of such vast antiquity, putting it in a modern mincing machine, dividing it among so many supposed writers, and settling the exact parts of it written by each! Is there any ancient writing that might not yield a similar result if the same ingenuity were exercised upon it?

To judge of the source of writings by apparent varieties of style, and call in a different writer for every such variety, is to commit oneself to a very precarious rule. There are doubtless cases where the diversity of style is so marked that the inference is justified, but in these the evidence is unmistakably clear. Often the evidence against identity of authorship *appears* very clear, while it is absolutely worthless. Suppose that three thousand years hence an English book should be found, consisting, first, of an eloquent exposition of a parliamentary budget; secondly, a scheme for Home Rule in Ireland; thirdly, a dissertation on

Homer; and fourthly, essays on the "Impregnable Rock of Holy Scripture"—how convincingly might the critics of the day demonstrate, beyond possibility of contradiction, that the book could not be the work of the single man who bore the name of William E. Gladstone! In like manner, it might be made very plain that Milton could never have written both "L'Allegro" and "Il Penseroso," or "Paradise Lost" and the "Defence of the English People." Cowper could not have written "John Gilpin" and "God moves in a mysterious way." Samuel Rutherford could not have written his "Letters" and his "Divine Right of Church Government." Moreover, in the course of years a writer may change his style, even when his subject is the same. The earlier essays of Mr. Carlyle show no traces of that most quaint, terse, graphic style which became one of his outstanding characteristics in later years. Perhaps the most remarkable instance of change of style in a great writer is that of Jeremy Bentham. In Sir James Mackintosh's Dissertation prefixed to the *Encyclopædia Britannica* (eighth edition) he says: "The style of Mr. Bentham underwent a more remarkable revolution than perhaps befell that of any other celebrated writer. In his early works, it was clear, free, spirited, often and seasonably eloquent. . . . He gradually ceased to use words for conveying his thoughts to others, but merely employed them as a short hand to preserve his meaning for his own purpose. It is no wonder that his language thus became obscure and repulsive. Though many of his technical terms are in themselves exact and pithy, yet the overflow of his vast nomenclature was enough to darken his whole diction."

If we compare the criticism of the Book of Joshua with that (let us say) of Genesis, the difference in the clearness of the conclusions is very great. By far the most striking basis of the criticism of Genesis is the feature that was noticed first—the occurrence of different Divine names, Elohim and Jehovah, in different portions of the book. Now, although it is held that the *combined* JE document was used in compiling Joshua, there is no trace of this distinction of names in that book. Nor is there much trace of other distinctions found in Genesis. So that it is no great wonder that Canon Driver is uncertain whether, after all, that was the document that was used in compiling Joshua. Then, as to the grounds on which the Deuteronomist is supposed to have had a share in the book. Wherever anything is said indicating that under Joshua the Divine purposes and ordinances enjoined by God on Moses were fulfilled, that is referred to the Deuteronomist writer, as if it would have been unnatural for an ordinary historian to call attention to such a circumstance. For instance, the remark of Rahab that as soon as the Canaanites heard what God had done to Egypt, and to the two kings of the Amorites on the other side of Jordan, their hearts fainted, is referred to the Deuteronomist, as if it had rather been an idea of his than a statement of Rahab's. It is strange that Canon Driver should not have seen that this is the very hinge of Rahab's speech, because it gives us the explanation of the remarkable faith that had taken possession of her polluted heart. The truth is, we can hardly conceive that any part of the book should have been written by one who did not connect Joshua with Moses, and both of them with the patriarchs, and who was not impressed by the vital connection of the earlier with the later transactions, and likewise by the single Divine purpose running through the whole history.

But we are far from thinking that there is no foundation for any of the conclusions of the critics regarding the Book of Joshua. What seems their great weakness is the confidence with which they assign this part to one writer and that part to another, and bring down the composition of the book to a late period of the history. That various earlier documents were made use of by the author of the book seems very plain. For instance, in the account of the crossing of the Jordan, use seems to have been made of two documents, not always agreeing in minute details, and pieced together in a primitive fashion characteristic of a very early period of literary composition. The record of the delimitation of the possessions of the several tribes must have been taken from the report of the men that were sent to survey the country, but it is not a complete record. There are other traces of different documents in other parts of the book, but any diversities between them are quite insignificant, and in no degree impair its historical trustworthiness.

As to the hand of a reviser or revisers in the book, we see no difficulty in allowing for such. We can conceive an authorized reviser expanding speeches, but thoroughly in the line of the speakers, or inserting explanatory remarks as to places, or as to practices that had prevailed "unto this day." But it is atrocious to be told of revisers colouring statements and modifying facts in the interests of religious parties, or even in the interest of truth itself. Any alterations in the way of revision seem to have been very limited, otherwise we should not find in the existing text those awkward joinings of different documents which are not in perfect accord. Whoever the revisers were, they seem to have judged it best to leave these things as they found them, rather than incur the responsibility of altering what had already been written.

It has generally been assumed by spiritual expositors that there must be something profoundly symbolical in a book that narrates the work of Joshua, or Jesus, the first, so far as we know, to bear the name that is " above every name." The subject is considered with some fulness in Pearson's " Exposition of the Creed," and various points of resemblance, not all equally valid,[1] are noted between Joshua and Jesus.

The one point of resemblance on which we seem to be warranted to lay much stress is, that Joshua gave the people REST. Again and again we read— " The land rested from war " (xi. 23), " The land had rest from war " (xiv. 15), " The Lord gave them rest round about " (xxi. 44), " The Lord your God hath given rest unto your brethren " (xxii. 4), " The Lord had given rest unto Israel from all their enemies round about " (xxiii. 1). That was Joshua's great achievement, as the instrument of God's purpose. Yet

---

[1] " The hand of Moses and Aaron brought the people out of Egypt, but left them in the wilderness, and could not seat them in Canaan. . . . Joshua, the successor, only could effect that in which Moses failed. . . . The death of Moses and the succession of Joshua pre-signified the continuance of the law till Jesus came. . . . Moses must die that Joshua might succeed. . . . If we look on Joshua as the judge and ruler of Israel, there is scarce an action which is not predictive of our Saviour. He begins his office at the banks of the Jordan where Christ is baptized, and enters upon the public exercise of his prophetical office. He chooseth there twelve men out of the people to carry twelve stones over with them ; as our Jesus thence began to choose His twelve apostles. . . . It hath been observed that the saving Rahab the harlot alive foretold what Jesus once should speak to the Jews—' Verily I say unto you, that the publicans and the harlots go into the kingdom of God before you.' . . ."

in Hebrews we read that this was not the real rest—it was only a symbol of it: "If Joshua had given them rest, then would God not afterward have spoken of another day." The real rest was the rest arising from faith in Jesus Christ. Many persons look on Joshua as a somewhat dry book, full of geographical names, as unsuggestive as they are hard and unfamiliar. Yet on every one of the places so named faith may see inscribed, as in letters from heaven, the sweet word REST. Each of these places became a home for men who had been wandering for some forty years in a waste howling wilderness. At last they reached a spot where they did not fear the long familiar summons to "arise and depart." The sickly mother, the consumptive maiden, the paralysed old man might rest in peace, no longer terrified at the prospect of journeys which only increased their ailments and aggravated their sufferings.

The spiritual lesson of this book then is, that in Jesus Christ there is rest for the pilgrim. It is no slight or unevangelical lesson. It is the echo of His own glorious words, "Come unto Me, all ye that labour and are heavy laden, and I will give you rest." Whosoever is weary—whether under the burden of care, or the sense of guilt, or the bitterness of disappointment, or the anguish of a broken heart, or the conviction that all is vanity—the message of this book to him is,— "There remaineth a rest to the people of God." Even now, the rest of faith; and hereafter, that rest of which the voice from heaven proclaimed—"Blessed are the dead which die in the Lord from henceforth: yea, saith the Spirit, that they may rest from their labours; and their works do follow them."

CHAPTER II.

JOSHUA'S ANTECEDENTS

FOUR hundred years is a long way to go back in tracing a pedigree. Joshua's might have been traced much farther back than that—back to Noah, or for that matter to Adam; but Israelites usually counted it enough to begin with that son of Jacob who was the head of their tribe. It could be no small gratification to Joshua that he had Joseph for his ancestor, and that of the two sons of Joseph he was sprung from the one whom the dying Jacob so expressly placed before the other as the heir of the richer blessing (1 Chron. vii. 20-27). It is remarkable that the descendants of Joseph attached no consequence to the fact that on the side of Joseph's wife they were sprung from one of the highest functionaries of Egypt (Gen. xli. 45), any more than the children of Mered, of the tribe of Judah, whose wife, Bithiah, was a daughter of Pharaoh (1 Chron. iv. 18), gained rank in Israel from the royal blood of their mother. The glory of high connections with the heathen counted for nothing; it was entirely eclipsed by the glory of the chosen seed. To be of the household of God was higher than to be born of kings.

Joshua appears to have come of the principal family of the tribe, for his grandfather, Elishama (1 Chron. vii. 26), was captain and head of his tribe (Num. i. 10, ii. 18), and in the order of march through the wilderness marched at the head of the forty thousand five hundred men that constituted the great tribe of Ephraim; while his son, Nun, and his grandson, Joshua, would of course march beside him. Not only was Elishama at the head of the tribe, but apparently also of the whole "camp of Ephraim," which, besides his own tribe, embraced Manasseh and Benjamin, being the whole descendants of Rachel (Num. ii. 24). Under their charge in all likelihood was a remarkable relic that had been brought very carefully from Egypt—the bones of Joseph (Exod. xiii. 19). Great must have been the respect paid to the coffin which contained the embalmed body of the Governor of Egypt, and which was never lost sight of during all the period of the wanderings, till at length it was solemnly deposited in its resting-place at Shechem (Josh. xxiv. 32). Young Joshua, grandson of the prince of the tribe, must have known it well. For Joshua was himself cast in the mould of Joseph, an ardent, courageous, God-fearing, patriotic youth. Very interesting to him it must have been to recall the romance of Joseph's life, his grievous wrongs and trials, his gentle spirit under them all, his patient and invincible faith, his lofty purity and self-control, his intense devotion to duty, and finally his marvellous exaltation and blessed experience as the saviour of his brethren! And that coffin must have seemed to Joshua ever to preach this sermon,—" God will surely visit you." With Joseph, young Joshua believed profoundly in his nation, because he believed profoundly in his nation's God; he felt that no other people in the world could have such a destiny, or could be so worthy of the service of his life.

This sense of Israel's relation to God raised in him an enthusiastic patriotism, and soon brought him under the notice of Moses, who quickly discerned in the grandson a spirit more congenial to his own than that of either the father or the grandfather. Not even Moses himself had a warmer love than Joshua for Israel, or a more ardent desire to serve the people that had such a blessed destiny. In all likelihood the first impression Joshua made on Moses might have been described in the words—" It came to pass that the soul of Moses was knit with the soul of Joshua, and Moses loved him as his own soul."

In no other way can we account for the extraordinary mark of confidence with which Joshua was honoured when he was selected in the early days of the wilderness sojourn, not only to repel the attack which the Amalekites had made upon Israel, but to choose the men by whom this was to be done. Why pass over father and grandfather, if this youth, Joshua, had not already displayed qualities that fitted him for this difficult task better than either of them? We cannot but note, in passing, the proof we have of the contemporaneousness of the history, that no mention is made of the reasons why Joshua of all men was appointed to this command. If the history was written near the time, with Joshua's splendid career fresh in the minds of the people, the reasons would be notorious and did not need to be given ; if it was written long afterwards, what more natural than that something should be said to explain the remarkable choice ?

On whatever grounds Joshua was appointed, the result amply vindicated the selection. On Joshua's part there is none of that hesitation in accepting his work which was shown even by Moses himself when he got his commission at the burning bush. He seems to have accepted the appointment with humble faith and spirited enthusiasm, and prepared at once for the perilous enterprise.

And he had little enough time to prepare, for a new attack of the Amalekites was to be made next day. We may conceive him, after prayer to his Lord, setting out with a few chosen comrades to invite volunteers to join his corps, rousing their enthusiasm by picturing the dastardly attack that the Amalekites had made on the sick and infirm (Deut. xxv. 17, 18), and scattering their fears by recalling the promise to Abraham, "I will bless them that bless thee, and curse him that curseth thee." That Moses knew him to be a man of faith whose trust was in the living God was shown by his promise to stand next morning on the hill top with the rod of God in his hand. Yes, the rod of God! Had not Joshua seen it stretched out over the Red Sea, first to make a passage for Israel, and thereafter to bring back the waters on Pharaoh's host? Was he not just the man to value aright that symbol of Divine power? The troop selected by Joshua may have been small as the band of Gideon, but if it was as full of faith and courage it was abundantly able for its work!

The Amalekites are sometimes supposed to have been descendants of an Amalek who was the grandson of Esau (Gen. xxxvi. 12), but the name is much older (Gen. xiv. 7), and was applied at an early period to the inhabitants of the tract of country stretching southwards from the Dead Sea to the peninsula of Sinai. Whatever may have been their origin, they were old inhabitants of the wilderness, well acquainted probably with every mountain and valley, and well skilled in that Bedouin style of warfare which even practised troops are little able to meet. They were therefore very formidable opponents to the raw levy of

Israelites, who could be but little acquainted with weapons of war, and were wholly unaccustomed to battle.

The Amalekites could not have been ignorant of the advantage of a good position, and they probably occupied a post not easy to attack and carry. Evidently the battle was a serious one. The practised and skilful tactics of the Amalekites were more than a match for the youthful valour of Joshua and his comrades; but as often as the uplifted rod of Moses was seen on the top of the neighbouring hill, new life and courage rushed into the souls of the Israelites, and for the time the Amalekites retreated before them. Hour after hour the battle raged, till the arm of Moses became too weary to hold up the rod. A stone had to be found for him to sit on, and his comrades, Aaron and Hur, had to hold up his hands. But even then, though the advantage was on the side of Joshua, it was sunset before Amalek was thoroughly defeated. The issue of the battle was no longer doubtful—" Joshua discomfited Amalek and his people with the edge of the sword" (Exod. xvii. 13).

It was a memorable victory, due in effect to the hand of God as really as the destruction of the Egyptians had been, but due instrumentally to the faith and fortitude of Joshua and his troop, whose ardour could not be quenched by the ever-resumed onslaughts of Amalek. And when the fight was over, Joshua could not but be the hero of the camp and the nation, as really as David after the combat with Goliath. Congratulations must have poured on him from every quarter, and not only on him, but on his father and grandfather as well. To Joshua these would come with mingled feelings; gratification at having been able to do such a service for his people, and gratitude for the presence of Him by whom alone he had prevailed. "Not unto us, Lord, not unto us, but to Thy name be the glory." It was a splendid beginning for Israel's wilderness history, if only it had been followed up by the people in a kindred spirit. But there were not many Joshuas in the camp, and the spirit did not spread.

It is remarkable what a hold that incident at Rephidim has taken on the Christian imagination. Age after age, for more than three thousand years, its influence has been felt. Nor can it ever cease to impress believing men that, so long as Moses holds out his rod, so long as active trust is placed in the power and presence of the Most High in the great battle with sin and evil, Israel must prevail; but if this trust should fail, if Moses should let down his rod, Amalek will conquer. It was well that Moses was instructed to write the transaction in a book and rehearse it before Joshua. Well also that it should be commemorated by another memorial, an altar to the Lord with the name of "Jehovah-nissi," the Lord my banner. How often has faith looked out towards that unknown mountain where Aaron and Hur held up the weary arms of Moses, and what a new thrill of courage and hope has the spectacle sent through hearts often "faint yet pursuing"! Happily on Joshua the effect was wholesome; a less spiritual man would have been puffed up by his remarkable victory; but in him its only effect, as was shown by the whole tenor of his future life, was a firmer trust in God, and a deeper determination to wait only on Him.

It was no wonder that after this Joshua was selected by Moses to be his personal comrade and attendant in connection with that most solemn of all his duties—the receiving of the law on the top of the mount. Here again was a most distinguished honour for so young a man. Aaron, Nadab, and Abihu, with seventy of the elders, were summoned to ascend to a certain height and worship afar off; while Moses, accompanied by Joshua, went up into the mount of God (Exod. xxiv. 13). What became of Joshua while Moses was in immediate fellowship with God is not very apparent. The first impression we derive from the narrative is that he was with Moses all the time, for when Moses begins his descent Joshua is at his side (Exod. xxxii. 17). Yet we cannot suppose that in that most solemn transaction of Moses with Jehovah when the law was given any third party was present. On a careful study of the narrative throughout it will probably be seen that when, after going up a certain distance in company with Aaron and his sons and the seventy elders, Moses was called to a higher part of the mount, Joshua accompanied Moses (Exod. xxiv. 13), and that he was with Moses during the six days when the glory of God abode on Mount Sinai and a cloud covered the mount (ver. 15); but that when God again, after these six days, called to Moses to ascend still higher, and Moses "went into the midst of the cloud, and gat him up to the mount" (ver. 18), Joshua remained behind. His place of rest would thus be half-way between the spot where the elders saw God's glory and the summit where God talked with Moses. But the remarkable thing is, that from that place Joshua would seem never to have moved all the forty days and forty nights when Moses was with God. We can hardly conceive a case of more remarkable obedience, a more striking instance of the quiet waiting of faith. To a youth of his spirit and habits the restraint must have been somewhat trying. We know that Aaron did not remain long on the hill, for he was at hand when the people cried for "gods to go before them" (Exod. xxxii. 1). Impatience of God's slow methods had been a snare to the fathers—to Abraham and Sarah in the matter of Hagar; to Rachel when she raised the petulant cry, "Give me children, or else I die"; to Jacob when the promises seemed broken to atoms, and "all things" seemed "against him." Joseph alone had stood the trial of patience, and now Joshua showed himself of the like spirit. The word of Moses to him was like an anchor holding the ship firmly against the force of wind and tide. What a solemn time it must have been, and what a precious lesson it must have taught him for the whole future of his life!

More than three thousand years have sped away, but have the servants of God on an average reached the measure of Joshua's patience? Prayers unanswered, promises unfulfilled, sickness protracted during weary years of pain, disappointments and trials coming in troops as if all God's waves and billows were passing over them, active persecution bringing all the devices of torture to bear upon them,—how have such things tried the patience, the waiting power of the servants of God! But let them remember that if the trial be severe the recompense is great, and that in the end nothing will grieve them more than to have distrusted their master and thought it possible that His promises would fail. "God is not unrighteous to forget." Richard Cecil tells that once, when walking with his little son, he bade him wait for him at a certain gate till he should return. He thought he would be back in a few minutes, but meanwhile an unexpected occurrence constrained him to go into the city, where, under an engrossing piece of business, he remained all day utterly forgetful of his charge to the boy. On his return at night to his suburban home, the boy was nowhere to be found. In a moment the order to remain at the gate flashed on his father's memory. Was it possible he should still be there? He hurried back and found him—he had been told to wait till his father returned, and he had done as he had been told. The boy that could act thus must have been made of no common stuff. So are they who can say, "I waited patiently for the Lord, and He inclined unto me, and heard my cry."

At last Joshua rejoins his master, and they proceed towards the foot of the mount. As they approach the camp, a noise is heard from afar. His military instinct finds an explanation,—"There is a noise of war in the camp." No, says the more experienced Moses; it is neither the shout of victors nor of vanquished, it is the noise of singing I hear; and so it was. For when they reached the camp, the people were at the very height of the idolatrous revelling that followed the construction and worship of the golden calf, and the sounds that fell on the ears of Moses and Joshua were the bacchanalian shouts of unholy and shameful riot. What a contrast to the solemn and holy scene on the top! What a gulf lies between the holy will of God and the polluted passions of men!

During the painful scenes that ensued, Joshua continued in faithful attendance on Moses; and when Moses removed the tabernacle (the temporary structure hitherto used for sacred services) and placed it outside the camp, Joshua was with him, and departed not out of the tabernacle (Exod. xxxiii. 11). We are not told whether he ascended the mount the second time with

Moses, but it is likely that he did. At all events he was much with Moses at this early and susceptible period of his life. The young man did not recoil from the company of the old, nor did he who had been commander in the battle of Rephidim shrink from the duty of a servant. Deeper and deeper, as he kept company with Moses, must have been his impression of his wisdom, his faith, his loyalty to God, and his entire devotion to the welfare of his people; and stronger and stronger must have waxed his own desire that if ever he should be called to a similar service he might show the same spirit and fulfil the same high end!

The next time that Joshua comes into notice is not so flattering to himself. It is on that occasion when the Spirit descended on the seventy elders that had been appointed to assist Moses, and they prophesied round about the tabernacle. Two of the seventy were not with the rest, but nevertheless they got the spirit and were prophesying in the camp. The military instinct of Joshua was hurt at the irregularity, and his concern for the honour of Moses was roused by their apparent indifference to the presence of their head. He hurried to inform Moses, not doubting but he would interfere to correct the irregularity. But the narrow spirit of youth met with a memorable rebuke from the larger and more noble spirit of the leader,—" Enviest thou for my sake? Would God that all the Lord's people were prophets, and that the Lord would put His Spirit upon them!"

Not long after this Joshua was appointed to another memorable service. After the law-giving had been brought to an end, and the host of Israel had removed from the mountain to the borders of the promised land, he was appointed one of the twelve spies that were sent forward to explore the country. Formerly his name had been Oshea; it was now changed to Jehoshua or Joshua. The changing of the name was in itself significant, and still more the character of the change, by which a syllable of the Divine name was inserted in it. For, by the practice of the nation, the changing of a name denoted a man's entrance on a new chapter of his history, or his coming out before the world in a new character. So it was when Abram's name was changed to Abraham, Sarai's to Sarah, and Jacob's to Israel; so also when Simon became Cephas, and Saul Paul. But the new name given to Joshua was in itself more remarkable—Joshua, that is, Jehovah saves: in the New Testament, Jesus. No doubt it looked back on the victory of Rephidim when the Lord wrought such a deliverance in Israel through Joshua. But it indicated that the feature that had appeared at Rephidim would continue to characterise him during his life. It was a testimony from Moses, and from Him who inspired Moses, to the character of Joshua, as it had come out during all the close intercourse of Moses with him. And it invested Joshua with a dignity that ought to have raised him very highly in the eyes of the other spies, and of all the congregation of Israel. Who could be more worthy of their respect than the young man who had shown himself so faithful in all his previous history and who had now received a name that indicated that it would be the distinction of his life, like Him whom he prefigured, to lead his people to the enjoyment of God's salvation?

The forty days spent by the twelve men in exploring the land were a great contrast to the forty days spent by Joshua on the mount. All was inactivity and patient waiting in the one case; all was activity and bustle in the other. For there is a time to work and a time to rest. If at the one period Joshua had to put a restraint on his natural activity, at the other he could give it full swing.

Apart from its more immediate object, this early tour through Palestine must have been one of surpassing interest. To witness each spot that had been made memorable and classical by the lives of his forefathers; to sit by the well of Beersheba, and recall all that had happened there; to repose under Abraham's oak at Mamre; to bow at the cave of Machpelah; to recall the visits of angels at Bethel, and the ladder which had been seen going up to heaven,—was not only most thrilling, but to a man of Joshua's faith most inspiring; because every spot that had such associations was a witness that God had given them the land, and a proof that even though the sons of Anak were there, and their cities were walled up to heaven, the God of Abraham and Isaac and Jacob would be faithful to His promise, and, if the people would only trust Him, would right speedily place them in full possession.

Caleb and Joshua were the only two men whose faith stood the test of this survey; the rest were thoroughly cowed by the greatness of the difficulties. And Caleb seems to have been the foremost of the two, for in some places he is named as if he stood alone. Probably he was the one who came forward and spoke; but even if Joshua's faith was not so strong at first, it was no dishonour to be indebted to the greater courage and confidence of his brother.

We can hardly doubt that in their long marches and quiet encampments the twelve men had many a discussion as to what they would advise, and that the ten felt themselves beaten both in argument and in faith by the two. Long before they returned to the camp of Israel they had taken their sides, and by the sides they had taken they were determined to abide.

When they come back, the ten open the business and give their decided judgment against any attempt to take possession of the land. Impatient of their misrepresentations, Caleb perhaps strikes in, repudiates the notion that the people are not able to take possession, and urges them in God's name to go up at once. But it is easier far to stir up discontent and fear than to stimulate faith. The cry of the congregation, "Up, make us a captain, and let us return to Egypt," shows how strongly the tide of unbelief is flowing. Moses and Aaron are overwhelmed. The two leaders fall on their faces before the congregation. But neither the cry of the congregation nor the attitude of Moses and Aaron daunts the two faithful spies. With clothes rent they rush in, renewing their commendations of the land, laying hold of the Almighty Protector, and scorning the opposition of the inhabitants, whose hearts were cowed with terror and whose defence was departed from them. It was a fine spectacle,—the two against the million—the little remnant "faithful found among the faithless." But it was all in vain. "All the congregation bade stone them with stones." And in their impulsive and excitable temper the horrible cry would have been obeyed had not the glory of the Lord shone out and arrested the infatuated people (Num. xiv. 10).

For this shameless sin the penalty was very heavy. The congregation were to wander in the wilderness for forty years till all that generation should die off; the ten unfaithful spies were to die at once of a plague before the Lord; and not one of the generation that left Egypt was to enter the promised land. How easily can

God defeat the purposes of man! Where is now the proposal to make a captain and return to Egypt? "How art thou fallen from heaven, O Lucifer, son of the morning!"

Joshua and Caleb are doubly honoured; their lives are preserved when the other ten die of the plague; and they alone, of all the grown men of that generation, are to be allowed to enter and obtain homes in the land of promise.

For eight-and-thirty years we hear nothing more of Joshua. Like Moses, he has an interesting youth, then a long burial in the wilderness, and then he emerges from his obscurity and does a great work, second only to that of Moses himself. The first mention of him after his long eclipse is immediately before the death of Moses. God virtually appoints him to be his successor, and directs both of them to present themselves in the tabernacle of the congregation (Deut. xxxi. 14). And Moses calls him to his office, gives him a charge and says, "Be strong and of a good courage: for thou shalt bring the children of Israel into the land which I sware unto them: and I will be with thee" (Deut. xxxi. 23).

We might earnestly desire, in entering on the study of Joshua's life, to draw aside the veil that covers the eight-and-thirty years, and see how he was further prepared for his great work. We might like to look into his heart, and see after what fashion this man was made to whom the destruction of the Canaanites was entrusted. A religious warrior is a peculiar character; a Gustavus Adolphus, an Oliver Cromwell, a Henry Havelock, a General Gordon; Joshua was of the same mould, and we should have liked to know him more intimately; but this is denied to us. He stands out to us simply as one of the military heroes of the faith. In depth, in steadiness, in endurance, his faith was not excelled by that of Abraham or of Moses himself. The one conviction that dominated all in him was, that he was called by God to his work. If that work was often repulsive, let us not on that account withhold our admiration from the man who never conferred with flesh and blood, and who was never appalled either by danger or difficulty, for he "saw Him who is invisible."

CHAPTER III.

A SUCCESSOR TO MOSES.

JOSHUA i. 2.

THERE are some men to whom it is almost impossible to find successors. Men of imperial mould; Nature's primates, head and shoulders above other men, born to take the lead. Not only possessed of great gifts originally, but placed by Providence in situations that have wonderfully expanded their capacity and made their five talents ten. Called to be leaders of great movements, champions of commanding interests, often gifted with an imposing presence, and with a magnetic power that subdues opposition and kindles enthusiasm as if by magic. What a bereavement when such men are suddenly removed! How poor in comparison those who come next them, and from among whom successors have to be chosen! When the Hebrews mourned the death of Samson, the difference in physical strength between him and his brethren could not have appeared greater than the intellectual and moral gulf appears between a great king of men, suddenly removed, and the bereaved children that bend helpless over his grave.

A feeling of this sort must have spread itself through the host of Israel when it was known that Moses was dead. Speculation as to his successor there could be none, for not only had God designated Joshua, but before he died Moses had laid his hands upon him, and the people had acknowledged him as their coming leader. And Joshua had already achieved a record of no common order, and had been favoured with high tokens of the Divine approval. Yet what a descent it must have seemed from Moses to Joshua! From the man who had so often been face to face with God, who had commanded the sea to make a way for the redeemed of the Lord to pass over, who had been their legislator and their judge ever since they were children, to whom they had gone in every difficulty, and who for wisdom and disinterestedness had gained the profound confidence of every one of them ;—what a descent, we say, to this son of Nun, known hitherto as but the servant of Moses—an intrepid soldier, no doubt, and a man of unfaltering faith, but whose name seemed as if it could not couple with that of their imperial leader!

Well though Joshua did his work in after life, and bright though the lustre of his name ultimately became, he never attained to the rank of Moses. While the name of Moses is constantly reappearing in the prophets, in the psalms, in the gospels, in the epistles, and in the apocalypse, that of Joshua is not found out of the historical books except in the speech of Stephen and that well-known passage in the Hebrews (iv. 8), where the received version perplexes us by translating it Jesus. But it was no disparagement of him that he was so far surpassed by the man to whom, under God, the very existence of the nation was due. And in some respects, Joshua is a more useful example to us than Moses. Moses seems to stand half-way in heaven, almost beyond reach of imitation. Joshua is more on our own level. If not a man of surpassing genius, he commends himself as having made the best possible use of his talents, and done his part carefully and well.

The remark has been made that eras of great creative vigour are often succeeded by periods dull and common place. The history of letters and of the fine arts shows that bursts of artistic splendour like the Renaissance, or of literary originality like the Augustan age in Roman or the Elizabethan in English literature, are not followed by periods of equal lustre. And the same phenomenon has often been found in the Christian Church. In more senses than one the Apostles had no successors. Who in all the sub-apostolic age was worthy even to untie the latchet of Peter, or John, or Paul? The inferiority is so manifest that had there been nothing else to guide the Church in framing the canon of the New Testament, the difference between the writings of the Apostles and their companions on the one hand, and of men like Barnabas, Clement of Rome, Polycarp, Ignatius, and Hermes on the other, would have sufficed to settle the question. So also at the era of the Reformation. Hardly a country but had its star or its galaxy of the first magnitude. Luther and Melancthon, Calvin and Coligny, Farel and Viret, John à-Lasco and John Knox, Latimer and Cranmer,—what incomparable men they were! But in the age that followed what names can we find to couple with theirs?

Of other sections of the Church the same remark has been made, and sometimes it has been turned to an unfair use. If in the second generation, after a great outburst of power and grace, there are few or no men of equal calibre, it does not follow that the glory has departed, and that the Church is to droop her head, and wonder to what unworthy course on her part the degeneracy is to be ascribed. We are not to expect in such a case that the laws of nature will be set aside to gratify our pride. We are to recognise a state of things which God has ordained for wise purposes, although it may not be flattering to us. We are to place ourselves in the attitude in which Joshua was called to place himself when the curt announcement of the text as to Moses was followed by an equally curt order to him—" Moses My servant is dead; now therefore arise."

The question for Joshua is not whether he is a fit person to succeed Moses. His mental exercise is not to compare himself with Moses, and note the innumerable points of inferiority on every side. His attitude is not to bow down his head like a bulrush, mourning over the departed glory of Israel, grieving for the mighty dead, on whose like neither he nor his people will ever look again. If there ever was a time when it might seem excusable for a bereaved nation and a bereaved servant to abandon themselves to a sense of helplessness, it was on the death of Moses. But even at that supreme moment the command to Joshua is, " Now therefore arise." Gird yourself for the new duties and responsibilities that have come upon you. Do not worry yourself with asking whether you are capable of doing these duties, or with vainly looking within yourself for the gifts and qualities which marked your predecessor. It is enough for you that God in His providence calls you to take the place of the departed. If He has called you, He will equip you. It is not His way to send men a warfare on their own charges. The work to which He calls you is not yours but His. Remember He is far more interested in its success than you can be. Think not of yourself, but of Him, and go forth under the motto, " We will rejoice in Thy salvation, and in the name of our God we will set up our banners.'

In many different situations of life we may hear the same exhortation that was now addressed to Joshua. A wise, considerate, and honoured father is removed, and the eldest son, a mere stripling, is called to take his place, perhaps in the mercantile office or place of business, certainly in the domestic circle. He is called to be the comforter and adviser of his widowed mother, and the example and helper of his brothers and sisters. Well for him when he hears a voice from heaven, "Your father is dead; now therefore arise!" Rouse yourself for the duties that now devolve upon you; onerous they may be and beyond your strength, but not on that account to be evaded or repudiated; rather to be looked on as spurs provided and designed by God, that you may apply yourself with heart and soul to your duties, in the belief that faithful and patient application shall not be without its reward!

Or it may be that the summons comes to some young minister as successor to a father in Israel, whose ripe gifts and fragrant character have won the confidence and the admiration of all. Or to some teacher in a Sunday-school, where the man of weight, of wise counsel, and holy influence has been suddenly snatched away. But be the occasion what it may, the removal of any man of ripe character and gifts always comes to the survivor with the Divine summons, " Now therefore arise!" That is the one way in which you must try to improve this dispensation; the world is poorer for the loss of his gifts—learn you to make the most of yours!

It was no mean impression of Moses that God meant to convey by the designation, " Moses My servant." It was not a high-sounding title, certainly. A great contrast to the long list of honourable titles sometimes engraved on men's coffins or on their tombs, or proclaimed by royal herald or king-at-arms over departed kings or nobles. One of the greatest of men has no handle to his name—he is simply Moses. He has no titles of rank or office—he is simply "My servant." But true greatness is "when unadorned adorned the most." Moses is a real man, a man of real greatness; there is no occasion therefore to deck him out in tinsel and gilt; he is gold to the core.

But think what is really implied in this designation, "My servant." Even if Moses had not been God's servant in a sense and in a degree in which few other men ever were, it would have been a glorious thing to obtain that simple appellation. True indeed, the term "servant of God" is such a hackneyed one, and often so little represents what it really means, that we need to pause and think of its full import. There may be much honour in being a servant. Even in our families and factories a model servant is a rare and precious treasure. For a real servant is one that has the interest of his master as thoroughly at heart as his own, and never scruples, at any sacrifice of personal interest or feeling, to do all that he can for his master's welfare. A true servant is one of whom his master may say, "There is absolutely no need for me to remind him what my interest requires; he is always thinking of my interest, always on the alert to attend to it, and there is not a single thing I possess that is not safe in his hands."

Does God possess many such servants? Who among us can suppose God saying this of him? Yet this was the character of Moses, and in God's eyes it invested him with singular honour. It was his distinction that he was "faithful in all his house." His own will was thoroughly subdued to the will of God. The people of whom God gave him charge were dear to him as a right hand or a right eye. All personal interests and ambitions were put far from him. To aggrandise himself or to aggrandise his house never entered into his thoughts. Never was self more thoroughly crucified in any man's breast. Beautiful and delightful in God's eyes must have seemed this quality in Moses,—his absolute disinterestedness, his sensibility to every hint of his Master's will, his consecration of all he was and had to God, and to his people for God's sake!

It was thus no unsuggestive word that God used of Moses, when he told Joshua that "His servant" was dead. It was a significant indication of what God had valued in Moses and now expected of Joshua. The one thing for Joshua to remember about Moses is, that he was the servant of God. Let him take pains to be the same; let him have his ear as open as that of Moses to every intimation of God's will, his will as prompt to respond, and his hand as quick to obey.

Was not this view of the glory of Moses as God's servant a foreshadow of what was afterwards taught more fully and on a wider scale by our Lord? "The Son of man came not to be ministered unto, but to minister, and to give His life a ransom for many." Jesus sought to reverse the natural notions of men as to what constitutes greatness, when He taught that, instead of being measured by the number of servants who wait on us, it is measured rather by the number of persons to whom we become servants. And if it was a mark of Christ's own humiliation that "He took on Him the form of a servant," did not this redound to His highest glory? Was it not for this that God highly exalted Him and gave Him a name that is above every name? Happy they who are content to be GOD's SERVANTS in whatsoever sphere of life He may place them; seeking not their own, but always intent upon their Master's business!

And now Joshua must succeed Moses and be God's servant as he was. He must aim at this as the one distinction of his life; he must seek in every action to know what God would have him to do. Happy man if he can carry out this ideal of life! No conflicting interests or passions will distract his soul. His eye being single, his whole body will be full of light. The power that nerves his arm will not be more remarkable than the peace that dwells in his soul. He will show to all future generations the power of a "lost will,"— not the suppression of all desire, according to the Buddhist's idea of bliss, but all lawful natural desires in happy and harmonious action, because subject to the wise, holy, and loving guidance of the will of God.

Thus we see among the other paradoxes of His government, how God uses death to promote life. The death of the eminent, the aged, the men of brilliant gifts makes way for others, and stimulates their activity and growth. When the champion of the forest falls the younger trees around it are brought more into contact with the sunshine and fresh air, and push up into taller and more fully developed forms. If none of the younger growth attains the size of the champion, a great many may be advanced to a higher average of size and beauty. If in the second generation of any great religious movement few or none can match the "mighties" of the previous age, there may be a general elevation, a rise of level, an increase of efficiency among the rank and file.

In many ways death enters into God's plans. Not

only does it make way for the younger men,[1] but it has a solemnizing and quickening effect on all who are not hardened and dulled by the wear and tear of life.

What a memorable event in the spiritual history of families is the first sudden affliction, the first breach in the circle of loving hearts! First, the new experience of intense tender longing, baffled by the inexorable conditions of death; then the vivid vision of eternity, the reality of the unseen flashing on them with living and awful power, and giving an immeasurable importance to the question of salvation; then the drawing closer to one another, the forswearing of all animosities and jealousies, the cordial desire for unbroken peace and constant co-operation; and if it be the father or the mother that has been taken, the ambition to be useful,—to be a help not a burden to the surviving parent, and to do what little they can of what used to be their father's or their mother's work. Death becomes actually a quickener of the vital energies; instead of a withering influence, it drops like the gentle dew, and becomes the minister of life.

And death is not alone among the destructive agencies that are so often directed to life-giving ends. What a remarkable place is that which is occupied by Pain

---

[1] 'Can death itself when seen in the light of this truth [the adjustment of every being in animated nature to every other] be denied to be an evidence of benevolence? I think not. The law of animal generation makes necessary the law of animal death, if the largest amount of animal happiness is to be secured. If there had been less death there must also have been less life, and what life there was must have been poorer and meaner. Death is a condition of the prolificness of nature, the multiplicity of species, the succession of generations, the co-existence of the young and the old; and these things, it cannot reasonably be doubted, add immensely to the sum of animal happiness."—FLINT's "Theism," p. 251.

among God's instruments of good! How many are there who, looking back on their lives, have to confess, with a mixture of sadness and of joy, that it is their times of greatest suffering that have been the most decisive in their lives,—marked by their best resolutions,—followed by their greatest advance! And it sometimes would seem as if the acuter the suffering the greater the blessing. How near God seems at times to come to the height of cruelty when really He is overflowing with love! He seems to select the very tenderest spots on which to inflict His blows, the very tenderest and purest affections of the heart. It is a wonderful triumph of faith and submission when the sufferer stands firm and tranquil amidst it all. And still more when he can find consolation in the analogy which was supplied by God's own act,—"He that spared not His own Son, but delivered Him up for us all, how shall He not with Him also freely give us all things?"

And this brings us to our last application. Our Lord Himself, by a beautiful analogy in nature, showed the connection, in the very highest sense, between death and life—"Except a grain of wheat fall into the earth and die, it abideth alone; but if it die it beareth much fruit." "Without shedding of blood there is no remission of sin." When Jesus died at Calvary, the headquarters of death became the nursery of life. The place of a skull, like the prophet's valley of dry bones, gave birth to an exceeding great army of living men. Among the wonders that will bring glory to God in the highest throughout eternity, the greatest will be this evolution of good from evil, of happiness from pain, of life from death. And even when the end comes, and death is swallowed up of victory, and death and hell are cast into the lake of fire, there will abide with the glorified a lively sense of the infinite blessing that came to them from God through the repulsive channel of death, finding its highest expression in that anthem of the redeemed—" THOU WAST SLAIN, AND HAST REDEEMED US TO GOD BY THY BLOOD."

CHAPTER IV.

JOSHUA'S CALL.

Joshua i. 2—5.

JOSHUA has heard the Divine voice summoning him to the attitude of activity—" Arise!" Directions follow immediately as to the course which his activity is to take. His first step is to be a very pronounced one—"Go over this Jordan": enter the land, not by yourself, or with a handful of comrades, as you did forty years ago, but "thou and all this people." Take the bold step, cross the river; and when you are across the river, take possession of the country which I now give to your people. The time has come for decided action; it is for you to show the way, and summon your people to follow.

It was a very solemn and striking moment, second only in interest to that when, forty years before, their fathers had stood at the edge of the sea, with the host of Pharaoh hurrying on behind. At length the hour has come to take possession of the inheritance! At length the promise made so many hundred years ago to Abraham, Isaac, and Jacob is ripe for fulfilment! You, children of Israel, have seen that God is in no haste to fulfil His promises, and your hearts may have known much of the sickness of hope deferred. But now you are to see that after all God is faithful. He never forgets. He makes no mistakes. His delays are all designed for good, either to chasten or to try, and thus confirm and bless His people. He will now bring forth your righteousness as the light and your judgment as the noon-day.

There were two things that might make Joshua and the people hesitate to cross the Jordan. In the first place, the river was in flood ; it was the time when the Jordan overflowed its banks (Josh. iii. 15), and, being a rapid river, crossing it in such circumstances might well seem out of the question. But in the second place, to cross the Jordan was to throw down the gauntlet to the enemy. It was a declaration of war, and a challenge to them to do their worst. It was a signal for them to assemble, fight for their hearths and homes, and strain every nerve to annihilate this invader who made such a bold claim to their possessions. All the children of Anak whom Joshua had seen on his former visit would now range themselves against Israel; all the seven nations would muster their bravest forces, and the contest would not be like Joshua's battle with Amalek, finished in a single day, but a long succession of battles, in which all the resources of power and skill, of craft and cunning would be brought to bear against Israel. According to appearances, nothing short of this would be the result of compliance with the command, "Go over this Jordan."

On the one hand, therefore, compliance was physically impossible, and on the other, even if possible, it would have been fearfully perilous. But it is never God's method to give impossible commands. The very fact of His commanding anything is a proof of His readiness to make it possible, nay, to make it easy and simple to those who have faith to attempt it. " Stretch out thy hand," said Christ to the man with the withered hand.

"Stretch out my hand?" the man might have said in astonishment,—"why, it is the very thing I am unable to do." "Rise up and walk," said Peter to the lame man at the Beautiful gate. "How can I do that?" he might have replied; "don't you see that I have no use of my limbs?" But in these cases the helpless men had faith in those who bade them exert themselves; they believed that if they tried they would be helped, and helped accordingly they were. So too in the present case. Joshua knew that he and the host could not have crossed the Jordan as it then was by any contrivance in his power; but he knew that it was God's command, and he was sure that He would provide the means. He felt as if God and the people were in partnership, each equally interested in the result, and equally desirous to bring it about. Whatever it was necessary for God to do he was assured would be done, provided he and the people entered into the Divine plan, and threw all their energies into the work. Not a word of remonstrance did Joshua offer, not a word of explanation of the Divine plan did he ask; he acted as a servant should;

> "His not to make reply,
> His not to reason why;"

his only to trust and obey.

This faith in Divine power qualifying feeble mortals for the hardest tasks has originated some of the noblest enterprises in the history of the world. It was a Divine voice Columbus seemed to hear bidding him cross the wild Atlantic, for he desired to bring the natives of the distant shores beyond it into the pale of the Church; and it was his faith that sustained him when his crew became mutinous and his life was not safe for an hour. It was a Divine voice Livingstone seemed to hear bidding him cross Africa, strike up into the heart of the continent, examine its structure, and throw it open from shore to shore; and never was there a faith stronger or steadier than that which bore him on through fever and famine, through pain and sickness, through disappointment and anguish, and, even when the cold hand of death was on him, would not let him rest until his work was done.

Often in the spiritual warfare it is useful to apply this principle. Are we called to believe? Are we called to make ourselves a new heart and a new spirit? Are we summoned to fight, to wrestle, to overcome? Certainly we are. But is not this to tantalize us by ordering us to do what we cannot do? Is not this like telling a sick man to get well, or a decrepit old creature to skip and frisk like a child? It would be so if the principle of partnership between God and us did not come into play. Faith says, God is my partner in this matter. Partners even in an ordinary business put their resources together, each doing what his special abilities fit him for. In the partnership which faith establishes between God and you, the resources of the infinite Partner become available for the needs of the finite. It is God's part to give orders, it is your part to execute them, and it is God's part to strengthen you so to do. It is this that makes the command reasonable, "Work out your salvation with fear and trembling; for it is God that worketh in you both to will and to do of His good pleasure." Faith rejoices in the partnership, and goes forward in the confidence that the strength of the Almighty will help its weakness, not by one sudden leap, but by that steady growth in grace that makes the path of the just like the shining light, that shineth more and more unto the perfect day.

It was a great thing for God to announce that He was now in the act of turning His old, old promise into reality,—that the land pledged to Abraham centuries ago was now at length to become the possession of his descendants. But the gift could be of no avail unless it was actually appropriated. God gave the people the right to the land; but their own energy, made effectual through His grace, could alone secure the possession. In a remarkable way they were made to feel that, while the land was God's gift, the appropriation and enjoyment of the gift must come through their own exertions. Just as in a higher sphere we know that our salvation is wholly the gift of God; and yet the getting hold of this gift, the getting linked to Christ, the entrance as it were into the marriage covenant with Him involves the active exertion of our own will and energy, and the gift never can be ours if we fail thus to appropriate it.

As soon as God mentions the land, He expatiates on its amplitude and its boundaries. It was designed to be both a comfortable and an ample possession. In point of extent it was a spacious region,—" from the wilderness and this Lebanon, even unto the great river, the river Euphrates, all the land of the Hittites, and unto the great sea, towards the going down of the sun." And it was not merely bits or corners of this land that were to be theirs, they were not designed to share it with other occupants, but "every place that the sole of your foot shall tread upon, to you have I given it, as I spake unto Moses." It was in no meagre or stingy spirit that God was now to fulfil His ancient promise, but in a way corresponding to the essential bountifulness of His nature. For it is a delightful truth that God's heart is large and liberal, and that

He delights in large and bountiful gifts. Has He not made this plain to all in the arrangements of nature ? What more lavish than the gift of light, ever streaming from the sun in silver showers ? What more abundant than the fresh air that, like an inexhaustible ocean, encompasses our globe, or the rivers that carry their fresh and fertilizing treasures unweariedly through every meadow ? What more productive than the vegetable soil that under favourable conditions teems with fruits and flowers and the elements of food for the use and enjoyment of man ?

And when we turn to God's provision in grace we find glorious proofs of the same abundance and generosity. We see this symbolized by the activity and generosity of our Lord, as He went about " preaching the gospel of the kingdom, and healing all manner of sickness and all manner of disease among the people." We understand the spiritual reality of which this was the symbol, when we call to mind the Divine generosity that receives the vilest sinners ; the efficacy of the blood that cleanses from all sin ; the power of the Spirit that sanctifies soul, body, and spirit; the wisdom of the providence that makes all things work together for good ; the glory of the love that makes us now " sons of God, and it doth not yet appear what we shall be ; but we know that when He shall appear we shall be like Him, for we shall see Him as He is." And once more it appears in the glory and amplitude of the inheritance, of which the land of Canaan was but the type, prepared of God's infinite bounty for all who are His children by faith. Our Father's house is both large and well furnished ; it is a house of many mansions ; and the inheritance which He has promised is incorruptible and undefiled and fadeth not away.

It is a grand truth, of which we never can make too much, this bountifulness of God, and the delight which He has in being bountiful. It is emphatically a truth for faith to apprehend and enjoy, because appearances are so often against it. Appearances were fearfully against it while the Israelites were groaning in their Egyptian bondage, and hardly less so, despite the manna and the water from the rock, during the forty years' wandering in the desert. But that was a period of correction and of training, and in such circumstances lavish bounty was out of the question.

The most bountiful man on earth could not pour out all the liberality of his heart on the inmates of a hospital for the sick ; he may give all that sick men need, but he must wait till they are well before he can give full scope to his generosity. While we are in the body we are like patients in a hospital, and the kindest feelings from God toward us must often take the form of bitter medicines, painful operations, close restraint, stinted diet, and it may be silence and darkness. But wait till we are well, and then we shall see what God hath prepared for him that waiteth for Him ! Wait till we go over Jordan and take possession of the land ! Two things will be seen in the clearest light— the supreme bountifulness of God, and the sinfulness of that impatient and suspicious spirit to which we are so prone. What a humiliation, if humiliation be possible in heaven, to discover that all the time when we were fretting and grumbling, God was working out His plans of supreme beneficence and love, waiting only till we should come of age to make us heirs of the universe !

It is natural to ask why, if the boundaries of the promised land were so extensive, if they reached so far on the north-east as the Euphrates, and if they extended from Lebanon on the north to the confines of Egypt on the south, there should have been any difficulty about the two and a half tribes occupying the land east of the Jordan, where only by a special permission they obtained their settlement. For it is plain from the narrative that it was contrary to God's first intention, so to speak, that they should settle there, and that the land west of the Jordan was that to which the promise was held specially to apply. It will hardly do to say, as some have said, that the extension of the land to the Euphrates was a figure of speech, a poetical fringe or ornament as it were, intended to show that places adjacent to the land of Israel would share in some degree the radiance of its light and the influence of the Divine presence among its people. For the promise of God was really of the nature of a charter, and figures of poetry are not suitable in charters. It is rather to be understood that, in the *final* purpose of God, the possession included the whole of the ample domain contained within the specified boundaries, but that at first it would be confined within a narrower space. If the people should prove faithful to the covenant, the wider dominion would one day be conferred on them; but they were to start and get consolidated in a narrower territory. And the narrower space was that which had already been consecrated by the residence of the fathers Abraham, Isaac, and Jacob. The country west of Jordan was the land of *their* pilgrimage; and even when Lot and Abraham had to separate, it was not proposed that either should cross the river. The little strip lying between the Jordan and the sea was judged most suitable for the preparatory stage of Israel's history; but had the nation served God with fidelity, their country would have been extended—as in the days of David and Solomon it really was—to the dimensions of an empire. The rule afterwards announced was to be virtually brought into operation—"To him that hath shall be given." Hence the view taken of the settlement of the two and a half tribes east of the Jordan. It was not illegitimate ; it was not inconsistent with the covenant made with the fathers ; but it was for the time inexpedient, seeing that it exposed them to risks, both material and spiritual, which it would have been better for them to avoid.

One geographical expression, in the delimitation of the country, demands a brief explanation. While the country is defined as embracing the whole territory from Lebanon to the Euphrates, it is also defined as consisting in that direction of "all the land of the Hittites." But were not the Hittites one of the seven nations whose land was promised to Abraham and the fathers, and not even the first in the enumeration of these? Why should this great north-eastern section of the promised domain be designated "the land of the Hittites"?

The time was when it was a charge against the accuracy of the Scripture record that it ascribed to the Hittites this extensive dominion. That time has passed away, inasmuch as, within quite recent years, the discovery has been made that in those distant times a great Hittite empire did exist in the very region specified, between Lebanon and the Euphrates. The discovery is based on twofold data: references in the Egyptian and other monuments to a powerful people, called the Khita (Hittites), with whom even the great kings of Egypt had long and bloody wars ; and inscriptions in the Hittite language found in Hamah,

Aleppo, and other places in Syria. There is still much obscurity resting on the history of this people. That the Hittites proper prevailed so extensively has been doubted by some; a Hittite confederacy has been supposed, and sometimes a Hittite aristocracy exercising control over a great empire. The only point which it is necessary to dwell on here is, that in representing the tract between Lebanon and Euphrates as equivalent to "all the land of the Hittites," the author of the Book of Joshua made a statement which has been abundantly verified by recent research.[1]

To encourage and animate Joshua to undertake the work and position of Moses it is very graciously promised—" There shall not any man be able to stand before thee all the days of thy life : as I was with Moses, so will I be with thee : I will not fail thee, nor forsake thee." The invariable success promised was a greater boon than the greatest conquerors had been able to secure. Uniform success is a thing hardly known to captains of great expeditions, even though in the end they may prevail. But the promise to Joshua is, that all his enemies shall flee before him. None of his battles shall be even neutral, his opponents must always give way.[2] No son of Anak shall be able to oppose his onward march; no giant, like Og King of Bashan, shall terrify either him or his troops. He will "onward still to victory go,"—the Lord of hosts ever with him, the God of Jacob ever his defence.

---

[1] See "The Empire of the Hittites." By William Wright, D.D., F.R.G.S. London, 1886.

[2] The promise is not inconsistent with the fact that Joshua's troops were defeated by the men of Ai. In such promises there is an implied condition of steadfast regard to God's will on the part of those who receive them, and this condition was violated at Ai, not by Joshua, indeed, but by one of his people.

And this was no vague, indefinite assurance. It was sharply defined by a well-known example in the immediate past—" As I was with Moses, so I will be with thee." In what a remarkable variety of dangers and trials God was with Moses! Now he had to confront the grandest monarch on earth, supported by the strongest armies, and upheld by what claimed to be the mightest gods. Again he had to deal with an apostate people, mad upon idols, and afterwards with an excited mob, ready to stone him. Anon he had to overcome the forces of nature and bend them to his purposes ; to call water from the rock, to sweeten the bitter fountain, to heal the fiery bite, to cure his sister's leprous body, to bring down bread from heaven, and people the air with flocks of birds. Moreover, he had to be the messenger of the covenant between God and Israel, to unfold God's law in its length and breadth and in all its variety of application, and to obtain from the people a hearty compliance—" All that the Lord hath said unto us, that will we do." What a marvellous work Moses did! What a testimony his life presented to the reality of the Divine presence and guidance, and what a solid and indefeasible ground of trust God gave to Joshua when He said, " As I was with Moses, so will I be with thee."

And this is crowned with the further assurance, " I will not fail thee, nor forsake thee,"—an assurance which is extended in the Epistle to the Hebrews to all who believe. We are so apt to view these promises as just beautiful expressions that we need to pause and think what they really mean. A promise of Divine presence, Divine protection and guidance and blessing all the days of our life, is surely a treasure of inexpressible value. It is no slight matter to realize that this is in God's heart—that He has a constant, unvarying feeling of love toward us, and readiness to help; but we must believe this in order to get the benefit of it; and, moreover, He must be left to determine the time, the manner, and the form in which His help is to come. Alas for the unbelief, the suspicion, the fear that is so prone to eat out the spirit of trust, and in our trials and difficulties make us tremble as if we were alone! What a profound peace, what calm enjoyment and blessed hope fall to the lot of those who can believe in a God ever near, and in His unfailing faithfulness and love! Was it not the secret alike of David's calmness, of our Lord's serenity, and of the cheerful composure of many a martyr and many a common man and woman who have gone through life undisturbed and happy, that they could say—" I have set the Lord always before me; because He is at my right hand, I shall not be moved"? God grant us all that, like Abraham, we may "stagger not at the promise of God through unbelief, but that being strong in faith we may give glory to God, and believe that what He hath promised He is able also to perform."

CHAPTER V.

JOSHUA'S ENCOURAGEMENT.

Joshua i. 6—9.

GOD has promised to be with Joshua, but Joshua must strive to act like one in partnership with God. And that He may do so, God has just two things to press on him: in the first place, to be strong and of a good courage; and in the second place, to make the book of the law his continual study and guide. In this way he shall be able to achieve the specific purpose to which he is called, to divide the land for an inheritance to the people, as God hath sworn to their fathers; and likewise, more generally, to fulfil the conditions of a successful life—" then shalt thou make thy way prosperous, and then thou shalt have good success."

First, Joshua must be strong and very courageous. But are strength and courage really within our own power? Is strength not absolutely a Divine gift, and as dependent on God in its ordinary degrees as it was in the case of Samson in its highest degree? No doubt in a sense it is so; and yet the amount even of our bodily strength is not wholly beyond our own control. As bodily strength is undoubtedly weakened by careless living, by excess of eating and drinking, by all irregular habits, by the breathing of foul air, by indolence and self-indulgence of every kind, so undoubtedly it is increased and promoted by attention to the simple laws of health, by activity and exercise, by sleep and sabbatic rest, by the moderate use of wholesome food, as well as by abstinence from hurtful drinks and drugs And surely the duty of being strong, in so far as such things can give strength, is of far more importance than many think; for if we can thus maintain and increase our strength we shall be able to serve both God and man much better and longer than we could otherwise have done. On the other hand, the feebleness and fitfulness and querulousness often due to preventible illness must increase the trouble which we give to others, and lessen the beneficent activity and the brightening influence of our own lives.

But in Joshua's case is was no doubt strength and courage of soul that was mainly meant. Even that is not wholly independent of the ordinary conditions of the body. On the other hand, there are no doubt memorable cases where the elasticity and power of the spirit have been in the very inverse ratio to the strength of the body. By cheerful views of life and duty, natural depression has been counteracted, and the soul filled with hope and joy. "The joy of the Lord," said Nehemiah, "is the strength of His people." Fellowship with God, as our reconciled God and Father in Christ, is a source of perpetual strength. Who does not know the strengthening and animating influence of the presence even of a friend, when we find his fresh and joyous temperament playing on us in some season of depression? The radiance of his face, the cheeriness of his voice, the elasticity of his movements seem to infuse new hope and courage into the jaded soul.

When he is gone, we try to shake off the despondent feeling that has seized us, and gird ourselves anew for the battle of life. And if such an effect can be produced by fellowship with a fellow-creature, how much more by fellowship with the infinite God!—especially when it is His work we are trying to do, and when we have all His promises of help to rest on. "God is near thee, therefore cheer thee" is a perpetual solace and stimulus to the Christian soul.

But even men who are full of Christian courage need props and bulwarks in the hour of trial. Ezra and Nehemiah were bold, but they had ways of stimulating their courage, which they sometimes needed to fall back on, and they could find allies in unlikely quarters. Ezra could draw courage even from his shame, and Nehemiah from his very pride. "I was ashamed," said Ezra, "to require of the king a band of soldiers and horsemen to help us against the enemy in the way;" therefore he determined to face the danger with no help but the unseen help of God. And when Nehemiah's life was in danger from the cunning devices of the enemy, and his friends advised him to hide himself, he repelled the advice with high-minded scorn—"Should such a man as I flee?"

But there is no source of courage like that which flows from the consciousness of serving God, and the consequent assurance that He will sustain and help His servants. Brief ejaculatory prayers, constantly dropping from their lips, often bring the courage which is needed. "Now, therefore, O God, strengthen my hands," was Nehemiah's habitual exclamation when faintness of heart came over him. No doubt it was Joshua's too, as it has always been of the best of God's servants. Again and again, amid the murderous threats of cannibals in the New Hebrides, the missionary Paton must have sunk into despair but for his firm belief in the protection of God.

The other counsel to Joshua was to follow in all things the instructions of Moses, and for this end, not to let "the book of the law depart out of his mouth, but to meditate on it day and night, that he might observe to do all that was written therein."

For Joshua was called to be the executor of Moses, as it were, not to start on an independent career of his own; and that particular call he most humbly and cheerfully accepted. Instead of breaking with the past, he was delighted to build on it as his foundation, and carry it out to its predestined issues. It was no part of his work to improve on what Moses had done; he was simply to accept it and carry it out. He had his brief, he had his instructions, and these it was his one business to fulfil. No puritan ever accepted God's revelation with more profound and unquestioning reverence than Joshua accepted the law of Moses. No Oliver Cromwell or General Gordon ever recognised more absolutely his duty to carry out the plan of another, and, undisturbed himself, leave the issue in His hands. He was to be a very incarnation of Moses, and was so to meditate on his law day and night that his mind should be saturated with its contents.

This, indeed, was a necessity for Joshua, because he required to have a clear perception of the great purpose of God regarding Israel. Why had God taken the unusual course of entering into covenant with a single family out of the mass of mankind? A purpose deliberately formed and clung to for more than four hundred years must be a grand object in the Divine mind. It was Joshua's part to keep the people in mind of the solemnity and grandeur of their mission and to call them to a corresponding mode of life. What can more effectually give dignity and self-respect to men than to find that they have a part in the grand purposes of God? To find that God is not asleep; that He has neither given up the world to chance nor bound it with a chain of irreversible law, but that He calls us to be fellow-workers with Him in a great plan which shall in the end tend gloriously to advance the highest welfare of man?

This habit of meditation on the law which Joshua was instructed to practise was of great value to one who was to lead a busy life. No mere cursory perusal of a book of law can secure the ends for which it is given. The memory is treacherous, the heart is careless, and the power of worldly objects to withdraw attention is proverbial. We must be continually in contact with the Book of God. The practice enjoined on Joshua has kept its ground among a limited class during all the intervening generations. In every age of the Church it has been impressed on all devout and earnest hearts that there can be no spiritual prosperity and progress without daily meditation on the Word of God. It would be hard to believe in the genuine Christianity of any one who did not make a practice morning and evening of bringing his soul into contact with some portion of that Word. And wherever an eminent degree of piety has been reached, we shall find that an eminently close study of the Word has been practised. Where the habit is perfunctory, the tendency is to omit the meditation and to be content with the reading. Even in pious families there is a risk that the reading of the Scriptures morning and evening may push the duty of meditation aside, though even then we are not to despise the benefit that arises from the familiarity gained with their contents.

But, on the other hand, the instances are numberless of men attaining to great intimacy with the Divine will and to a large conformity to it, through meditation on the Scriptures. To many the daily portion comes fresh as the manna gathered each morning at the door of Israel's camp. Think of men like George Müller of Bristol reading the Bible from beginning to end as many as a hundred times, and finding it more fresh and interesting at each successive perusal. Think of Livingstone reading it right on four times when detained at Manyuema, and Stanley three times during his Emin expedition. What resources must be in it, what hidden freshness, what power to feed and revive the soul! The sad thing is that the practice is so rare. Listen to the prophet-like rebuke of Edward Irving to the generation of his time: "Who feels the sublime dignity there is in a fresh saying descended from the porch of heaven? Who feels the awful weight there is in the least iota that hath dropped from the lips of God? Who feels the thrilling fear or trembling hope there is in words whereon the eternal destinies of himself do hang? Who feels the swelling tide of gratitude within his breast for redemption and salvation, instead of flat despair and everlasting retribution? . . . This book, the offspring of the Divine mind and the perfection of heavenly wisdom is permitted to lie from day to day, perhaps from week to week, unheeded and unperused; never welcome to our happy, healthy, and energetic moods; admitted, if admitted at all, in seasons of weakness, feeblemindedness, and disabling sorrow. . . . Oh, if books had but tongues to speak their wrongs, then might this book exclaim, Hear, O heavens, and give ear, O earth! I came from the love and embrace of God, and mute nature, to whom I brought no boon, did me rightful homage. . . . I set open to you the gates of salvation and the way of eternal life, heretofore unknown. . . . But ye requited me with no welcome, ye held no festivity on my arrival; ye sequester me from happiness and heroism, closeting me with sickness and infirmity; ye make not of me, nor use me as your guide to wisdom and prudence, but press me into your list of duties, and withdraw me to a mere corner of your time, and most of you set me at nought and utterly disregard me. . . . If you had entertained me, I should have possessed you of the peace which I had with God when I was with Him and was daily His delight rejoicing always before Him. . . . Because I have called and ye refused . . . I also will laugh at your calamity and mock when your fear cometh."[1]

It is no excuse for neglecting this habitual reading of the Book of God that He places us now more under the action of principles than the discipline of details. For the glory of principles is that they have a bearing on every detail of our life. "Whatsoever ye do in word or in deed, do all in the name of the Lord Jesus, giving thanks unto God and the Father by Him." What could be more comprehensive than this principle of action—a principle that extends to "whatsoever we do"? There is not a moment of our waking life, not an action great or small we ever perform where the influence of this wide precept ought not to be felt. And how can it become thus pervasive unless we make it a subject of continual meditation?

---

[1] "For the Oracles of God: four Orations." Pp. 3—6.

In the case of Joshua, all the strenuous exhortations to him to be strong and of a good courage, and to meditate on the Divine law as given by Moses by day and by night, were designed to qualify him for his great work—"to divide the land for an inheritance to the people as God had sworn to their fathers." First of all, the land had to be conquered; and there is no difficulty in seeing how necessary it was for one who had this task on hand to be strong and of a good courage, and to meditate on God's law. Then the land had to be divided, and the people settled in their new life, and Joshua had to initiate them, as it were, in that life; he had to bind on their consciences the conditions on which the land was to be enjoyed, and start them in the performance of the duties, moral, social and religious, which the Divine constitution required. Here lay the most difficult part of his task. To conquer the country required but the talent of a military commander; to divide the country was pretty much an affair of trigonometry; but to settle them in a higher sense, to create a moral affinity between them and their God, to turn their hearts to the covenant of their fathers, to wean them from their old idolatries and establish them in such habits of obedience and trust that the doing of God's will would become to them a second nature,—here was the difficulty for Joshua. They had not only to be planted physically in groups over the country, but they had to be married to it morally, otherwise they had no security of tenure, but were liable to summary eviction. It was no land of rest for idolaters; all depended on the character they attained; loyalty to God was the one condition of a happy settlement; let them begin to trifle with the claims of Jehovah, punishment and suffering, to be followed finally by dispersion and captivity, was the inevitable result.

It was thus that Joshua had to justify his name,—to show that he was worthy to be called by the name of Jesus. The work of Jesus may be said to have been symbolized both by that of Moses and that of Joshua. Moses symbolized the Redeemer in rescuing the people from Egypt and their miserable bondage there; as "Christ hath redeemed us from the curse of the law." Joshua symbolized Him as He renews our hearts and makes us "meet to be partakers of the inheritance of the saints in light." For there are conditions moral and spiritual essential to our dwelling in the heavenly Canaan. "Lord, who shall abide in Thy tabernacle? and who shall dwell in Thy holy hill? He that hath clean hands, and a pure heart; who hath not lifted up his soul to vanity, nor sworn deceitfully." The atmosphere of heaven is too pure to be breathed by the unregenerate and unsanctified. There must be an adaptation between the character of the inhabitant and the place of his habitation. "Verily, verily, I say unto you, Except a man be born of water and of the Spirit, he cannot see the kingdom of God."

Thus we see the connection between Joshua's devotion to the book of the law, and success in the great work of his life—"then thou shalt make thy way prosperous, and then thou shalt have good success." No doubt he would have the appearance of success if he simply cleared out the inhabitants who were so degraded by sin that God was compelled to sweep them off, and settled His people in their room. But that, after all, was but a small matter unless accompanied by something more. It would not secure the people from at last sharing the fate of the old inhabitants; so far at least that though they should not be exterminated, yet they would be scattered over the face of the globe. How could Joshua get rid of these ominous words in the song of Moses to which they had so lately listened?—"They provoked Him to jealousy with strange gods, with abominations provoked they Him to anger. They sacrified to devils, not to God; to gods whom they knew not, to new gods that came newly up, whom your fathers feared not. . . . And He said, I will hide My face from them, I will see what their end shall be: for they are a very froward generation, children in whom is no faith." But even if in the end of the day it should come to this, nevertheless Joshua might so move and impress the people for the time being, that in the immediate future all would be well, and the dreaded consummation would be put off to a distant day.

And so at all times, in dealing with human beings, we can obtain no adequate and satisfying success unless their hearts are turned to God. Your children may be great scholars, or successful merchants, or distinguished authors, or brilliant artists, or even statesmen; what does it come to if they are dead to God, and have no living fellowship with Jesus Christ? Your congregation may be large and influential, and wealthy, and liberal; what if they are worldly, proud, and contentious? We must aim at far deeper effects, effects not to be found without the Spirit of God. The more we labour in this spirit, the more shall our way be made prosperous, the better shall be our success. "For them that honour Me I will honour; but they that despise Me shall be lightly esteemed."

CHAPTER VI.

JOSHUA'S CHARGE TO THE PEOPLE.

JOSHUA i. 10—18.

GOD has spoken to Joshua; it is now Joshua's part to speak to the people. The crossing of the Jordan must be set about at once, and in earnest, and all the risks and responsibilities involved in that step firmly and fearlessly encountered.

And in the steps taken by Joshua for this purpose we see, what we so often see, how the natural must be exhausted before the supernatural is brought in. Thus, in communicating with the people through the *shoterim*, or officers, the first order which he gives is to "command the people to prepare them victuals." "Victuals" denotes the natural products of the country, and is evidently used in opposition to "manna." In another passage we read that "the manna ceased on the very morning after they had eaten of the old corn of the land" (chap. v. 12). This may have been a considerable time before, for the conquest of Sihon and Og would give the people possession of ample stores of food out of the old corn of the land. The manna was a provision for the desert only, where few or no natural supplies of food could be found. But the very day when natural stores become available, the manna is discontinued. One cannot but contrast the carefully limited use of the supernatural in Scripture with its arbitrary and unstinted employment in mythical or fictional writings. Often in such cases it is brought in with a wanton profusion, simply to excite wonder, sometimes to gratify the love of the grotesque, not because natural means could not have accomplished what was sought, but through sheer love of revelling in the supernatural. In Scripture the natural is never superseded when it is capable of either helping or accomplishing the end. The east wind helps to dry the Red Sea, although the rod of Moses has to be stretched out for the completion of the work. The angel of God knocks Peter's chains from his limbs and opens the prison gates for him, but leaves him to find his way thereafter as best he can. So now. It is now in the power of the people to prepare them victuals, and though God might easily feed them as He has fed them miraculously for forty years, He leaves them to find food for themselves. In all cases the co-operation of the Divine and the human is carried out with an instructive combination of generosity and economy; man is never to be idle; alike in the affairs of the temporal and the spiritual life, the Divine energy always stimulates to activity, never lulls to sleep.

A little explanation is needed respecting the time when Joshua said the Jordan must be crossed—" within three days." If the narrative of the first two chapters be taken in chronological order, more than three days must have elapsed between the issuing of this order and the crossing of the river, because it is expressly stated that the two spies who were sent to examine Jericho hid themselves for three days in the mountains, and thereafter recrossed the Jordan and returned to

Joshua (ii. 22). But it is quite in accordance with the practice of Scripture narrative to introduce an episode out of its chronological place so that it may not break up the main record. It is now generally held that the spies were sent off before Joshua issued this order to the people, because it is not likely that he would have committed himself to a particular day before he got the information which he expected the spies to bring. In any case, it is plain that no needless delay was allowed. Half a week more and Jordan would be crossed, although the means of crossing it had not yet been made apparent; and then the people would be actually in their own inheritance, within the very country which in the dim ages of the past had been promised to their fathers.

Yes, the people generally; but already an arrangement had been made for the Reubenites, the Gadites, and the half-tribe of Manasseh on the east side of the river. How, then, were they to act in the present crisis? That had been determined between them and Moses when they got leave to occupy the lands of Sihon and Og, on account of their suitableness for their abundant flocks and herds. It had been arranged then that, leaving their cattle and their children, a portion of the men likewise, the rest would cross the river with their brethren and take their share of the toils and risks of the conquest of Western Canaan. All that Joshua needs to do now is to remind them of this arrangement. Happily there was no reluctance on their part to fulfil it. There was no going back from their word, even though they might have found a loophole of escape. They might have said that as the conquest of Sihon and Og had been accomplished so easily, so the conquest of the western tribes would be equally simple. Or they might have said that the nine tribes and a half could furnish quite a large enough army to dispossess the Canaanites. Or they might have discovered that their wives and children were exposed to dangers they had not apprehended, and that it would be necessary for the entire body of the men to remain and protect them. But they fell back on no such after thought. They kept their word at no small cost of toil and danger, and furnished thereby a perpetual lesson for those who, having made a promise under pressure, are tempted to resile from it when the pressure is removed. Fidelity to engagements is a noble quality, just as laxity in regard to them is a miserable sin. Even Pagan Rome could boast of a Regulus who kept his oath by returning to Carthage, though it was to encounter a miserable death. In the fifteenth psalm it is a feature in the portrait of the man who is to abide in God's tabernacle and dwell in His holy hill, that he " sweareth to his own hurt, and changeth not."

One arrangement was made by these transjordanic tribes that was perfectly reasonable—a portion of the men remained to guard their families and their property. The number that passed over was forty thousand (Josh. iv. 13), whereas the entire number of men capable of bearing arms (dividing Manasseh into two) was a hundred and ten thousand (Num. xxvi. 7, 18, and 34). But the contingent actually sent was amply sufficient to redeem the promise, and, consisting probably of picked men, was no doubt a very efficient portion of the force. The actual fighting force of the other tribes would probably be in the same proportion to the whole; and there, too, a section would have to be left to guard the women, children, and flocks, so that in point of fact the labours and dangers of the conquest were about equally divided between all the tribes.

Here, then, was an edifying spectacle : those who had been first provided for did not forget those who had not yet obtained any settlement ; but held themselves bound to assist their brethren until they should be as comfortably settled as themselves.

It was a grand testimony against selfishness, a grand assertion of brotherhood, a beautiful manifestation of loyalty and public spirit; and, we may add, an instructive exhibition of the working of the method by which God's providence seeks to provide for the dissemination of many blessings among the children of men. It was an act of socialism, without the drawbacks which most forms of socialism involve.

God has allowed many differences in the lots of mankind, bestowing on some ample means, for which they toiled not neither did they spin ; bestowing, often on the same individuals, a higher position in life, with corresponding social influence ; setting some nations in the van of the world's march, bestowing on some churches very special advantages and means of influence ; and it is a great question that arises—what obligations rest on these favoured individuals and communities ? Does God lay any duty on them toward the rest of mankind?

The inquiry in its full scope is too wide for our limits ; let us restrict ourselves to the element in respect of which the transjordanic tribes had the advantage of the others—the element of time. What do those who have received their benefits early owe to those who are behind them in time ?

The question leads us first to the family constitution, but there is really no question here. The obligations of parents to their children are the obligations of those who have already got their settlement to those who have not; of those who have already got means, and strength, and experience, and wisdom to those who have not yet had time to acquire them. It is only the vilest of our race that refuse to own their obligations here, and this only after their nature has been perverted and demonized by vice. To all others it is an obligation which amply repays itself. The affection between parent and child in every well-ordered house sweetens the toil that often falls so heavily on the elders; while the pleasure of seeing their children filling stations of respectability and usefulness, and the enjoyment of their affection, even after they have gone out into the world, amply repay their past labours, and greatly enrich the joys of life.

We advance to the relation of the rich to the poor, especially of those who are born to riches to those who are born to obscurity and toil. Had the providence of God no purpose in this arrangement? You who come into the world amid luxury and splendour, who have never required to work for a single comfort, who have the means of gratifying expensive tastes, and who grudge no expenditure on the objects of your fancy:—was it meant that you were to sustain no relation of help and sympathy to the poor, especially your neighbours, your tenants, or your workpeople? Do you fulfil the obligations of life when, pouring into your coffers the fruits of other men's toil, you hurry off to the resorts of wealth and fashion, intent only on your own enjoyment, and without a thought of the toiling multitude you leave at home? Is it right of you to leave deserving people to fall peradventure into starvation and despair, without so much as turning a finger to prevent it? What are you doing for the widows and orphans? Selfish and sinful beings! let these old Hebrews read you a lesson of condemnation!

They could not selfishly enjoy their comfortable homes till they had done their part on behalf of their brethren, for wherever there is a brotherly heart a poor brother's welfare is as dear as one's own.

Then there is the case of nations, and pre-eminently of our own. Some races attain to civilization, and order, and good government sooner than others. They have all the benefit of settled institutions and enlightened opinion, of discoveries in the arts and sciences, and of the manifold comforts and blessings with which life is thus enriched, while other nations are sunk in barbarism and convulsed by disorder. But how much more prone are such nations to claim the rights of superiority than to play the part of the elder brother! We are thankful for the great good that has been done in India, and in other countries controlled by the older nations. But even in the case of India, how many have gone there not to benefit the natives, but with the hope of enriching themselves. How ready have many been to indulge their own vices at the cost of the natives, and how little has it pained them to see them becoming the slaves of new vices that have sunk them lower than before. Our Indian opium traffic, and our drink traffic generally among native races—what is their testimony to our brotherly feeling? What are we to think of the white traders among the South Sea islands, stealing and robbing and murdering their feebler fellow-creatures? What are we to think of the traffic in slaves, and the inconceivable brutalities with which it is carried on? Or what are we to think of our traders at home, sending out in almost uncountable profusion the rum, and the gin, and the other drinks by which the poor weak natives are at once enticed, enslaved, and destroyed? Is there any development in selfishness that has ever been heard of more heartless and horrible ? Why can't they let them alone, if they will not try to benefit them ? What can come to any man in the end but the well-merited punishment of those who out of sheer greed have made miserable savages tenfold more the children of hell than before ?

We pass over the case of the early settlers in colonies, because there is hardly any obligation more generally recognised than that of such settlers to lend a helping hand to new arrivals. We go on to the case of Churches. The light of saving truth has come to some lands before others. We in this country have had our Christianity for centuries, and in these recent years have had so lively a dispensation of the gospel of Christ that many have felt more than ever His power to forgive, to comfort, to lift us up and bless us. Have we no duty to those parts of the earth which are still in the shadow of death ? If we are not actually settled in the Promised Land, we are as good as settled, because we have the Divine promise, and we believe in that promise. But what of those who are yet "without Christ, alienated from the commonwealth of Israel, and strangers to the covenants of promise, having no hope, and without God in the world" ? Have we no responsibility for them ? Have we no interest in that Divine plan which seeks to use those who first receive the light as instruments of imparting it to the rest ? Infidels object that Christianity cannot be of God, because if Christianity furnishes the only Divine remedy for sin it would have been diffused as widely as the evil for which it is the cure. Our reply is, that God's plan is to give the light first to some, and to charge them to give it freely and cordially to others. We say, moreover, that this plan is a wholesome one for those who are called to work it, because it draws out and strengthens what is best and noblest in them, and because it tends to form very loving bonds between those who give and those who get the benefit. But what if the first recipients of the light fold their hands, content to have got the blessing themselves, and decline to do their part in sending it to the rest? Surely there is here no ordinary combination of sins! Indolence and selfishness at the root, and, with these, a want of all public spirit and beneficent activity; and, moreover, not mere neglect but contempt of the Divine plan by which God has sought the universal diffusion of the blessing. Again we say, look to these men of Reuben, Gad, and Manasseh. They were not the *élite* of the race of Israel. Their fathers, at least in the case of Reuben and Dan, were not among the more honoured of the sons of Jacob. And yet they had the grace to think of their brethren, when so many among us are utterly careless of ours. And not only to think of them, but to go over the Jordan and fight for them, possibly die for them; nor would they think of returning to the comfort of their homes till they had seen their brethren in the west settled in theirs.

And this readiness of Reuben, Gad, and the half-tribe of Manasseh to fulfil the engagement under which they had come to Moses, was not the only gratifying occurrence which Joshua met with on announcing the impending crossing of the Jordan. For the whole people declared very cordially their acceptance of Joshua as their leader, vowed to him the most explicit fidelity, declared their purpose to pay him the same honour as they had paid to Moses, and denounced a sentence of death against any one that would not hearken to his words in all that he commanded them.

Joshua, in fact, obtained from them a promise of loyalty beyond what they had ever given to Moses till close on his death. It was the great trial of Moses that the people so habitually complained of him and worried him, embittering his life by ascribing to him even the natural hardships of the wilderness, as well as the troubles that sprang directly from their sins. It is the unwillingness of his people to trust him, after all he has sacrificed for them, that gives such a pathetic interest to the life of Moses, and makes him, more than perhaps any other Old Testament prophet, so striking an example of unrequited affection. After crossing the Red Sea, all the marvels of that deliverance from Pharaoh of which he had been the instrument are swallowed up and forgotten by the little inconveniences of the journey. And afterwards, when they are doomed to the forty years' wandering, they are ready enough to blame him for it, forgetting how he fell down before God and pled for them when God threatened to destroy them. Moreover, his enactments against the idolatry they loved so well made him any-thing but popular, to say nothing of the burdensome ceremonial which he enjoined them to observe. The time of real loyalty to Moses was just the little period before his death, when he led them against Sihon and Og, and a great stretch of fertile and beautiful land fell into their hands. Moses had just gained the greatest victory of his life, he had just become master of the hearts of his people, when he was called away. For Moses at last did gain the people's hearts, and those to whom Joshua appealed could say without irony or sarcasm, "According as we hearkened unto Moses in all things, so will we hearken unto thee."

In point of fact a great change had been effected on

the people at last. Moses had laboured, and Joshua now entered into his labours. The same thing has often occurred in history, and notably in our own. In civil life how much do we owe to the noble champions of freedom of other days, through whose patriotism, courage, and self-denial the hard fight was fought and the victory won that enables us to sit under our vine and under our fig tree. In ecclesiastical life was it not the blood of the martyrs and the struggles of those of whom the world was not worthy, who wandered in deserts and in mountains and in dens and caves of the earth, that won for us the freedom and the peace in which we now rejoice? What blessings we owe to those that have gone before us! And how can we better discharge our obligations to them than by hastening to the aid of those who have but emerged from the period of struggle and suffering, like the Christians of Madagascar or of Uganda, whose fearful sufferings and awful deaths under the merciless rule of heathen kings made Christendom stand aghast, and drew a wail of anguish from her bosom?

The unanimity of the people in their loyalty to Joshua is a touching sight. So far as appears there was not one discordant note in that harmonious burst of loyalty. No Korah, Dathan, or Abiram rose up to decline his rule and embarrass him in his new position. It is a beautiful sight, the united loyalty of a great nation. Nothing more beautiful has ever been known in the long reign of Queen Victoria than the crowding of her people in hundreds of thousands to witness her procession to St. Paul's on that morning when she went to return thanks for the rescue of her eldest son from the very jaws of death. Not one discordant note was uttered, not one disloyal feeling was known; the vast multitude were animated by the spirit of sympathy and affection for one who had tried to do her duty as a queen and as a mother. It was a sight not unlike to this that was seen in the streets of New York at the centennial celebration of the inauguration of George Washington as first President of the United States. One was thrilled by the thought that not only the multitude that thronged the streets, but the representatives of the whole nation, gathered in their churches throughout the land, were animated by a common sentiment of gratitude to the man whose wisdom and courage had laid the foundation of all the prosperity and blessing of the last hundred years. Are not such scenes the pattern of that spirit of loyalty which the entire race of man owes to Him who by His blood redeemed the world, and whose rule and influence, if the world would but accept of it, are so beneficent and so blessed? Yet how far are we from such a state! How few are the hearts that throb with true loyalty to the Saviour, and whose most fervent aspiration for the world is, that it would only throw down its weapons of rebellion, and give to him its hearty allegiance! Strange that the Old Testament Joshua should have got at once what eighteen hundred years have failed to bring to the New Testament Jesus! God hasten the day of universal light and universal love, when He shall reign from sea to sea, and from the river to the ends of the earth!

> "One song employs all nations, and all cry
> 'Worthy the Lamb, for He was slain for us'!
> The dwellers in the vales and on the rocks
> Shout to each other, and the mountain tops
> From distant mountains catch the flying joy,
> Till nation after nation taught the strain
> Earth rolls the rapturous Hosanna round."

CHAPTER VII.

THE SPIES IN JERICHO.

JOSHUA ii.

IT was not long ere Joshua found an occasion not only for the exercise of that courage to which he had been so emphatically called both by God and the people, but for calling on others to practise the same manly virtue. For the duty which he laid on the two spies—detectives we should now call them—to enter Jericho and bring a report of its condition, was perhaps the most perilous to which it was possible for men to be called. It was like sending them into a den of lions, and expecting them to return safe and sound. Evidently he was happy in finding two men ready for the duty and the risk. Young men they are called further on (vi. 23), and it is quite likely that they were leading men in their tribes. No doubt they might disguise themselves, they might divest themselves of anything in dress that was characteristically Hebrew, they might put on the clothes of neighbouring peasants, and carry a basket of produce for sale in the city; and as for language, they might be able to use the Canaanite dialect and imitate the Canaanite accent. But if they did try any such disguise, they must have known that it would be of doubtful efficacy; the officials of Jericho could not fail to be keenly on the watch, and no disguise could hide the Hebrew features, or divest them wholly of the air of foreigners. Nevertheless the two men had courage for the risky enterprise. Doubtless it was the courage that sprang from faith; it was in God's service they went, and God's protection would not fail them. To be able to find agents so willing and so suitable was a proof to Joshua that God had already begun to fulfil His promises.

Joshua had been a spy himself, and it was natural enough that he should think of the same mode of reconnoitring the country, now that they were again on the eve of making the entrance into it which they should have made nearly forty years before. There is no reason to think that in taking this step Joshua acted presumptuously, proceeding on his own counsel when he should have sought counsel of God. For Joshua might rightly infer that he ought to take this course inasmuch as it had been followed before with God's approval in the case of the twelve. Its purpose was twofold—to obtain information and confirmation. Information as to the actual condition and spirit of the Canaanites, as to the view they took of the approaching invasion of the Israelites, and the impression that had been made on them by all the remarkable things that had happened in the desert; and confirmation, —new proof for his own people that God was with them, fresh encouragement to go up bravely to the attack, and fresh assurance that not one word would ever fail them of all the things which the Lord had promised.

We follow the two men as they leave Shittim, so named from the masses of bright acacia which shed their glory over the plain; then cross the river at "the fords," which, flooded though they were, were still practicable for swimmers; enter the gates of Jericho, and move along the streets. In such a city as Jericho, and among such an immoral people as the Canaanites, it was not strange that they should fall in with a woman of Rahab's occupation, and should receive an invitation to her house. Some commentators have tried to make out that she was not so bad as she is represented, but only an innkeeper; but the meaning of the word both here and as translated in Heb. xi. and James ii. is beyond contradiction. Others have supposed that she was one of the harlot-priestesses of Ashtoreth, but in that case she would have had her dwelling in the precincts of a temple, not in an out-of-the-way place on the walls of the city. We are to remember that in the degraded condition of public opinion in Canaan, as indeed much later in the case of the Hetairai of Athens, her occupation was not regarded as disgraceful, neither did it banish her from her family, nor break up the bonds of interest and affection between them, as it must do in every moral community.[1] It was not accompanied with that self-contempt and self-loathing which in other circumstances are its fruits. We may quite easily understand how the spies might enter her house simply

---

[1] It is somewhat remarkable that the present village of Riha, at or near the site of the ancient Jericho, is noted for its licentiousness. The men, it is said, wink at the infidelity of the women, a trait of character singularly at variance with the customs of the Bedouin. "At our encampment over 'Ain Terâbeh (says Robinson) the night before we reached this place, we overheard our Arabs asking the Khatib for a paper or written charm to protect them from the women of Jericho; and from their conversation it seemed that illicit intercourse between the latter and strangers that come here is regarded as a matter of course. Strange that the inhabitants of the valley should have retained this character from the earliest ages; and that the sins of Sodom and Gomorrah should still flourish upon the same accursed soil."—"Researches in Palestine," i. 553.

for the purpose of getting the information they desired, as modern detectives when tracking out crime so often find it necessary to win the confidence and worm out the secrets of members of the same wretched class. But the emissaries of Joshua were in too serious peril, in too devout a mood, and in too high-strung a state of nerve to be at the mercy of any Delilah that might wish to lure them to careless pleasure. Their faith, their honour, their patriotism, and their regard to their leader Joshua, all demanded the extremest circumspection and self-control; they were, like Peter, walking on the sea; unless they kept their eye on their Divine protector, their courage and presence of mind would fail them, they would be at the mercy of their foes.

Whether disguised or not, the two men had evidently been noticed and suspected when they entered the city, which they seem to have done in the dusk of evening. But, happily for them, the streets of Jericho were not patrolled by policemen ready to pounce on suspicious persons, and run them in for judicial examination. The king or burgomaster of the place seems to have been the only person with whom it lay to deal with them. Whoever had detected them, after following them to Rahab's house, had then to resort to the king's residence and give their information to him. Rahab had an inkling of what was likely to follow, and being determined to save the men, she hid them on the roof of the house, and covered them with stalks of flax, stored there for domestic use. When, after some interval, the king's messengers came, commanding her to bring them forth since they were Israelites come to search the city, she was ready with her plausible tale. Two men had indeed come to her, but she could not tell who they were,—it was no business of hers to be inquisitive about them; the men had left just before the gates were shut, and doubtless, if they were alert and pursued after them, they would overtake them, for they could not be far off. The king's messengers had not half the wit of the woman; they took her at her word, made no search of her house, but set out on the wild-goose chase on which she had sent them. Sense and spirit failed them alike.

We are not prepared for the remarkable development of her faith that followed. This first Canaanite across the Jordan with whom the Israelites met was no ordinary person. Rays of Divine light had entered that unhallowed soul, not to be driven back, not to be hidden under a bushel, but to be welcomed, and ultimately improved and followed. Our minds are carried forward to what was so impressive in the days of our Lord, when the publicans and the harlots entered into the kingdom before the scribes and the pharisees. We are called to admire the riches of the grace of God, who does not scorn the moral leper, but many a time lays His hand upon him, and says "I will, be thou clean." "They shall come from the east, and from the west, and from the north, and from the south, and shall enter into the kingdom of heaven; but the children of the kingdom shall be cast into outer darkness; there shall be weeping and gnashing of teeth."

In the first place, Rahab made a most explicit confession of her faith, not only in Jehovah as the God of the Hebrews, but in Him as the one only God of heaven and earth. It would have been nothing had she been willing to give to the Hebrew God a place, a high place, or even the highest place among the gods. Her faith went much further. "The Lord your God, He is God in heaven above and in earth beneath."

This is an exclusive faith—Baal and Ashtoreth are nowhere. What a remarkable conviction to take hold of such a mind! All the traditions of her youth, all the opinions of her neighbours, all the terrors of her priests set at nought, swept clean off the board, in face of the overwhelming evidence of the sole Godhead of Jehovah!

Again, she explained the reason for this faith. "We have heard how the Lord dried up the water of the Red Sea for you, when ye came out of Egypt; and what ye did unto the two kings of the Amorites, that were on the other side Jordan, Sihon and Og, whom ye utterly destroyed." The woman has had an eye to see and an ear to hear. She has not gazed in stupid amazement on the marvellous tokens of Divine power displayed before the world, nor accepted the sophistry of sceptics referring all these marvels to accidental thunderstorms and earthquakes and high winds. She knew better than to suppose that a nation of slaves by their own resources could have eluded all the might of Pharaoh, subsisted for forty years in the wilderness, and annihilated the forces of such renowned potentates as Sihon and Og. She was no philosopher, and could not have reasoned on the doctrine of causation, but her common sense taught her that you cannot have extraordinary effects without corresponding causes. It is one of the great weaknesses of modern unbelief that with all its pretensions to philosophy, it is constantly accepting effects without an adequate cause. Jesus Christ, though He revolutionized the world, though He founded an empire to which that of the Cæsars is not for a moment to be compared, though all that were about Him admitted His supernatural power and person, after all, was nothing but a man. The gospel that has brought peace and joy to so many weary hearts, that has transformed the slaves of sin into children of heaven, that has turned cannibals into saints, and fashioned so many an angelic character out of the rude blocks of humanity, is but a cunningly devised fable. What contempt for such sophistries, such vain explanations of facts patent to all would this poor woman have shown! How does she rebuke the many that keep pottering in poor natural explanations of plain supernatural facts, instead of manfully admitting that it is the Arm of God that has been revealed, and the Voice of God that has spoken!

Further, Rahab informed the spies that when they heard these things the inhabitants of the land had become faint, their hearts melted, and there remained no more courage in them because of the Israelites. For they felt that the tremendous Power that had desolated Egypt and dried up the sea, that had crushed Sihon King of the Amorites and Og King of Bashan like nuts under the feet of a giant, was now close upon themselves. What could they do to arrest the march of such a power, and avert the ruin which it was sure to inflict? They had neither resource nor refuge—their hearts melted in them. It is when Divine Power draws near to men, or when men draw near to Divine Power that they get the right measure of its dimensions and the right sense of their own impotence. Caligula could scoff at the gods at a distance, but in any calamity no man was more prostrate with terror. It is easy for the atheist or the agnostic to assume a bold front when God is far off, but woe betide him when He draws near in war, in pestilence, or in death!

If we ask, How could Rahab have such a faith and yet be a harlot? or how could she have such faith in

God and yet utter that tissue of falsehoods about the spies with which she deluded the messengers of the king? we answer that light comes but gradually and slowly to persons like Rahab. The conscience is but gradually enlightened. How many men have been slaveholders after they were Christians! Worse than that, did not the godly John Newton, one of the two authors of the Olney hymns, continue for some time in the slave trade, conveying cargoes of his fellow-creatures stolen from their homes, before he awoke to to a sense of its infamy? Are there no persons among us calling themselves Christians engaged in traffic that brings awful destruction to the bodies and souls of their fellow-men? That Rahab should have continued as she was after she threw in her lot with God's people is inconceivable; but there can be no doubt how she was living when she first comes into Bible history. And as to her falsehoods, though some have excused lying when practised in order to save life, we do not vindicate her on that ground. All falsehood, especially what is spoken to those who have a right to trust us, must be offensive to the God of truth, and the nearer men get to the Divine image, through the growing closeness of their Divine fellowship, the more do they recoil from it. Rahab was yet in the outermost circle of the Church, just touching the boundary; the nearer she got to the centre the more would she recoil alike from the foulness and the falseness of her early years.

We have to notice further in Rahab a determination to throw in her lot with the people of God. In spirit she had ceased to be a Canaanite and become an Israelite. She showed this by taking the side of the spies against the king, and exposing herself to certain and awful punishment if it had been found out that they were in her house. And her confidential conversation with them before she sent them away, her cordial recognition of their God, her expression of assurance that the land would be theirs, and her request for the protection of herself and her relations when the Israelites should become masters of Jericho, all indicated one who desired to renounce the fellowship of her own people and cast in her lot with the children of God. That she was wholly blameless in the way in which she went about this, in favouring the spies against her own nation in this underhand way, we will not affirm; but one cannot look for a high sense of honour in such a woman. Still, whatever may be said against her, the fact of her remarkable faith remains conspicuous and beyond dispute, all the more striking, too, that she is the last person in whom we should have expected to find anything of the kind. That faith beyond doubt was destined to expand and fructify in her heart, giving birth to virtues and graces that made her after life a great contrast to what it had been. No doubt the words of the Apostle might afterwards have been applied to her—"Such were some of you; but ye are washed, but ye are sanctified, but ye are justified in the name of the Lord Jesus, and by the Spirit of the Lord."

And yet, though her faith may at this time have been but as a grain of mustard seed, we see two effects of it that are not to be despised. One was her protection of the Lord's people, as represented by the spies; the other was her concern for her own relations. Father, mother, brothers, and sisters and all that they had, were dear to her, and she took measures for their safety when the destruction of Jericho should come. She exacted an oath of the two spies, and asked a pledge of them, that they would all be spared when the crisis of the city arrived. And the men passed their oath and arranged for the protection of the family. No doubt it may be said that it was only their temporal welfare about which she expressed concern, and for which she made provision. But what more could she have been expected to do at that moment? What more could the two spies have engaged to secure? It was plain enough that if they were ever to obtain further benefit from fellowship with God's people, their lives must be preserved in the first instance from the universal destruction which was impending. Her anxiety for her family, like her anxiety for herself, may even then have begun to extend beyond things seen and temporal, and a fair vision of peace and joy may have begun to flit across her fancy at the thought of the vile and degrading idolatry of the Canaanites being displaced in them by the service of a God of holiness and of love. But neither was she far enough advanced to be able as yet to give expression to this hope, nor were the spies the persons to whom it would naturally have been communicated. The usual order in the Christian life is, that as anxiety about ourselves begins in a sense of personal danger and a desire for deliverance therefrom, so spiritual anxiety about the objects of our affection has usually the same beginning. But as it would be a miserable thing for the new life to stand still as soon as our personal safety was secured, so it would be a wretched affection that sought nothing more on behalf of our dearest friends. When, by accepting Christ, we get the blessing of personal safety, we only reach a height from which we see how many other things we need. We become ashamed of our unholy passions, our selfish hearts, our godless ways, and we aspire, with an ardour which the world cannot understand, to purity and unselfishness and consecration to God. For our friends we desire the same; we feel for them as for ourselves, that the bondage and pollution of sin are degrading, and that there can be neither peace, nor happiness, nor real dignity for the soul until it is created anew after the image of God.

Some commentators have laid considerable stress on the line of scarlet thread that was to be displayed in the window by which the spies had been let down, as a token and remembrance that that house was to be spared when the victorious army should enter Jericho. In that scarlet thread they have seen an emblem of atonement, an emblem of the blood of Christ by which sinners are redeemed. To us it seems more likely that, in fixing on this as the pledge of safety, the spies had in view the blood sprinkled on the lintels and door posts of the Hebrew houses in Egypt by which the destroying angel was guided to pass them by. The scarlet rope had some resemblance to blood, and for this reason its special purpose might be more readily apprehended. Obviously the spies had no time to go into elaborate explanations at the moment. It is to be observed that, as the window looked to the outside of the city, the cord would be observed by the Israelites and the house recognised as they marched round and round, according to the instructions of Joshua. Not a man of all the host but would see it again and again, as they performed their singular march, and would mark the position of the house so carefully that its inmates, gathered together like the family of Noah in the ark, would be preserved in perfect safety.

The stratagem of Rahab, and the mode of flight which she recommended to the spies, fruits of woman's ready wit and intuitive judgment, were both successful. She reminds us of the self-possession of Jael, or of Abigail, the wife of Nabal. In the dark, the spies escaped to the mountain,—the rugged rampart which bounded the valley of the Jordan on the west. Hiding in its sequestered crevices for three days, till the pursuit of the Jerichonians was over, they stole out under cover of darkness, recrossed the Jordan, told Joshua of their stirring and strange adventure, and wound up with the remark that the hearts of the people of the country were melting because of them. How often is this true, though unbelief cannot see it! When Jesus told His disciples that He beheld Satan fall as lightning from heaven, He taught us that those who set themselves against Him and His cause are fallen powers, no longer flushed with victory and hope, but defeated and dejected, and consciously unable to overcome the heaven-aided forces that are against them. Well for all Christian philanthropists and missionaries of the Cross, and brave assailants of lust and greed and vice and error, to bear this in mind! The cause of darkness never can triumph in the end, it has no power to rally and rush against the truth; if only the servants of Christ would be strong and of a good courage, they too would find that the boldest champions of the world do faint because of them.

When the spies return to Joshua and tell him all that has befallen them, he accepts their adventure as a token for good. They have not given him any hint how Jericho is to be taken; but, what is better, they have shown him that the outstretched arm of God has been seen by the heathen, and that the inhabitants of the country are paralysed on account of it. The two spies were a great contrast to the ten that accompanied

Joshua and Caleb so long before: the ten declared the land unassailable; the two looked on it as already conquered—" The Lord hath delivered into our hands all the land." Children of Israel, you must not be outdone in faith by a harlot; believe that God is with you, go up, and possess the land!

CHAPTER VIII.

JORDAN REACHED.

Joshua iii. 1—7.

THE host of Israel had been encamped for some time at Shittim on the east side of the river Jordan. It is well to understand the geographical position. The Jordan has its rise beyond the northern boundary of Palestine in three sources, the most interesting and beautiful of the three being one in the neighbourhood of Cæsarea Philippi. The three streamlets unite in the little lake now called Huleh, but Merom in Bible times. Issuing from Merom in a single stream the Jordan flows on to the lake of Galilee or Gennesareth, and from thence, in a singularly winding course, to the Dead Sea. Its course between the lake of Galilee and the Dead Sea is through a kind of ravine within a ravine; the outer ravine is the valley or plain of Jordan, now called by the Arabs El Ghor, which is about six miles in width at its northern part, and considerably more at its southern, where the Israelites now were. Within this "El Ghor" is a narrower ravine about three-quarters of a mile in width, in the inner part of which flows the river, its breadth varying from twenty to sixty yards. Some travellers say that the Jordan does not now rise so high as formerly, but others tell us they have seen it overflowing its banks at the corresponding season. But "the plain" is not fertilized by the rising waters: hence the reason why the banks of the river are not studded with towns as in Egypt. It is quite possible, however, that in the days of Abraham and Lot artificial irrigation was made use of: hence the description given of it then that it was "like the land of Egypt" (Gen. xiii. 10). If it be remarked as strange that Jordan should have overflowed his banks "in time of harvest" (Josh. iii. 15) when usually rain does not fall in Palestine, it is to be remembered that all the sources of the Jordan are fountains, and that fountains do not usually feel the effects of the rain until some time after it has fallen. The harvest referred to is the barley harvest, and near Jericho that harvest must have occurred earlier than throughout the country on account of the greater heat.

The host of Israel lay encamped at Shittim, or Abel Shittim, "the meadow or moist place of the acacias," somewhere in the Arboth-Moab or fields of Moab. The exact spot is unknown, but it was near the foot of the Moabite mountains, where the streams, coming down from the heights on their way to the Jordan, caused a luxuriant growth of acacias, such as are still found in some of the adjacent parts. Sunk as this part of the plain is far below the level of the Mediterranean, and enclosed by the mountains behind it as by the walls of a furnace, it possesses an almost tropical climate which, though agreeable enough in winter and early spring, would have been unbearable to the Israelites in the height of summer. It was while Israel "abode in Shittim," during the lifetime of Moses, that they were seduced by the Moabites to join in the idolatrous revels of Baal-peor and punished with the plague. The acacia groves gave facilities for the unhallowed revelling. That chastisement had brought them into a better spirit, and now they were prepared for better things.

The Jordan was not crossed then by bridges nor by ferry boats; the only way of crossing was by fords. The ford nearest to Jericho, now called El Mashra'a, is well known; it was the ford the Israelites would have used had the river been fordable; and perhaps the tradition is correct that there the crossing actually took place. When the spies crossed and recrossed the river it must have been by swimming, as it was too deep for wading at the time; but though this mode of crossing was possible for individuals, it was manifestly out of the question for a host. That the Israelites could by no possibility cross at that season must have been the forlorn hope of the people of Jericho; possibly they smiled at the folly of Joshua in choosing such a time of the year, and asked in derision, How is he ever to get over?

The appointed day for leaving Shittim has come, and Joshua, determined to lose no time, rises "early in the morning." Nor is it without a purpose that so often in the Old Testament narrative, when men of might commence some great undertaking, we are told that it was early in the morning. In all hot climates work in the open air, if done at all, must be done early in the morning or in the evening. But, besides this, morning is the appropriate time for men of great energy and decision to be astir; and it readily connects itself with the New Testament text—"Not slothful in business, fervent in spirit, serving the Lord." The benefits of an early start for all kinds of successful work are in the proverbs of all nations; and we may add that few have reached a high position in the Christian life who could not say, in the spirit of the hymn, "early in the morning my song shall rise to Thee." Nor can it easily be understood how under other conditions the precept could be fulfilled—"Whatsoever thy hand findeth to do, do it with thy might."

From Shittim to the banks of the Jordan is an easy journey of a few miles, the road being all over level ground, so that the march was probably finished before the sun had risen high. However strong their faith, it could not be without a certain tremor of heart that the people would behold the swollen river, and mark the walls and towers of Jericho a few miles beyond. Three days are to be allowed, if not for physical, certainly for moral and spiritual preparation for the crossing of the river. The three days are probably the same as those adverted to before (chap. i. 3), just as the order to select twelve men to set up twelve stones (chap. iii. 12) is probably the same as that more fully detailed in chap. iv. 2. The host is assembled in orderly array on the east bank of the Jordan, when the officers pass through to give instructions as to their further procedure. Three such instructions are given.

First, they are to follow the ark. Whenever they see the priests that bear it in motion, they are to move from their places and follow it. There was no longer the pillar of fire to guide them—that was a wilderness-symbol of God's presence, now superseded by a more permanent symbol—the ark. Both symbols represented the same great truth—the gracious presence and guidance of God, and both called the people to the same duty and privilege, and to the same assurance of absolute safety so long as they followed the Lord. Familiar sights are apt to lose their significance, and the people must have become so familiar with the

wilderness-pillar that they would hardly think what
it meant. Now a different symbol is brought forward.
The ark carried in solemn procession by the priests is
now the appointed token of God's guidance, and therefore the object to be unhesitatingly followed. A blessed
truth for all time was clearly shadowed forth. Follow
God implicitly and unhesitatingly in every time of
danger, and you are safe. Set aside the counsels of
casuistry, of fear, and of worldly wisdom; find out
God's will and follow it through good report and
through evil report, and you will be right. It was thus
that Joshua and Caleb did, and counselled the people
to do, when they came back from exploring the land;
and now these two were reaping the benefit; while the
generation, that would have been comfortably settled
in the land if they had done the same, had perished in
the wilderness on account of their unbelief.

Secondly, a span of two thousand cubits was to be
left between the people and the ark. Some have thought
that this was designed as a token of reverence; but
this is not the reason assigned. Had it been designed
as a token of reverence, it would have been prescribed
long before, as soon as the ark was constructed, and
began to be carried with the host through the wilderness.
The intention was, "that ye may know the way by
which you must go" (ver. 4). If this arrangement had
not been made, the course of the ark through the flat
plains of the Jordan would not have been visible to the
mass of the host, but only to those in the immediate
neighbourhood, and the people would have been liable
to straggle and fall into confusion, if not to diverge
altogether. In all cases, when we are looking out for
Divine guidance, it is of supreme importance that there
be nothing in the way to obscure the object or to

distort our vision. Alas, how often is this direction disregarded! How often do we allow our prejudices, or our wishes, or our worldly interests to come between us and the Divine direction we profess to desire! At some turn of our life we feel that we ought not to take a decisive step without asking guidance from above. But our own wishes bear strongly in a particular direction, and we are only too prone to conclude that God is in favour of our plan. We do not act honestly; we lay stress on all that is in favour of what we like; we think little of considerations of the opposite kind. And when we announce our decision, if the matter concern others, we are at pains to tell them that we have made it matter of prayer. But why make it matter of prayer if we do so with prejudiced minds? It is only when our eye is single that the whole body is full of light. This clear space of two thousand cubits between the people and the ark deserves to be remembered. Let us have a like clear space morally between us and God when we go to ask His counsel, lest peradventure we not only mistake His directions, but bring disaster on ourselves and dishonour on His name.

Thirdly, the people were instructed,—" Sanctify yourselves, for to-morrow the Lord will do wonders among you." It is an instinct of our nature that when we are to meet with some one of superior worldly rank preparation must be made for the meeting. When Joseph was summoned into the presence of Pharaoh, and they brought him hastily out of the dungeon, "he shaved himself, and changed his raiment, and came in unto Pharaoh." The poorest subject of the realm would try to wear his best and to look his best in the presence of his sovereign. But while "man looketh on the outward appearance the Lord looketh on the heart."

And our very instincts teach us, that the heart needs to be prepared when God is drawing near. It is not in our ordinary careless mood that we ought to stand before Him who "sets our iniquities before Him, our secret sins in the light of His countenance." Grant that we can neither atone for our sin, nor cleanse our hearts without His grace; nevertheless, in God's presence everything that is possible ought to be done to remove the abominable thing which He hates, so that He may not be affronted and offended by its presence. Most appropriate, therefore, was Joshua's counsel,—" Sanctify yourselves, for to-morrow the Lord will do wonders among you." He will surpass all that your eyes have seen since that night, much to be remembered, when He divided the sea. He will give you a token of His love and care that will amaze you, much though you have seen of it in the wilderness, and in the country of Sihon and Og. Expect great things, prepare for great things; and let the chief of your preparations be to sanctify yourselves, for " the foolish shall not stand in His sight, and He hateth all workers of iniquity."

Next day (compare ver. 5, " to-morrow," and ver. 7, "this day ") Joshua turns to the priests and bids them "take up the ark of the covenant." The priests obey; " they take up the ark, and go before the people."

Shall we take notice of the assertion of some that all those parts of the narrative which refer to priests and religious service were introduced by a writer bent on glorifying the priesthood? Or must we repel the insinuation that the introduction of the ark, and the miraculous effects ascribed to its presence, are mere myths? If they are mere myths, they are certainly myths of a very peculiar kind. Twice only in this book is the ark associated with miraculous events—at the crossing of the Jordan and at the taking of Jericho. If these were myths, why was the myth confined to these two occasions? When mythical writers find a remarkable talisman they introduce it at all sorts of times. Why was the ark not brought to the siege of Ai? Why was it absent from the battles of Bethhoron and Merom? Why was its presence restricted to the Jordan and Jericho, unless it was God's purpose to inspire confidence at first through the visible symbol of His presence, but leave the people afterwards to infer His presence by faith?

The taking up of the ark by the priests was a decisive step. There could be no resiling now from the course entered on. The priests with the ark must advance, and it will be seen whether Joshua has been uttering words without foundation, or whether he has been speaking in the name of God. Shall mere natural forces be brought into play, or shall the supernatural might of heaven come to the conflict, and show that God is faithful to His promise?

Let us put ourselves in Joshua's position. We do not know in what manner the communications were carried on between him and Jehovah of which we have the record under the words "the Lord spake unto Joshua." Was it by an audible voice? Or was it by impressions on Joshua's mind of a kind that could not have originated with himself, but that were plainly the result of Divine influence? In any case, they were such as to convey to Joshua a very clear knowledge of the Divine will. Yet even in the best of men nature is not so thoroughly subdued in such circumstances but that the shadow of anxiety and fear is liable to flit across them. They crave something like a personal pledge that all will go well. Hence the seasonableness of the assurance now given to Joshua—" This day will I begin to magnify thee in the sight of all Israel, that they may know that, as I was with Moses, so I will be with thee." How full and manifold the assurance! First, I will magnify thee. I will endue thee with supernatural might, and that will give you authority and weight, corresponding to the position in which you stand. Further, this shall be but the beginning of a process which will be renewed as often as there is occasion for it. "This day I will *begin.*" You are not to go a warfare on your own charges, but "as your days, so shall your strength be." Moreover, this exaltation of your person and office will take place "in the sight of all Israel," so that no man of them shall ever be justified in refusing you allegiance and obedience. And to sum up—you shall be just as Moses was; the resources of My might will be as available for you as they were for him. After this, what misgivings could Joshua have? Could he doubt the generosity, the kindness, the considerateness of his Master? Here was a promise for life; and no doubt the more he put it to the test in after years the more trustworthy did he find it, and the more convincing was the proof it supplied of the mindfulness of God.

It is an experience which has been often repeated in the case of those who have had to undertake difficult work for their Master. Of all our misapprehensions, the most baseless and the most pernicious is, that God does not care much about us, and that we have not much to look for from Him. It is a misapprehension which dishonours God greatly, and which He is ever showing Himself most desirous to remove. It stands fearfully in the way of that spirit of trust by which God is so much honoured, and which He is ever desirous that we should show. And those who have trusted God, and have gone forward to their work in His strength, have always found delightful evidence that their trust has not been in vain. What is the testimony of our great Christian philanthropists, our most successful missionaries, and other devoted Christian workers? Led to undertake enterprises far beyond their strength, and undergo responsibilities far beyond their means, we know not a single case in which they have not had ample proof of the mindfulness of their Master, and found occasion to wonder at the considerateness and the bountifulness which He has brought to bear upon their position. And is it not strange that we should be so slow to learn how infinite God is in goodness? That we should have no difficulty in believing in the goodness of a parent or of some kind friend who has always been ready to help us in our times of need, but so slow to realize this in regard to God, though we are constantly acknowledging in words that He is the best as well as the greatest of beings? It is a happy era in one's spiritual history when one escapes from one's contracted views of the love and liberality of God, and begins to realize that " as far as heaven is above the earth, so far are His ways above our ways, and His thoughts above our thoughts "; and when one comes to find that in one's times of need, whether arising from one's personal condition or from the requirements of public service, one may go to God for encouragement and help with more certainty of being well received than one may go to the best and kindest of friends.

It is sometimes said that the Old Testament presents us with a somewhat limited view of God's love. Certainly it is in the New Testament that we see it placed in the brightest of all lights—the Cross, and that we find the argument in its most irresistible form—" He that spared not His own Son, but delivered Him up for us all, how shall He not, with Him also, freely give us all things ? " But one must have read the Old Testament in a very careless spirit if one has not been struck with its frequent and most impressive revelations of God's goodness. What scenes of gracious intercourse with His servants does it not present from first to last, what outpourings of affection, what yearnings of a father's heart I If there were many in Old Testament times whom these revelations left as heedless as they found them, there were certainly some whom they filled with wonder and roused to words of glowing gratitude. The Bible is not wont to repeat the same thought in the same words. But there is one truth and one only which we find repeated again and again in the Old Testament, in the same words, as if the writers were never weary of them—" For His mercy endureth for ever." Not only is it the refrain of a whole psalm (cxxxvi.), but we find it at the beginning of three other psalms (cvi., cvii., cxviii.), we find it in David's song of dedication when the ark was brought up to Jerusalem (1 Chron. xvi. 34), and we find also that on the same occasion a body of men, Heman and Jeduthun and others, were told off expressly "to give thanks to the Lord, because His mercy endureth for ever " (1 Chron. xvi. 41). This, indeed, is the great truth which gives the Old Testament its highest interest and beauty. In the New Testament, in its evangelical setting, it shines with incomparable brightness. Vividly realized, it makes the Christian's cup to flow over ; as it fills him likewise with the hope of a joy to come—" a joy unspeakable and full of glory.'

CHAPTER IX.

JORDAN DIVIDED.

JOSHUA iii.

AT Joshua's command, the priests carrying the ark are again in motion. Bearing the sacred vessel on their shoulders, they make straight for the bank of the river. "The exact spot is unknown; it certainly cannot be that which the Greek tradition has fixed, where the eastern banks are sheer precipices of ten or fifteen feet high. Probably it was either immediately above or below, where the cliffs break away; above at the fords, or below where the river assumes a tamer character on its way to the Dead Sea."[1] Following the priests, at the interval of a full half-mile, was the host of Israel. "*There* was the mailed warrior with sword and shield, and the aged patriarch, trembling on his staff. Anxious mothers and timid maidens were there, and helpless infants of a day old; and there, too, were flocks and herds and all the possessions of a great nation migrating westward in search of a home. Before them lay their promised inheritance,

> 'While Jordan rolled between,'

full to the brim, and overflowing all its banks. Nevertheless, through it lies their road, and God commands the march. The priests take up the sacred ark and

---

[1] Stanley's "Sinai and Palestine," p. 303.

bear it boldly down to the brink ; when lo! 'the waters which came down from above stood and rose up upon a heap very far from the city Adam, that is before Zaretan: and those that came down toward the sea of the plain, even the Salt Sea, failed, and were cut off: and the people passed over right against Jericho.' And thus, too, has all-conquering faith carried the thousand times ten thousand of God's people in triumph through the Jordan of death to the Canaan of eternal rest."[1]

The description of the parting of the waters is clear enough in the main, though somewhat obscure in detail. The obscurity arises from the meaningless expression in the Authorized Version, "very far from the city Adam, which is beside Zaretan." The Revised rendering gives a much more natural meaning—"rose up in one heap, very far off, at Adam, the city that is beside Zarethan." The names Adam and Zaretan occur nowhere else in Scripture, nor are they mentioned by Josephus; some think we have a relic of Adam in the first part of ed-Damieh, the name of a ford, and others, following the rendering of the Septuagint, which has ἕως μέρους Καριαθιαρίμ, consider the final "arim" to be equivalent to "adim" or "adam," the Hebrew letter "r" being almost the same as "d." What we are taught is, that the waters were cut off from the descending river a long way up, while down below the whole channel was laid bare as far as the Dead Sea. The miracle involved an accumulation of water in the upper reaches of the river, and as it was obviously undesirable that this should continue for a long time, enough of the channel was laid bare to enable the great host to cross rapidly in a broad belt, and without excitement or con-

---

[1] "Land and Book," vol. ii., pp. 460-61.

fusion. The sceptical objection is completely obviated that it was physically impossible for so vast a host to make the passage in a short time.

As soon as the waters began to retreat, after the feet of the priests were planted in them, the priests passed on to the middle of the channel, and stood there "firm, on dry ground," until all the people were passed clean over. The vast host crossed at once, and drew up on the opposite bank. That no attempt was made by the men of Jericho, which was only about five miles off, to attack them and stop their passage, can be explained only on the supposition that they were stricken with panic. One inhabitant undoubtedly heard of the passage without surprise. Rahab could feel no astonishment that the arm of God should thus be made bare before the people whom He was pledged to protect and guide. As little could she wonder at the paralysis which had petrified her own people.

The priests passed on before the people, and stood firm in the midst of the river until the whole host had passed. It was both a becoming thing that they should go before, and that they should stand so firm. It is not always that either priests or Christian ministers have set the example of going before in any hazardous undertaking. They have not always moved so steadily in the van of great movements, nor stood so firmly in the midst of the river. What shall we say of those whose idea, whether of Hebrew priesthood or of Christian ministry, has been that of a mere office, that of men ordained to perform certain mechanical functions, in whom personal character and personal example signified little or nothing? Is it not infinitely nearer to the Bible view that the ministers of religion are the leaders of the people, and that they ought as such to be ever foremost in zeal, in holiness, in self-denial, in victory over the world, the flesh, and the devil? And of all men ought they not to stand firm? Where are Mr. Byends, and Mr. Facing-Both-Ways, and Mr. Worldly-Wiseman more out of place than in the ministry? Where does even the world look more for consistency and devotion and fearless regard to the will of God? What should we think of an army where the officers counted it enough to see to the drill and discipline of the men, and in the hour of battle confined themselves to mere mechanical duties, and were outstripped in self-denial, in courage, in dash and daring by the commonest of their soldiers? Happy the Church where the officers are officers indeed! Feeling ever that their place is in the front rank of the battle and in the vanguard of every perilous enterprise, and that it is their part to set the men an example of unwavering firmness even when the missiles of death are whistling or bursting on every side!

Who shall try to picture the feelings of the people during that memorable crossing? The outstretched arm of God was even more visibly shown than in the crossing of the Red Sea, for in that case a natural cause, the strong east wind, contributed something to the effect, while in this case no secondary cause was employed, the drying up of the channel being due solely to miracle. Who among all that host could fail to feel that God was with them? And how solemn yet cheering must the thought have been alike to the men of war looking forward to scenes of danger and death, and to the women and children, and the aged and infirm, dreading otherwise lest they should be trampled down amid the tumult! But of all whose hearts were moved by the marvellous transaction,

Joshua must have been pre-eminent. "As I was with Moses, so I will be with thee." At the dividing of the sea the leadership of Moses began, and they were all baptized unto him in the cloud and in the sea. And now, in like manner, the leadership of Joshua begins at the dividing of the river, and baptism unto Joshua takes the place of baptism unto Moses. A new chapter of an illustrious history begins as its predecessor had begun, but not to be marred and rendered abortive by unbelief and disobedience like the last. How true God has been to His word! What wonders He has done among the people! What honour He has put upon Joshua! How worthy He is to be praised! Will disloyalty to Him ever occur again, will this marvellous deed be forgotten, and the miserable gods of the heathen be preferred to Jehovah? Will any future prophet have cause to say, "O Ephraim, what shall I do unto thee? O Judah, what shall I do unto thee? For your goodness is as a morning cloud, and as the early dew, it goeth away"?

It is to be especially remarked that God took into His own hands the prescription of the method by which this great event was to be commemorated. It seems as if He could not trust the people to do it in a way that would be free from objection and from evil tendency. It was assumed that the event was worthy of special commemoration. True, indeed, there had been no special commemoration of the passage of the sea, but then the Passover was instituted so near to that event that it might serve as a memorial of it as well as of the protection of the Israelites when the firstborn of the Egyptians was slain. And generally the people had been taught, what their own hearts in some degree recognised, that great mercies should be specially commemorated. The Divine method of commemorating the drying up of the Jordan was a very simple one. In the first place, twelve men were selected, one from every tribe, to do the prescribed work. The democratic constitution of the nation was recognised—each tribe was to take part in it; and as it was a matter in which all were concerned, each person was to take part in the election of the representative of his tribe. Then each of these twelve representatives was to take from the bed of the river, from the place where the priests had stood with the ark, a stone, probably as large as he could carry. The twelve stones were to be carried to the place where the host lodged that night, and to be erected as a standing memorial of the miracle. It was a very simple memorial, but it was all that was needed. It was not like the proud temples or glorious pyramids of Egypt, reared as these were to give glory to man more than to God. It was like Jacob's pillar before, or Samuel's Ebenezer afterwards; void of every ornament or marking that could magnify man, and designed for one single purpose—to recall the goodness of God.

It would appear, from chap. iv. 9, that two sets of stones were set up, Joshua, following the spirit of the Divine direction, having caused a second set to be erected in the middle of the river on the spot where the priests had stood. Some have supposed that that verse is an interpolation of later date; but, as it occurs in all the manuscripts, and as it is expressly stated in the Septuagint and Vulgate versions that this was a different transaction from the other, we must accept it as such. The one memorial stood on the spot where the ark had indicated the presence of God, the other where the first encampment of the host had shown God's faithfulness to His word. Both seemed to proclaim the great truth afterwards brought out in the exquisite words of the psalm—" God is our refuge and our strength ; a very present help in time of trouble." They might not be needed so much for the generation that experienced the deliverance ; but in future generations they would excite the curiosity of the children, and thus afford an opportunity to the parents to rehearse the transactions of that day, and thrill their hearts with the sense of God's mercy.

Among devout Israelites, that day was never forgotten. The crossing of the Jordan was coupled with the crossing of the sea, as the two crowning tokens of God's mercy in the history of Israel, and the most remarkable exhibitions of that Divine power which had been so often shown among them. In that wailing song, the seventy-fourth psalm, where God's wonderful works of old are contrasted in a very sad spirit with the unmitigated desolations that met the writer's eye, almost in the same breath in which he extols the miracle of the sea, " Thou didst divide the sea by Thy strength," he gives thanks for the miracle of the river, " Thou didst cleave the fountain and the flood : Thou driedst up mighty rivers." And in a song, not of wailing, but of triumph, the hundred and fourteenth psalm, we have the same combination :—

> "When Israel went forth out of Egypt,
> The house of Jacob from a people of strange language;
> Judah became His sanctuary
> Israel His dominion.
> The sea saw it, and fled ;
> Jordan was driven back.
> The mountains skipped like rams,
> The little hills like lambs.
> What aileth thee, O thou sea, that thou fleest ?
> Thou Jordan, that thou turnest back ?

> Ye mountains, that ye skip like rams;
> Ye little hills like lambs?
> Tremble, thou earth, at the presence of the Lord,
> At the presence of the God of Jacob;
> Which turned the rock into a pool of water,
> The flint into a fountain of waters."

The point of this psalm lies in the first verse—in the reference to the time " when Israel came out of Egypt, the house of Jacob from a people of strange language." Israel on that occasion gave a signal proof of his trust in God. At God's bidding, and with none but God to trust in, he turned his back on Egypt, and made for the wilderness. It was a delight to God to receive this mark of trust and obedience, and in recognition of it the mightiest masses and forces of nature were moved or arrested. The mountains and hills skipped like living creatures, and the sea saw it and fled. It seemed as if God could not do too much for His people. It was the same spirit that was shown when they followed Joshua to the river. They showed that they trusted God. They renounced the visible and the tangible for the invisible and the spiritual. They rose up at Joshua's command, or rather at the command of God by Joshua; and, pleased with this mark of trust, God caused the waters of the Jordan to part asunder. Surely there is something pathetic in this; the Almighty is so pleased when His children trust Him, that to serve them the strongest forces are moved about as if they were but feathers.

In many ways the truth has been exemplified in later times. When a young convert, at home or abroad, takes up decided ground for Christ, coming out from the world and becoming separate, very blessed tokens of God's nearness and of God's interest are usually given him. And Churches that at the call of Christ surrender their worldly advantages, receive tokens of spiritual blessing that infinitely outweigh in sweetness and in spiritual value all that they lose. "Them that honour Me, I will honour."

Occurrences of more recent times show clearly that God did well in taking into His own hands the prescription of the way in which the crossing of the Jordan was to be commemorated. Tradition has it that it was at the same place where Joshua crossed that Jesus was baptized by John. That may well be doubted, for the Bethabara where John was baptizing was probably at a higher point of the river. But it is quite possible that it was at this spot that Elijah's mantle smote the river, and he and his servant passed over on dry ground. Holding that all these events occurred at the same place, tradition has called in the aid of superstition, and given a sacred character to the waters of the river at this spot. Many have seen, and every one has read of the pilgrimage to the Jordan, performed every spring, from which many hope to reap such advantage. "In the mosaics of the earliest churches at Rome and Ravenna," says Dean Stanley, "before Christian and pagan art were yet divided, the Jordan appears as a river god pouring his streams out of his urn. The first Christian emperor had always hoped to receive his long-deferred baptism in the Jordan, up to the moment when the hand of death struck him at Nicomedia. . . . Protestants, as well as Greeks and Latins, have delighted to carry off its waters for the same sacred purpose to the remotest regions of the West."

No doubt the expectation of spiritual benefit from the waters of the Jordan is one cause of the annual pilgrimage thither, and of the strange scene that presents itself when the pilgrims are bathing. It seems impossible for man, except under the influence of the strongest spiritual views, to avoid the belief that somehow mechanical means may give rise to spiritual results. There is nothing from which he is naturally more averse than spiritual activity. Any amount of mechanical service he will often render to save him from spiritual exercise. Symbols without number he will willingly provide, if he thereby escape the necessity of going into the immediate presence of God, and worshipping Him who is a Spirit in spirit and in truth. But can mechanical service or material symbols be anything but an evil, if the would-be worshipper is thereby prevented from recognising the necessity of a heart-to-heart fellowship with the living God? Must we not be in living touch with God if the stream of Divine influence is to reach our hearts, and we are to be changed into His image? In the Psalms, which express the very essence of Hebrew devotion, spiritual contact with God is the only source of blessing. "O God, Thou art my God; early will I seek Thee: my soul thirsteth for Thee, my flesh longeth for Thee in a dry and thirsty land, where there is no water. To see Thy power and Thy glory, so as I have seen Thee in the sanctuary."

Thus it was that by God's prescription the twelve plain stones taken out of the Jordan were the only memorial of the great deliverance. There was no likeness on them of the Divine Being by whom the miracle had been performed. There was nothing to encourage acts of reverence or worship directed toward the memorial. Twelve rough stones, with no sculptured figures or symbols, not even dressed by hammer and chisel, but simply as they were taken out of the river, were the memorial. They were adapted for one purpose, and for one only: "When your children shall ask their fathers in time to come, saying, What mean these stones? then ye shall let your children know, saying, Israel came over this Jordan on dry land. For the Lord your God dried up the waters of the Jordan from before you, until ye were passed over, as the Lord your God did to the Red Sea, which He dried up from before us, until we were gone over: that all the people of the earth might know the hand of the Lord, that it is mighty: **that ye might fear the Lord your God for ever.**"

CHAPTER X.

CIRCUMCISION AND PASSOVER—MANNA AND CORN.

JOSHUA v. 1—12.

THE first two facts recorded in this chapter seem to be closely connected with each other. One is, that when all the Amorite and Canaanite kings on the west side of the Jordan heard of the miraculous drying up of the waters and the passage of the Israelites, "their heart melted, neither was there spirit in them any more." The other is, that the opportunity was taken then and there to circumcise the whole of the generation that had been born after leaving Egypt. But for the fact recorded in the first verse, it would have been the most unsuitable time that could be conceived for administering circumcision. The whole male population would have been rendered helpless for the time, and an invitation would have been given to the men of Jericho to commit such a massacre as in the like circumstances the sons of Jacob inflicted on the men of Shechem (Gen. xxxiv. 25). Why was not this business of circumcising performed while the host were lying inactive on the other side, and while the Jordan ran between Israel and his foes? It was because the kings of the Canaanites were petrified. It is true they plucked up courage by-and-by, and many of the kings entered into a league against Joshua. But this was after the affair of Ai, after the defeat of the Israelites before that city had showed that, as in the case of Achilles, there was a vulnerable spot somewhere, notwithstanding the protection of their God. Meanwhile the people of Jericho were paralysed, for though the whole male population of Israel under forty lay helpless in their tents, not a finger was raised by the enemy against them.

It is with no little surprise that we read that circumcision had been suspended during the long period of the wilderness sojourn. Why was this? Some have said that, owing to the circumstances in which the people were, it would not have been convenient, perhaps hardly possible, to administer the rite on the eighth day. Moving as they were from place to place, the administration of circumcision would often have caused so much pain and peril to the child, that it is no wonder it was delayed. And once delayed, it was delayed indefinitely. But this explanation is not sufficient. There were long, very long periods of rest, during which there could have been no difficulty. A better explanation, brought forward by Calvin, leads us to connect the suspension of circumcision with the punishment of the Israelites, and with the sentence that doomed them to wander forty years in the wilderness. When the worship of the golden calf took place, the nation was rejected, and the breaking by Moses of the two tables of stone seemed an appropriate sequel to the rupture of the covenant which their idolatry had caused. And though they were soon restored, they were not restored without certain drawbacks,—tokens of the Divine displeasure. Afterwards, at the great outburst of unbelief in connection with the report of the spies, the adult generation that had come out of Egypt were doomed to perish in the wilderness, and, with the exception of Joshua and Caleb, not one of them was permitted to enter the land of promise. Now, though it is not expressly stated, it seems probable that the suspension of circumcision was included in the punishment of their sins. They were not to be allowed to place on their children the sign and seal of a covenant which in spirit and in reality they had broken.

But it was not an abolition, but only a suspension of the sacrament for a time that took place. The time might come when it would be restored. The natural time for this would be the end of the forty years of chastisement. These forty years had now come to an end. Doubtless it would have been a great joy to Moses if it had been given him to see the restoration of circumcision, but that was not to take place until the people had set foot on Abraham's land. Now they have crossed the river. They have entered on the very land which God sware to Abraham and Isaac and Jacob to give it them. And the very first thing that is done after this is to give back to them the holy sign of the covenant, which was now administered to every man in the congregation who had not previously received it. We may well think of it as an occasion of great rejoicing. The visible token of his being one of God's children was now borne by every man and boy in the camp. In a sense they now served themselves heirs to the covenant made with their fathers, and might thus rest with firmer trust on the promise—" I will bless them that bless thee, and curse him that curseth thee."

Two other points in connection with this transaction demand a word of explanation. The first is the statement that "all the people that were born in the wilderness by the way as they came forth out of Egypt, them they had not circumcised" (ver. 5). If the view be correct that the suspension of circumcision was part of the punishment for their sins, the prohibition would not come into operation for some months, at all events, after the exodus from Egypt. We think, with Calvin, that for the sake of brevity the sacred historian makes a general statement without waiting to explain the exceptions to which it was subject. The other point needing explanation is the Lord's statement after the circumcision—" This day have I rolled the reproach of Egypt from off you. Wherefore the name of the place is called Gilgal (*i.e.*, Rolling) unto this day." How could the suspension of circumcision be called the reproach of Egypt? The words imply that, owing to the want of this sacrament, they had lain exposed to a reproach from the Egyptians, which was now rolled away. The brevity of the statement, and our ignorance of what the Egyptians were saying of the Israelites at the time, make the words difficult to understand. What seems most likely is, that when the Egyptians heard how God had all but repudiated them in the wilderness, and had withdrawn from them the sign of His covenant, they malignantly crowed over them, and denounced them as a worthless race, who had first rejected their lawful rulers in Egypt under pretext of religion, and, having shown their hypocrisy, were now scorned and cast off by the very God whom they had professed themselves so eager to serve. We may be sure that the Egyptians would not be slow to seize any pretext for denouncing the Israelites, and would be sure to make their jibes as sharp and as bitter as they could. But now the tables are turned on the Egyptians. The restoration of circumcision stamps this people once more as the people of God. The stupendous miracle just wrought in the dividing of the

Jordan indicates the kind of protection which their God and King is sure to extend to them. The name of Gilgal will be a perpetual testimony that the reproach of Egypt is rolled away.

Circumcision being now duly performed, the way was prepared for another holy rite for which the appointed season had arrived—the Passover. Some have supposed that the Passover as well as circumcision was suspended after the sentence of the forty years' wandering, the more especially that it was expressly enacted that no uncircumcised person was to eat the Passover. We know (Num. ix. 5) that the Passover was kept the second year after they left Egypt, but no other reference to it occurs in the history. On this, as on many other points connected with the wilderness history, we must be content to remain in ignorance. We are not even very sure how far the ordinary sacrifices were offered during that period. It is quite possible that the considerations that suspended the rite of circumcision applied to other ordinances. But whether or not the Passover was observed in the wilderness, we may easily understand that after being circumcised the people would observe it with a much happier and more satisfied feeling. There were many things to make this Passover memorable. The crossing of the Jordan was so like the crossing of the Red Sea that the celebration in Egypt could not fail to come back vividly to all the older people,—those that were under twenty at the exodus, to whom the sentence of exclusion from Canaan did not apply (Num. xiv. 29). Many of these must have looked on while their fathers sprinkled the lintels and door posts with the blood of the lamb, and must have listened to the awful death-cry of the firstborn of the Egyptians. They must have remembered well that memorable midnight when all were in such excitement marching away from Egypt; and not less vividly must they have remembered the terror that seized them when the Egyptian host was seen in pursuit; and then again the thrill of triumph with which they passed between the crystal walls, under the glow of the fiery pillar; and once more the triumphant notes of Miriam's timbrel and the voices of the women, "Sing unto the Lord, for He hath triumphed gloriously; the horse and his rider He hath cast into the sea." And now these days of glory were coming back! As surely as the passage of the sea had been followed by the destruction of the Egyptians, so surely would the passage of the Jordan be followed by the destruction of the Canaanites. Glorious things were spoken of the city of their God. The benediction of Moses was about to receive a new fulfilment—" Happy art thou, O Israel : who is like unto thee, O people saved by the Lord, the shield of thy help, and who is the sword of thy excellency! and thine enemies shall be found liars unto thee; and thou shalt tread upon their high places."

The remembrance of the past is often an excellent preparation for the trials of the future, and as often it proves a remarkable support under them. It was the very nature of the Passover to look back to the past, and to recall God's first great interposition on behalf of His people. It was a precious encouragement both to faith and hope. So also is our Christian Passover. It is a connecting link between the first and second comings of our Lord. The first coming lends support to faith, the second to hope. No exercise of soul can be more profitable than to go back to that memorable day when Christ our Passover was sacrificed for us. For then the price of redemption was paid in full, and the door of salvation flung wide open. Then the Son sealed His love by giving Himself to the cross for us. What blessing, whether for this life or the life to come, was not purchased by that transaction? Life may be dark and stormy, but hope foresees a bright to-morrow. "When Christ, who is our life, shall appear, then shall ye also appear with Him in glory."

Yet another incident is connected with this transition period of the history. "They did eat of the old corn of the land on the morrow after the passover, unleavened cakes, and parched corn in the selfsame day. And the manna ceased on the morrow after they had eaten of the old corn of the land; neither had the children of Israel manna any more; but they did eat of the fruit of the land of Canaan that year." It is not necessary to suppose that they did not partake at all of the fruits of the land till the morning after that Passover. The conquest of Sihon and Og must have put a large share of produce in their hands, and we can hardly suppose that they did not make some use of it. The narrative is so brief that it does not undertake to state every modification that may be applicable to its general statements. The main thing to be noticed is, that while the manna continued to descend, it was the staple article of food; but when the manna was withdrawn, the old corn and other fruits of the country took its place. In other words, the miracle was not continued when it ceased to be necessary. The manna had been a provision for the wilderness, where ordinary food in sufficient quantity could not be obtained; but now that they were in a land of fields and orchards and vineyards the manna was withdrawn.

We have already adverted to the Bible law of the supernatural. No sanction is given to the idea of a lavish and needless expenditure of supernatural power. A law of economy, we might almost say parsimony, prevails, side by side with the exercise of unbounded liberality. Jesus multiplies the loaves and fishes to feed the multitude, but He will not let one fragment be lost that remains after the feast. A similar law guides the economy of prayer. We have no right to ask that mercies may come to us through extraordinary channels, when it is in our power to get them by ordinary means. If it is in our power to procure bread by our labour, we dare not ask it to be sent direct. We are only too prone to make prayer at the eleventh hour an excuse for want of diligence or want of courage in what bears on the prosperity of the spiritual life. It may be that of His great generosity God sometimes blesses us, even though we have made a very inadequate use of the ordinary means. But on that we have no right to presume. We are fond of short and easy methods where the natural method would be long and laborious. But here certainly we find the working of natural law in the spiritual world. We cannot look for God's blessing without diligent use of God's appointed means.

More generally, this occurrence in the history of Israel, the cessation of one provision when another comes into operation, exemplifies a great law in providence by which the loss of one kind of advantage is compensated by the advent of another. In childhood and early youth we depend for our growth in knowledge on the instructions of our teachers. What puzzles us we refer to them, and they guide us through the difficulty. If they are wise teachers they will not tell us everything, but they will put us on the right method to find out. Still they are there as a court of appeal, so to speak, and we have always the satisfaction of a last resort. But the time comes when we bid farewell to teachers. Happily it is the time when the judgment becomes self-reliant, independent, penetrating. We are thrown mainly upon our own resources. And the very fact of our having to depend on our own judgment fosters and promotes independence, and fits us better for the responsibilities of life. When we become men we put away childish things. A habit of leaning on others keeps us children; but grappling with difficulties as we find them, and trying to make our way through them and over them, promotes manliness. The manna ceases, and we eat the fruit of the land.

So in family life. The affection that binds parents and children, brothers and sisters to one another in the family is both beautiful and delightful; and it were no wonder if, on the part of some, there were the desire that their intercourse should suffer no rude break, but go on unchanged for an indefinite time. But it is seldom God's will that family life shall remain unbroken. Often the interruption comes in the rudest and most terrible form—by the death of the head of the house. And the circumstances of the family may require that all who are capable of earning anything shall turn out to increase the family store. It is often a painful and distressing change. But at least it wakens up all who can do anything, it rescues them from the temptation of a slumbering, aimless life, and often draws out useful gifts that turn their lives into a real blessing. And there are other compensations. When Sarah died, Isaac was left with an empty heart; but when Rebecca came to him, he was comforted. The precise blank that death leaves may never be wholly filled, but the heart expands in other directions, and with new objects of affection the gnawing void ceases to be acutely felt. As old attachments are snapped, new are gradually formed. And even in old age a law of compensation often comes in; children and children's children bring new interests and pleasures, and the green hues of youth modify the grey of age.

Then there is the happy experience by which the advent of spiritual blessings compensates the loss of temporal. Nothing at first appears more desolate than loss of fortune, loss of health, or loss of some principal bodily sense—like sight or hearing. But in a Milton intellectual vigour, patriotic ardour, and poetic sensibility attain their noblest elevation, though

> "Cloud and ever-during dark
> Surrounds me, from the cheerful ways of men
> Cut off, and, for the book of knowledge fair,
> Presented with a universal blank
> Of nature's works, to me expunged and rased,
> And wisdom at one entrance quite shut out."

It is the total loss of hearing, the result of a sudden accident, that turns the slater, John Kitto, into a most instructive and interesting Oriental scholar and writer. How often temporal loss has proved in a higher sense spiritual gain, all Christian biography testifies. Such instances are not uncommon as that which the Rev. Charles Simeon gives, in speaking of some blind men from Edinburgh whom nearly a century ago he found at work in a country house in Scotland: "One of the blind men, on being interrogated with respect to his knowledge of spiritual things, answered, 'I never saw till I was blind; nor did I ever know contentment while I had my eyesight, as I do now that I have lost it; I can truly affirm, though few know how to credit me, that I would on no account change my present situation and circumstances with any that I ever enjoyed before I was blind.' He had enjoyed eyesight till twenty-five, and had been blind now about three years."[1]

Lastly, of all exchanges in room of old provisions the most striking is that which our Lord thus set forth : "It is expedient for you that I go away : for if I go not away, the Comforter will not come unto you ; but if I depart, I will send Him to you." If we should think of life, even the Christian life, as a mere time of enjoyment, albeit spiritual enjoyment, no statement could be more paradoxical or unpalatable. It is because life is a training school, and because what we most need in that school is the immediate action of the Divine Spirit on our spirits, purifying, elevating, strengthening, guiding all that is deepest in our nature, that our Lord's words are true. Very precious had been the manna that ceased when Jesus left. But more nourishing is the new corn with which the Spirit feeds us. Let us prize it greatly so long as we are in the flesh. We shall know the good of it when we enter on the next stage of our being. Then, in the fullest sense, the manna will cease, and we shall eat the corn of the land.

---

[1] "Life of Rev. Charles Simeon," p. 125.

CHAPTER XI.

THE CAPTAIN OF THE LORD'S HOST.

JOSHUA v. 13—15, vi. 1.

THE process of circumcision is over, and the men are well; the feast of unleavened bread has come to an end; all honour has been paid to these sacred ordinances according to the appointment of God; the manna has ceased, and the people are now depending on the corn of the land, of which, in all probability, they have but a limited supply. Everything points to the necessity of further action, but it is hard to say what the next step is to be. Naturally it would be the capture of Jericho. But this appears a Quixotic enterprise. The city is surrounded by a wall, and its gates are " straitly shut up," barred, and closely guarded to prevent the entrance of a single Israelite. Joshua himself is at a loss. No Divine communication has yet come to him, like that which came as to the crossing of the Jordan. See him walking all alone " by Jericho," as near the city as it is safe for him to go. With mind absorbed in thought and eyes fixed on the ground, he is pondering the situation, but unable to get light upon it, when something comes athwart his sphere of vision. He lifts his eyes, and right against him perceives a soldier, brandishing his sword.

A less courageous man would have been startled,

perhaps frightened. His first thought is, that it is an enemy. None of his own soldiers would have ventured there without his orders, or would have dared to take up such an attitude towards his commander-in-chief. With a soldier's presence of mind, instead of moving off, he assumes an aggressive attitude, challenges this warrior, and demands whether he is friend or foe. If friend, he must explain his presence; if foe, prepare for battle. Joshua is himself a thorough soldier, and will allow no one to occupy an ambiguous position. "And Joshua went unto him, and said unto him, Art thou for us, or for our adversaries?"

If the appearance of the soldier was a surprise, his answer to the question must have been a greater. "Nay; but as Captain of the host of the Lord am I now come." The "nay" deprecates his being either friend or foe in the common sense, but especially his being foe. His position and his office are far more exalted. As Captain of the host of the Lord, he is at the head, not of human armies, but of all the principalities and powers of heavenly places,—

> "The mighty regencies
> Of seraphim, and potentates and thrones."

And now the real situation flashes on Joshua. This soldier is no other than the Angel of the Covenant, the same who came to Abraham under the oak at Mamre, and that wrestled with Jacob on the banks of this very Jordan at Peniel. Joshua could not but remember, when God threatened to withdraw from Israel after the sin of the golden calf, and send some created angel to guide them through the wilderness, how earnestly Moses remonstrated, and how his whole soul was thrown into the pleading—" If Thy presence go not with us, carry me not up hence." He could not but remember the intense joy of Moses when this pleading proved successful—" My presence shall go with thee, and I will give thee rest." There could be little doubt in his mind who this " Captain of the host of Jehovah " was, and no hesitation on his part in yielding to Him the Divine honour due to the Most High. And then he must have felt warmly how very kind and seasonable this appearance was, just at the very moment when he was in so great perplexity, and when his path was utterly dark. It was a new proof that man's extremity is God's opportunity. It was just like what used to happen afterwards, when "the Word became flesh and dwelt among us," and was so promptly at hand for His disciples in all times of their tribulation. It was an anticipation of the scene when the ship was tossed so violently on the waves, and Jesus appeared with His " Peace, be still." Or, on that dreary morning, soon after the crucifixion, after they had spent the whole night on the lake and caught nothing, when Jesus came and brought the miraculous draught of fishes to their nets. It is the truth with which all His suffering and stricken children have been made so familiar in all ages of the Church's history :—that, however He may seem to hide Himself and stand afar off in times of trouble, He is in reality ever near, and can never forget that last assurance to His faithful people—" Lo, I am with you alway, even to the end of the world."

It is not likely that Joshua found any cause to discuss the question that modern criticism has so earnestly handled, whether this being that now appeared in human form really was Jehovah. And as little does it seem necessary for us to discuss it. There seems no good reason to reject the view that these theophanies, though not incarnations, were yet foreshadows of the incarnation,—hints of the mystery afterwards to be realized when Jesus was born of Mary. If these appearances looked like incarnations, it was incarnation after the pagan, not the Christian type; momentary alliances of the Divine being with the human form or appearance, assumed merely for the occasion, and capable of being thrown aside as rapidly as they were assumed. This might do very well to foreshadow the incarnation, but it fell a long way short of the incarnation itself. The Christian incarnation was after a type never dreamt of by the pagan mind. That the Son of God should be born of a woman, His body formed in the womb by the slow but wonderful process which "fashioned all His members in continuance, when as yet there was none of them" (Psalm cxxxix. 16), and that He should thus stand in relations to His fellow-men that could not be obliterated, was very wonderful; but most wonderful of all that the manhood once assumed could never be thrown off, but that the Son of God must continue to be the Son of man, in two distinct natures and one person for ever. The fact that all this has taken place is well fitted to give us unshaken confidence in the love and sympathy of our Elder Brother. For He is as really our Brother as He ever was in the days of His flesh, and as full of the care and thoughtful interest that the kindest of elder brothers takes in the sorrows and struggles of his younger brethren.

It has often been remarked as an instructive circumstance, that now, as on other occasions, the Angel of the Lord appeared in the character most adapted to the circumstances of His people. He appeared as a soldier with a drawn sword in His hand. A long course of fighting lay before the Israelites ere they could get possession of their land, and the sword in the hand of the Angel was an assurance that He would fight with them and for them. It was also a clear intimation that in the judgment of God, it was necessary to use the sword. But it was not the sword of the ambitious warrior who falls upon men simply because they are in his way, or because he covets their territories for his country. It was the judicial sword, demanding the death of men who had been tried for their sins, long warned, and at last judicially condemned. The iniquity of the Amorites was now full. We know what kind the people were who dwelt near Jericho four or five hundred years before, while the cities of Sodom and Gomorrah stood in the plain, cities that even then were reeking with the foulest corruption. It is true the judgment of God came down on these cities, but bare judgments have never reformed the world. The destruction of Sodom and Gomorrah removed the foulest stain-spot for the time, but it did not change the hearts nor the habits of the nations. It has seemed good to the Spirit of God to give us one glimpse of the foulness that had been reached at that early period, but not to multiply the filthy details at a future time,— after the long interval between Abraham and Joshua. But we know that if Sodom was bad, Jericho was no better. The country as a whole, which had now filled up its cup of iniquity, was no better. No wonder that the Angel bore a drawn sword in His hand. The long-suffering of the righteous God was exhausted, and Joshua and his people were the instruments by whom the judicial punishment was to be inflicted. The Captain of the Lord's host had drawn His sword from its scabbard to show that the judgment of that wicked people was to slumber no more.

It was not in this spirit nor in this attitude that the Angel of the Covenant had met with Jacob, centuries before, a little higher up the river, at the confluence of the Jabbok. Yet there was not a little that was similar in the two meetings. Like Joshua now, Jacob was then about to enter the land of promise. Like him, he was confronted by an enemy in possession, who, in Jacob's case, was bent on avenging the wrong of his youth. How that enemy was to be overcome Jacob knew not, just as Joshua knew not how Jericho was to be taken. But there was this difference between the two, that in Jacob's case the Angel dealt with him as an opponent; in Joshua's He avowed Himself a friend. The difference was no doubt due to the different dispositions of the two men. Jacob does not seem to have felt that it was only in God's name, and in God's strength, and under God's protection that he could enter Canaan; he appears to have been trusting too much to his own devices,— especially to the munificent present which he had forwarded to his brother. He must be taught the lesson "Not by might, nor by power, but by My Spirit, saith the Lord." At first Jacob dealt with his opponent simply as an obstructionist; then he discovered His Divine rank, and immediately he became the aggressor, and, spite of his dislocated thigh, held on to his opponent, declaring that he would not let Him go except He blessed him. It is otherwise with Joshua. He has no personal matter to settle with God before he is ready to advance into the land. He is in perplexity, and the Angel comes to relieve him. It is neither for reproof nor correction but simply for blessing that He is there.

The appearance of the Angel denoted a special method of communication with Joshua. We have already remarked that we do not know in what manner God's communications to His servant were made before. This incident shows that the ordinary method was not that of personal intercourse,—probably it was that of impressions made supernaturally on Joshua's mind. Why, then, is the method changed now? Why does this Warrior-angel present Himself in person? Probably because the way in which Jericho was to be taken was so extraordinary that, to encourage the faith of Joshua and the people, a special mode of announcement had to be used. One might have thought this unnecessary after the display of Divine power at the crossing of the Jordan. But steadiness of faith was no characteristic of the Israelites, and such as it was it was as liable to fail after crossing the Jordan as it had been after crossing the sea. Special means were taken to invigorate it and fit it for the coming strain. It was one of those rare occasions when a personal visit from the Angel of the Covenant was desirable. Something visible and tangible was needed, something which might be spoken of and readily understood by the people, and which could not possibly be gainsayed.

The moment that Joshua understood with whom he was conversing, he fell on his face, and offered to his visitor not only obeisance but worship, which the visitor did not decline. And then came a question indicating profound regard for his Lord's will, and readiness to do whatsoever he might be told—"What saith my Lord unto His servant?" It cannot but remind us of the question put by Saul to the Lord while yet lying on the ground on the way to Damascus—"Lord, what wilt Thou have me to do?" Joshua compares favourably with Moses at the burning bush, not only now, but throughout the whole interview. No word of remonstrance does he utter, no token of unwillingness or unbelief does he show. And it cannot be said that the instructions which the Angel gave him respecting the taking of Jericho were of a kind to be easily accepted. The course to be followed seemed to human wisdom the very essence of silliness. To all appearance there was not a vestige of adaptation of means to the end. Yet so admirable is the temper of Joshua, that he receives all with absolute and perfect submission. The question "What saith my Lord unto His servant?" is very far from mere matter of courtesy. It is a first principle with Joshua that when the mind of God is once indicated there is nothing for him but to obey. What is he that he should dare to criticise the plans of omnipotence? that he should propose to correct and improve the methods of Divine wisdom? Anything of the kind was alike preposterous and irreverent. "Let all the earth fear the Lord; let all the inhabitants of the world stand in awe of Him. For He spake, and it was done; He commanded, and it stood fast." "Thus saith the high and lofty One that inhabiteth eternity, and whose name is Holy: I dwell in the high and holy place, and with him also who is of a humble and contrite spirit, and who trembleth at My word."

The first answer to the question "What saith my Lord unto His servant?" is somewhat remarkable. "Put off thy shoes from off thy feet, for the place whereon thou standest is holy." Rationalists have explained this as meaning that this was an ancient shrine of the Canaanites, and therefore a place holy in the eyes of Israel; but such an idea needs no refutation. Others conceive it to mean that Joshua, having crossed the Jordan, had now set foot on the land promised to the fathers, and that the soil for that reason was called holy. But if that was the reason for his putting off his shoes, it is difficult to see how he could ever have been justified in again putting them on. And when God called to Moses out of the bush and bade him do the very same thing, it surely was not because the peninsula of Sinai was holy; it was because Moses stood in the immediate presence of the holy God. And it is simply to remind Joshua of the Divine presence that this command is given; and being given it is no sooner uttered than obeyed.

And then follow God's instructions for the taking of Jericho. Never was such a method propounded to reasonable man, or one more open to the objections and exceptions of worldly wisdom. No arrangement of his forces could have been more open to objection than that which God required of him. He was to march round Jericho once a day for six successive days, and seven times on the seventh day, the priests carrying the ark and blowing with trumpets, the men of war going before, and others following the ark, making a long narrow line round the place. We know that the city was provided with gates, like other fortified cities. What was there to prevent the men of Jericho from sallying out at each of the gates, breaking up the line of Israel into sections, separating them from each other, and inflicting dreadful slaughter on each? Such a march round the city seems to be the very way to invite a murderous attack. But it is the Divine command. And this process of surrounding the city is to be carried on in absolute silence on the part of the people, with no noise save the sounding of trumpets until a signal is given; then a great shout is to be raised, and the walls of Jericho are to fall down flat on the ground. Who would have thought it strange if Joshua had been somewhat staggered by so singular directions, and if, like Moses at the bush, he had suggested all manner of objections, and shown the greatest unwillingness to undertake the operation? The noble quality of his faith is shown in his raising no objection at all. After God has thus answered his question, " What saith my Lord unto His servant ? " he is just as docile and submissive as he was before. True faith is blind to everything except the Divine command. When God has given him his orders, he simply communicates them to the priests and to the people. He leaves the further development of the plan in God's hands, assured that He will not leave His purpose unfulfilled.

Nor do the priests or the people appear to have made any objection on their part. The plan no doubt exposed them to two things which men do not like, ridicule and danger. Possibly the ridicule was as hard to bear as the danger. God would protect them from the danger, but who would shield them from the ridicule? Even if at the end of the seven days, the promised result should take place, would it not be hard to make themselves for a whole week the sport of the men of Jericho, who would ask all that time whether they had lost their senses, whether they imagined that they would terrify them into surrender by the sound of their rams' horns? How often, especially in the case of young persons, do we find this dread of ridicule the greatest obstacle to Christian loyalty? And even where they have the strongest conviction that ere long the laugh, if laughter may be spoken of in the case, will be turned against their tormentors, and that it will be clearly seen who the men are whom the King delighteth to honour, what misery is caused for the time by ridicule, and how often do the young prove traitors to Christ rather than endure it? All the more remarkable is the steadiness of the priests and people on this occasion. We cannot think that this was due simply and solely to their loyalty to the leader to whom they had recently sworn allegiance. We cannot but believe that personal faith animated many of them, the same faith as that of Joshua himself. Their wilderness training and trials had not been in vain; the manifest interposition of God in the defeat of Sihon and Og had sunk into their hearts; the miraculous passage of the river had brought God very near to them; and it was doubtless in a large measure their conviction that He who had begun the work of conquest for them would carry it on to the end, that procured for Joshua's announcement the unanimous acquiescence and hearty support alike of priests and people.

And hence, too, the reason why, in the eleventh chapter of Hebrews, the falling down of the walls of Jericho is specially accounted for as the result of faith : " By faith the walls of Jericho fell down, after they were compassed about seven days " (ver. 30). The act of faith lay in the conviction that God, who had prescribed the method of attack, foolish though it seemed, would infallibly bring it to a successful issue. It was not merely Joshua's faith, but the priests' faith, and the people's faith, that shone in the transaction. Faith repelled the idea that the enemy would sally forth and break their ranks; it triumphed over the scorn and ridicule which would certainly be poured on them; it knew that God had given the directions, and it was convinced that He would bring all to a triumphant issue. Never had the spiritual thermometer risen so high in Israel, and seldom did it rise so high at any future period of their history. That singular week, spent in marching round Jericho again and again and again, was one of the most remarkable ever known; the people were near heaven, and the grace and peace of heaven seem to have rested on their hearts.

We sometimes speak of "ages of faith." There have been times when the disposition to believe in the unseen, in the presence and power of God, and in the certain success at last of all that is done in obedience to His will, has dominated whole communities, and led to a wonderful measure of holy obedience. Such a period was this age of Joshua. We cannot say, thinking of ourselves, that the present is an age of faith. Rather, on the part of the masses, it is an age when the secular, the visible, the present lords it over men's minds. Yet we are not left without splendid examples of faith. The missionary enterprise that contemplates the conquest of the whole world for Christ, because God has given to His Messiah the heathen for His inheritance and the uttermost part of the earth for His possession, and that looks forward to the day when this promise shall be fulfilled to the letter, is a fruit of faith. And the ready surrender of so many young lives for the world's evangelization, as missionaries, and teachers, and medical men and women, is a crowning proof that faith is not dead among us. Would only it were a faith that pervaded the whole community,—princes, priests, and people alike; and that there were a harmony among us in the attack on the strongholds of sin and Satan as great as there was in the host of Israel when the people, one in heart and one in hope, marched out, day after day, round the walls of Jericho!

CHAPTER XII.

THE FATE OF JERICHO.

Joshua vi. 8—27.

THE instructions of Joshua to the priests and the people are promptly obeyed. In the bright rays of the morning sun, on the day when Jericho is to be surrounded, the plain between the Jordan and Jericho, a space of some five miles, may be seen dotted over with the tents of Israel, arranged in that orderly manner which had been prescribed by Moses in the wilderness. The whole encampment is astir in the prospect of great events. The erect carriage, the flashing eye, the compressed lip of the soldiers show that something great and unusual is expected. By-and-by, there is a stir near the spot where the ark rests, and, borne on the shoulders of the priests, the sacred vessel is seen in motion in the direction of Jericho. Right in front of it are seven priests carrying trumpets of rams' horns, or, as some render it, jubilee horns. The procession of the ark halts a little, till a body of armed men advance and form in front of it. Others of the people take up their places in the rear. The seven priests sound their trumpets, and the procession moves on. Their course is round the walls of Jericho, far enough removed to be beyond the reach of the arrows of its defenders. Not a shout is raised. Not a sound is heard, save that of the trumpets of the seven priests.

At last the procession returns to the camp, leaving Jericho just as it found it. Next day the same process is repeated; and the next, and the next, on to the sixth. On the seventh day, the march begins early and is continued late. The spirits of the people are sustained during their weary, monotonous tramp by the expectation of a crisis. At length, when the seventh circuit has been made, the signal is given by Joshua. The air is rent with the shouts of the people and the noise of the trumpets, and immediately, all round, the wall falls flat to the ground, and the people march straight into the city. Paralysed with astonishment and terror, the inhabitants are unable to resist, and lie, men, women and children, at the mercy of their assailants. And the instructions to the Israelites are to destroy everything that is in the city, both man and woman, young and old, ox and sheep and ass, with the edge of the sword. As for the more solid part of the spoil, the silver and the gold and the vessels of brass and iron, they are "devoted" to the service of God (the Authorized translation unhappily uses the word "accursed"). No one is to appropriate a single article to his own use. An exception to the universal massacre was to take place only in the case of the harlot Rahab, who was to be saved, with all her relations, in accordance with the solemn promise of the spies.

There is no difficulty in perceiving the great lesson for all time to be derived from this extraordinary transaction, or the great law of the kingdom of God that was made so conspicuous by it. When we have clear indications of the Divine mind as to any course of action, we are to advance to it promptly and without fear, even though the means at our disposal appear utterly inadequate to the object sought to be gained. No man goeth a warfare at his own charges in the service of God. The resources of infinite power avail for that service, and they are sure to be brought into play if it be undertaken for God's glory, and in accordance with His will. Who could have supposed that the fishermen of Galilee would in the end triumph over all the might of kings and rulers; over all the influence of priesthoods and systems of worship enshrined in the traditions of centuries; over all the learning and intellect of the philosopher, and over all the prejudices and passions of the multitude? The secret lay manifestly in the promise of Jesus—"Lo, I am with you alway, even to the end of the world." Who could have thought that the efforts of a poor German student in Berlin, on behalf of some neglected children, would expand into the widespread and well-rooted "Inner Mission" of Wichern? Or that the concern of a prison chaplain for the welfare of some of the prisoners after their release would develop into the worldwide work of Fliedner? Or that the distress of a kind-hearted medical student in London for a batch of poor boys who "didn't live nowhere," and whose pale faces, as they lay on a cold night on the roof of a shed, stirred in him an irrepressible compassion, would give birth to one of the marvels of London philanthropy,—Dr. Barnardo's twenty institutions, caring for three to four thousand children, in connection with which the announcement could be made that no really destitute child was ever turned from its doors? When Carey on his shoemaker's stool contemplated the evangelization of India, there was as great a gulf between the end and the apparent means, as when the priests blew with their rams' horns round the walls of Jericho.

But Carey felt it to be a Divine command, and Joshua-like set himself to obey it, leaving to God from whom it came to furnish the power by which the work was to be done. And wherever there have been found men and women of strong faith in God, who have looked on His will as recorded in the Scriptures with as much reverence as if it had been announced personally to themselves, and who have set themselves to obey that will with a sense of its reality, and a faith in God's promised help, like that of Joshua as the priests marched round Jericho, the same result has been realized; before Zerubbabel the great mountain has become a plain, and success has been achieved worthy of the acknowledgment—" The Lord hath done great things for us, whereof we are glad."

Far more effectual has this brave and thorough method of doing the Divine will proved than all the contrivances of compromise and worldly wisdom. The attempt to serve two masters has never proved either dignified or permanently successful. " If the Lord be God, follow Him; but if Baal, then follow him;" but do not attempt to combine in one what will please God and Baal too. It is the single eye that is full of light, and full of blessing. If God really is our Master, all the resources of heaven and earth are at our back. If we are able to go forward in sole and simple reliance on His might, as David did in the conflict with Goliath, all will go well. If we waver in our trust in Him, if we fly to the resources of human policy, if we seek deliverance from present evil at whatever cost, we arrest, as it were, the electric current flowing from heaven, and become weak as other men. Still more if we are guilty of deceit and cunning. How different was David confronting Goliath, and

David feigning madness before King Achish! In the one case a noble hero, in the other a timid, faltering child. It is a dear price we pay for present safety or convenience when we forfeit the approval of our conscience and the favour of God. It is a sublime attitude that faith takes up even in the face of overwhelming danger—" Lord, it is nothing with Thee to help, whether with many, or with them that have no power: help us, O Lord our God; for we rest on Thee, and in Thy name we go against this multitude. O Lord, Thou art our God; let not man prevail AGAINST THEE" (2 Chron. xiv. 11).

This, however, is but one half the lesson of the siege of Jericho. The other and not less valuable lesson is, that in many good enterprises, all that is done may appear for a long time to be labour lost, and not to advance us by one step nearer to the object in view. For six days the priests carried the ark round Jericho, but not one stone was loosened from the walls, not by one iota did the defences seem to yield. Six times on the seventh day there was an equally complete want of result. Nay, the seventh perambulation on the seventh day appeared to be equally unsuccessful, until the very last moment; but when that moment came, the whole defences of the city came tumbling to the ground. It is often God's method to do a great deal of work unseen, and then on a sudden effect the consummation. And whenever we are working in accordance with God's will, it is our encouragement to believe that though our visible success is hardly appreciable, yet good and real work is done. For one day is with the Lord as a thousand years, and a thousand years as one day. Sometimes in a thousand years God does not seem to accomplish a good day's work, but at other times in a single day He does the work of a thousand years. The reformation of the Church in the Middle Ages,—how little progress it seemed to make during weary centuries; and even when victory seemed to be drawing nigh, how thoroughly was it arrested by the martyrdom of Huss and Jerome in Bohemia, the extinction of the light of Wicliffe in England, and the suppression of the Lollards in Scotland! And when in Providence some causes began to operate that seemed to have a bearing on the desired consummation, such as the invention of printing, the revival of learning, and the love of freedom, how feebly they seemed to operate in opposition to that overwhelming force which the Papacy had been accumulating for centuries, and which nothing seemed able to touch! But when Luther appeared, nailed his theses to the door of the church at Wittemberg, and took up the bold attitude of an out-and-out opponent to Rome, in one hour the Church was struck as with an earthquake; it reeled to its foundations, and half of the proud structure fell. The conflict with American slavery, how slowly it advanced for many a year, nay, at times it seemed to be even losing ground; till in the midst of the great Civil War the President signed a certain proclamation, and in one moment American slavery received its death blow. An eminent historian of England has a striking picture of the slow, steady, awful triumph of iniquity in the career of Cardinal Wolsey, and the sudden collapse of the structure built up so carefully by that wicked man. Speaking of the final retribution, he says: "The time of reckoning at length was arrived. Slowly the hand had crawled along the dial plate, slowly as if the event would never come, and wrong was heaped on wrong, and oppression cried, and it seemed as if no ear had heard its voice, till the measure of the wickedness was at length fulfilled; the finger touched the hour, and as the strokes of the great hammer rang out above the nation, in an instant the mighty fabric of iniquity was shivered to ruins."

It is the prerogative of faith to believe that the same law of Providence is ever in operation, and that the rapidity with which some great drama is to be wound up may be as striking as the slowness of its movement was trying in its earlier stages. May we not be living in an age destined to furnish another great example of this law? The years as they pass seem laden with great events, and we seem to hear the angel that hath power over fire calling to the angel with the sharp sickle,—"Thrust in thy sharp sickle, and gather the clusters of the vine of the earth, for the grapes thereof are fully ripe." We cannot tell but before a year ends some grand purpose of Providence shall be accomplished, the death blow given to some system of force or of fraud that has scourged the earth for centuries, or some great prophetic cycle completed for which Simeons and Annas have been watching more than they that watch for the morning. God hasten the day when on every side truth shall finally triumph over error, good over evil, peace over strife, love over selfishness, and order over confusion; and when from every section of God's great but scattered family the shout of triumph shall go up, "Alleluia: for the Lord God omnipotent reigneth."

But let us return to the narrative of the fall of Jericho, and advert to two of the difficulties that have occurred to many minds in connection with it; one of comparatively little moment, but another of far more serious import.

The lesser difficulty is connected with the order to march round Jericho for seven successive days. Was it not contrary to the spirit of the law to make no difference on the Sabbath? As the narrative reads we are led to think that the Sabbath was the last of the seven days, in which case, instead of a cessation of labour, there was an increase of it sevenfold. Possibly this may be a mistake; but at the least it seems as if, all days being treated alike, there was a neglect of the precept, "In it thou shalt not do any work."

To this it has usually been replied that the law of the Sabbath being only a matter of arrangement, and not founded on any unchangeable obligation, it was quite competent for God to suspend it or for a time repeal it, if occasion required. The present instance has been viewed as one of those exceptional occasions when the obligation to do no work was suspended for a time. But this is hardly a satisfactory explanation. Was it likely that immediately after God had so solemnly charged Joshua respecting the book of the law, that it was "not to depart out of his mouth, but he was to meditate therein day and night, to observe to do according to all that was written therein," that almost on the first occurrence of a public national interest He would direct him to disregard the law of the Sabbath? Or was it likely that now that the people were about to get possession of the land, under the most sacred obligation to frame both their national and their personal life by the Divine law, one of the most outstanding requirements of that law should be even temporarily superseded? We cannot help thinking that it is in another direction that we must look for the solution of this difficulty.

And what seems the just explanation is, that this

solemn procession of the ark was really an act of worship, a very public and solemn act of worship, and that therefore the labour which it involved was altogether justifiable, just as the Sabbath labour involved in the offering of the daily sacrifices could not be objected to. It was a very solemn and open demonstration of honour to that great Being in whom Israel trusted—of obedience to His word, and unfaltering confidence that He would show Himself the God of His chosen people. At every step of their march they might well have sung—" I will lift up mine eyes unto the hills, from whence cometh my help." The absurdity of their proceeding to the eye of flesh invested it with a high sanctity, because it testified to a conviction that the presence of that God who dwelt symbolically in the ark would more than compensate for all the feebleness and even apparent silliness of the plan. It was indeed an exception to the usual way of keeping the Sabbath, but an exception that maintained and exalted the honour of God. And, in a sense, it might be called resting, inasmuch as no aggressive operations of any kind were carried on ; it was simply a waiting on God, waiting till He should arise out of His place, and cause it to be seen that " Israel got not the land in possession by their own sword, neither did their own arm save them : but Thy right hand, and Thine arm, and the light of Thy countenance, because Thou hadst a favour unto them " (Psalm xliv. 3).

A more serious objection in the eyes of many is that which is founded on the promiscuous massacre of the people of Jericho, which, according to the narrative, the Israelites were ordered to make. And it is not wonderful that, with the remarkable sense of the sanctity of human life attained in our country and in our age, and the intense horror which we have at scenes of blood and death, the idea of this slaughter should excite a strong feeling of repugnance. For in truth human life has never been held so sacred among men as it is in these our days and in this our island, where by the mercy of God war and bloodshed have been unknown for nearly a century and a half. We must remember that three thousand years ago, and in the tumultuous regions of the East, such a sentiment was unknown. The massacre of one tribe by another was an event of frequent occurrence, and so little thought of that a year or two after its occurrence the survivors of the massacre might be found on perfectly good terms with those who had committed it. This of course does not affect the righteousness of the sentence executed on the men of Jericho, but it shows that as executioners of that sentence the Israelites were not exposed either to the harrowing or the hardening influence which would now be inseparable from such a work.

We reserve the general question for consideration further on.[1] We confine ourselves for the present to the inquiry, Why was Jericho singled out for treatment so specially severe? Not only were all its inhabitants put to the sword, as indeed the inhabitants of other cities were too, but the city was burnt with fire, and a special curse was pronounced upon any one that should set up its gates and its walls. Of only two other cities do we read that they were destroyed in this way—Ai and Hazor (viii. 28, xi. 13). And in regard to all the three we may see special considerations dictating Joshua's course. Jericho and Ai were the first two cities taken by him, and it may have been

---

[1] See Chapter XXXI., "Jehovah the Champion of Israel."

useful to set an example of severity in their case. Hazor was the centre of a conspiracy, and being situated in the extreme north, its fate might read a lesson to those who were too far from Jericho and Ai to see what had happened there. But in the case of Jericho there was another consideration. Gilgal, which Joshua had made his headquarters, was but three or four miles distant. At that place there were no doubt gathered a great part of the flocks and herds of the Israelites, with the women and children, as well as the ark and the sacred tabernacle. It was necessary to prevent the possibility of a fortress being again erected at Jericho. For if it should fall into the enemy's hands, it would endanger the very existence of Gilgal. We shall see in the after part of the narrative that the policy of sparing the towns even when the inhabitants were destroyed proved a mistake, and was very disastrous to the Israelites. We shall find that in very many cases, while Joshua was occupied elsewhere, the towns were taken possession of anew by the Canaanites, and new troubles befell the Israelites. For Joshua's conquest was not a complete subjugation, and much remained to be done by each tribe in its settlement in order to get quit of the old inhabitants. It was the failure of most of the tribes to do their part in this process that led to most of the troubles in the future history of Israel, both in the way of temptation to idolatry and in the form of actual war.

The only things saved from utter destruction at Jericho were the gold and the silver and other metallic substances, which were put into the treasury of the house of the Lord. The fact that the "house of the Lord," situated at this time at Gilgal, was an establishment of such size as to be able to employ all these things in its service refutes the assertion of those critics who would make out that at the settlement in Canaan there was no place that might be called emphatically "*the house of the Lord.*" It indicates that the arrangements for worship were on a large scale,—a fact which is confirmed afterwards by the circumstance that the Gibeonites were assigned by Joshua to be "hewers of wood and drawers of water *for the house of my God.*" If little is said about the arrangements for worship in the Book of Joshua, it is because the one object of the book is to record the settlement of the nation in the country. If it were true that the book was overhauled by some priestly writer who took every opportunity of magnifying his office, he must have done his work in a strange manner. We find in it such hints as we have noticed showing that the service of the sanctuary was not neglected, but we have none of those full or formal details that would have been given if a writer with such a purpose had worked over the book.

We hear of Jericho from time to time as a place of abode both in the Old Testament and in the New; but when Hiel the Bethelite rebuilt it with walls and gates, "he laid the foundation thereof in Abiram his firstborn, and set up the gates thereof in his youngest son Segub, according to the word of the Lord, which He spake by Joshua the son of Nun" (1 Kings xvi. 34). It was ordained that that first fortress which had withstood the people of God on the west of Jordan should remain a perpetual desolation. As the stones set up in the channel and on the banks of the river witnessed to future generations of God's care for His own people, so the stones of Jericho cast down and lying in ruined heaps were designed to testify to the dread retribution that overtook the guilty. The two great lessons of

Providence from Jericho are, the certainty of the reward of faith and obedience on the one hand, and of the punishment of wickedness on the other. The words which Balaam had proclaimed from the top of the mountain on the other side now received their first fulfilment :—

> "How goodly are thy tents, O Jacob,
> Thy tabernacles, O Israel! . . .
> God bringeth him forth out of Egypt,
> He hath, as it were, the strength of the wild **ox**;
> He shall eat up the nations his adversaries,
> And shall break their bones in pieces,
> **And smite them through with His arrows."**

CHAPTER XIII.

RAHAB SAVED.

Joshua vi. 17, 22—25.

IT has not been the lot of Rahab to share the devout interest which has been lavished on Mary Magdalene. Our Correggios, Titians, and Carlo Dolcis have not attempted to represent the spirit of contrition and devotion transfiguring the face of the Canaanite girl. And this is not surprising. Rahab had never seen the human face of Jesus, nor heard the words that dropped like honey from His lips. She had never come under that inexpressible charm which lay in the bearing of the living Jesus, the charm that made so remarkable a change not only on the "woman that was a sinner," but on Zaccheus, on Peter in the high priest's hall, on the penitent thief, and on Saul of Tarsus on the way to Damascus. For there was a wonderful power in the very looks and tones of Jesus to touch the heart, and thereby to throw a new light on all one's past life, making sin look black and odious, and inspiring an intense desire for resemblance to Him who was so much fairer than all the children of men. Rahab had never seen the Divine image in any purer form than it appeared in Joshua and men and women like-minded with him.

But though she was not one of those whose contrite and holy love painters delight to represent, she belonged to the same order, and in some respects is more remarkable than any of the New Testament penitents. For her light was much dimmer than theirs who lived in the days of the Son of man. She was utterly without support or sympathy from those among whom she lived, for with the exception of her own relations, who seem to have been influenced by herself, not a creature in Jericho shared her faith, or showed the slightest regard for the God of Israel.

But the time has now come for her to reap the reward of her faith and its works. In her case there was but a short interval between the sowing and the reaping. And God showed Himself able to do in her exceeding abundantly above what she could ask or think. For she was not only protected when Jericho and all its people were destroyed, but incorporated with the children of Israel. She became an heir of Abraham's blessing; she came among those "to whom pertained the adoption, and the glory, and the covenants, and the giving of the law, and the service of God, and the promises." An old tradition made her the wife of Joshua, but, according to the genealogies she married Salmon (Matt. i. 5), prince of the imperial tribe of Judah, great-grandfather of David, and ancestor of the Messiah. In the golden roll of the eleventh chapter of Hebrews, she is the only woman who shares with Sarah, the great mother of the nation, the honour of a place among the heroes of the faith. Such honours could not have been attained by her had she not been a changed character,—one of those who erewhile "had lain among the pots, but who became like the wings of a dove covered with silver and her feathers with yellow gold."

Very special mention is made of her in the narrative

of the destruction of Jericho. In the first place, before the overthrow of the city, Joshua gives particular instructions regarding her, accepting very readily the promise that had been made to her by the two spies. If Joshua had been a man of unreasonable temper, he might have refused to ratify their action in her case. He might have said that God had doomed the whole inhabitants of the city to destruction, and as no instructions had been given by Him to spare Rahab, she must share the doom of the rest. But Joshua at once recognised the propriety of an exception in favour of one who had shown such faith, and who had rendered such service to the spies and to the nation; and, moreover, he looked on the promise made by the spies as reasonable, for it would have been gross tyranny to send them on such an errand without power to make fair compensation for any assistance they might receive. Yet how often have promises made in danger been broken when the danger was past! Rahab must have known that had it been some Canaanite chief and not Joshua that had to decide her fate, he would have scorned the promise of the spies, and consigned her to the general doom. She must have been impressed with the honourable conduct of Joshua in so cordially endorsing the promise of the spies, and thought well of his religion on that account. Honour and religion go well together; meanness and religion breed contempt. We see meanness with a religious profession culminating in the treachery of Judas. We see honour in alliance with religion culminating in the Garden of Gethsemane, when the bleeding Sufferer rallied His fainting courage and stood firm to His undertaking—" The cup which My Father hath given Me, shall I not drink it?"

No doubt the scarlet cord was hung from her window, as had been arranged with the spies, and the Israelites, when they saw it, would be reminded of the blood of the lamb sprinkled on their door posts and lintels when the destroying angel passed through Egypt. It was the two men who had acted as spies that Joshua instructed to enter her house, and bring out the woman and all that she had. And a happy woman she no doubt was when she saw the faces of her old guests, and under their protection was brought out with all her kindred and all that she had and led to a place of safety. It is a blessed time, after you have stood fast to duty while many have failed, when the hour comes that brings you peace and blessing, while it carries confusion and misery to the faithless. How thankful one is at such a moment for the grace that enabled one to choose the right! With what awe one looks into the gulf on whose edge one stood, and thanks God for the grace that brought the victory! And how often is the welfare of a lifetime secured in some crisis by the firm attitude of an hour. What do we not gain by patience when we do the right and wait for the reward? One of the pictures in the Interpreter's House is that of "a little room where sat two little children, each in his chair. The name of the eldest was Passion, and of the other Patience. Passion seemed much discontent, but Patience was very quiet. Then asked Christian, What is the reason of the discontent of Passion? The Interpreter answered, The Governor of them would have them stay for his best things till the beginning of the next year; but he will have them all now; but Patience is willing to wait." How invaluable is the spirit that can wait till the beginning of the next year! And especially with reference to the awards of eternity. The rush for good things now, the desire at all hazards to gratify inclination as it rises, the impatience that will not wait till next year—how many lives they wreck, what misery they gender for eternity ! But when you do choose that good part that shall not be taken away, and count all things but loss for the excellency of the knowledge of Christ Jesus, what ecstatic bliss you make sure of in that solemn hour when the dead, small and great, shall stand before God; and, amid weeping and wailing inexpressible on the left hand, the Judge shall pronounce the words, " Come, ye blessed of My Father, inherit the kingdom prepared for you from the foundation of the world."

The case of Rahab was one of those where whole families were saved on account of the faith of one member. Such was the case of Noah, whose faith secured the exemption of himself and all his family from the flood. Such, hypothetically, was the case of Lot, whose whole family would have been preserved from the fire and brimstone, if only they had received his warning and left Sodom with him. On the other hand, there were cases, like that of Korah in the wilderness, and of Achan, near this very place, Jericho, where the sin of the father involved the death of the whole family. In the case of Rahab, we find a family saved, not through the faith of the head of the house, but of a member of it, and that member a woman. The head of a Hebrew house was eminently a representative man, and by a well-understood and recognised law his family were implicated in his acts, whether for good or for evil. But in this case the protector of the family, the member of it that determines the fate of the whole, is not the one whom the law recognises, but his child, his daughter. A woman occupies here a higher and more influential place, in relation to the rest of the family, than she has ever held at any previous time. The incident comes in as a kind of foreshadow of what was to be abundantly verified in after times. For it is in Christian times that woman has most conspicuously attained that position of high influence on the welfare of the family, and especially its eternal welfare, which Rahab showed in delivering her house from the destruction of Jericho.

At a very early period in the history of the Christian Church, the great influence of godly women on the welfare of their male relations began to be seen. About the fourth century we can hardly peruse the biography of any eminent Christian father, without being struck with the share which the prayers and efforts of some pious female relative had in his conversion. Monica, the mother of Augustine, is held in reverence all over Christendom for her tears and wrestling prayers on behalf of her son; and the name of Anthusa, the mother of Chrysostom, is hardly less venerable. Nonna, the mother of Gregory Nazianzen; Macrina and Emmelia, the mother and the grandmother of Basil the Great and Gregory of Nyssa, as well as their sister, also called Macrina; Theosebia too, the wife of Gregory, and Marallina, the sister of Ambrose, all share a similar renown. And in more recent times, how many are the cases where sisters and daughters have exercised a blessed influence on brothers and fathers! Every right-hearted sister has a peculiarly warm and tender interest in the welfare of her brothers. It is a feeling not to be neglected, but carefully nursed and deepened. This narrative shows it to be in the line of God's providence that sisters and daughters shall prove instruments of deliverance to their relations. It is blessed when they are so even in earthly things, but far more glorious when, through faith and prayer and unwearied interest, they are enabled to win them to Christ, and turn them into living epistles for Him.

It can hardly be necessary to dwell at length on the commentary which we find in the Epistle of James on the faith of Rahab. For it is not so much anything personal to her that he handles, but an important quality of all true faith, and of her faith as being true. "Was not Rahab the harlot justified by works when she had received the messengers, and had sent them out another way?" No intelligent person needs to be told that the view of justification here given is in no wise at variance with that of St. Paul. Paul's doctrine was propounded in the early years of the Church, when, in opposition to the notion prevalent among the Gentiles, it was necessary to show clearly that there was no justifying merit in works. The doctrine of James was propounded at a later period, when men, presuming on free grace, were beginning to get lax in their practice, and it was necessary to insist that faith could not be true faith if it was not accompanied by corresponding works. The case of Rahab is employed by St. James to illustrate this latter position. If Rahab had merely professed belief in the God of Israel as the only true God, and in the certainty that Israel would possess the land, according to God's promise, her faith would have been a barren or dead faith; in other words, it would have been no true faith at all. It was her taking up the cause of the spies, protecting them, endangering her life for them, and then devising and executing a scheme for their safety, that showed her faith to be living, and therefore real. Let it be true that faith is only the instrument of justification, that it possesses no merit, and that its value lies solely in its uniting us to Christ, so that we get justification and all other blessings from Him; still that which really unites us to Christ must be living. Dr. Chalmers used to sum up the whole doctrine in the formula, "We are justified by faith alone, but not by a faith which is alone."

But let us now advert to the reception of Rahab into the nation and church of the Israelites. "They brought out all her kindred, and left them without the camp of Israel.... And Joshua saved Rahab the harlot alive, and her father's household, and all that she had; and she dwelleth in Israel even unto this day; because she hid the messengers which Joshua sent to spy out Jericho." First, they left them without the camp. At first they could be treated only as unclean until the rites of purification should be performed. In the case of Rahab this was doubly necessary—owing to her race, and owing to her life. Thereafter they were admitted to the commonwealth of Israel, and had an interest in the covenants of promise. The ceremonial purification and the formal admission signified little, except in so far as they represented the washing of regeneration and the renewal of the Holy Ghost. Whether this vital change took place we are not told, but we seem justified in inferring it both from what we read in Hebrews and from the fact that Rahab was one of the ancestors of our Lord. It is interesting and instructive to think of her as exemplifying that law of grace by which the door of heaven is flung open even to the vilest sinner. "Where sin abounded grace did much more abound." When the enemy ensnares a woman, wiles her into the filthiest chambers of sin, and so enchains her there that she cannot escape, but must sink deeper and deeper in the mire, the case is truly hopeless. More rapidly and more thoroughly than in the case of a man, the leprosy spreads till every virtuous principle is rooted out, and every womanly feeling is displaced by the passions of a sensual reprobate. "Son of man, can these bones live?" Is there any art to breathe the breath of purity and pure love into that defiled soul? Can such a woman ever find her home on the mountains of spices, and hear a loving bridegroom say, "My love, my undefiled is but one"? It is just here that the religion of the Bible achieves its highest triumphs. We say the religion of the Bible, but we should rather say, that gracious Being whose grace the Bible untolds. "The things that are impossible with men are possible with God." Jesus Christ is the prince of life. Experience of His saving grace, living fellowship with Him, can so change "fornicators and idolaters, and adulterers and effeminate and abusers of themselves with mankind, and thieves and covetous and drunkards and revilers and extortioners," that it may be said of them, "But ye are washed, but ye are sanctified, but ye are justified in the name of the Lord Jesus, and by the Spirit of our God." Living faith in a living and loving Saviour can do all things.

Ten thousand times has this truth been illustrated in evangelistic addresses, in sermons, and in tracts innumerable from the case of the prodigal son. And what imagination can estimate the good which that parable has done? In this point of view it is strange that little use has been made of an Old Testament passage, in which the same truth is unfolded with touching beauty from the case of a faithless woman. We refer to the second chapter of Hosea. It is the case of a guilty and apparently shameless wife. Impelled by greed, meanest of all motives, she has gone after this lover and that, because they seemed able to gratify her love of finery and luxury, and all the vain show of the world. But the time comes when her eyes are opened, her lovers are brought to desolation, she sees that they have all been a lie and a deception, and that no real good has ever come to her save from the husband whom she has forsaken and insulted. And now when she turns to him she is simply overwhelmed by his graciousness and generosity. He does all that can be done to make her forget her past miseries, all her past life, and he succeeds. The valley of Achor becomes a door of hope; she is so transformed inwardly, and her outward surroundings are so changed, that "she sings as in the days of her youth." The happy feelings of her unpolluted childhood return to her, as if she had drunk the waters of Lethe, and she sings like a light-hearted girl once more. The allegory is hardly an allegory,—it is Divine love that has effected the change; that love that many waters cannot quench and floods cannot drown.

We wonder whether Rahab obtained much help in her new life from the fellowship of those among whom she came when she joined the Church. If the Church then was what the Church ever ought to be, if its outstanding members were like the three fair damsels, Prudence, Piety and Charity, in the Palace Beautiful, no doubt she would be helped greatly. But it is not very often that that emblem is realized. And strange to say, among the members of our Churches now, we usually find a very imperfect sense of the duty which they owe to those who come among them from without, and especially out of great wickedness. It is quite possible that Rahab was chilled by the coldness of some of her Hebrew sisters, looking on her as an intruder, looking on her as a reprobate, and grieved because their select society was broken in upon by this outlandish woman. And it is quite possible that she was disappointed to find that, though they were nominally the people of God, there was very little of what was divine or heavenly about them. So it often happens that what ought to be the greatest attraction in a Church, the character of its members, is the greatest repellant. If all sin-worn and world-worn souls, weary of the world's ways, and longing for a society more loving, more generous, more pure, more noble, could find in the Christian Church their ideal fulfilled, could find in the fellowship of Christians the reality of their dreams, how blessed would be the result! Alas, in too many cases they find the world's bitterness and meanness and selfishness reproduced under the flag of Christ! If all so-called Christians, it has been said, should live for but one year in accordance with the thirteenth chapter of 1st Corinthians, unbelief would vanish. Will the day ever be when every one that names the name of Christ shall be a living epistle, known and read of all men?

But, however she may have been affected by the spirit of those among whom she came, Rahab undoubtedly attained to a good degree before God, and a place of high honour in the Hebrew community. It was well for her that what at first arrested and impressed her was not anything in the people of Israel; it was the glorious attributes of their God. For this would preserve her substantially from disappointment. Men might change, or they might pass away, but God remained the same yesterday and to-day and for ever. If she kept looking to Him, admiring His grace and power, and drawing from His inexhaustible fulness, she would be able to verify one at least of the prophet's pictures: "Cursed be the man that trusteth in man, and maketh flesh his arm, and whose heart departeth from the Lord: for he shall be like the heath in the desert, and shall not see when good cometh; but shall inhabit the parched places in the wilderness, in a salt land and not inhabited. Blessed is the man that trusteth in the Lord, and whose hope the Lord is: for he shall be as a tree planted by the waters, and that spreadeth out her roots by the river, and shall not see when heat cometh, but her leaf shall be green; and shall not be careful in the year of drought, neither shall cease from yielding fruit."

CHAPTER XIV.

ACHAN'S TRESPASS.

Joshua vii.

A VESSEL in full sail scuds merrily over the waves. Everything betokens a successful and delightful voyage. The log has just been taken, marking an extraordinary run. The passengers are in the highest spirits, anticipating an early close of the voyage. Suddenly a shock is felt, and terror is seen on every face. The ship has struck on a rock. Not only is progress arrested, but it will be a mercy for crew and passengers if they can escape with their lives.

Not often so violently, but often as really, progress is arrested in many a good enterprise that seemed to be prospering to a wish. There may be no shock, but there is a stoppage of movement. The vital force that seemed to be carrying it on towards the desired consummation declines, and the work hangs fire. A mission that in its first stages was working out a beautiful transformation, becomes languid and advances no further. A Church, eminent for its zeal and spirituality, comes down to the ordinary level, and seems to lose its power. A family that promised well in infancy and childhood fails of its promise, its sons and daughters waver and fall. A similar result is often found in the undertakings of common life. Something mysterious arrests progress in business or causes a decline. In "enterprises of great pith and moment," "the currents turn awry, and lose the name of action."

In all such cases we naturally wonder what can be the cause. And very often our explanation is wide of the mark. In religious enterprises, we are apt to fall back on the sovereignty and inscrutability of God. "He moves in a mysterious way, His wonders to perform." It seems good to Him, for unknown purposes of His own, to subject us to disappointment and trial. We do not impugn either His wisdom or His goodness; all is for the best. But, for the most part, we fail to detect the real reason. That the fault should lie with ourselves is the last thing we think of. We search for it in every direction rather than at home. We are ingenious in devising far-off theories and explanations, while the real offender is close at hand—"*Israel hath sinned.*"

It was an unexpected obstacle of this kind that Joshua now encountered in his next step towards possessing the land. Let us endeavour to understand his position and his plan. Jericho lay in the valley of the Jordan, and its destruction secured nothing for Joshua save the possession of that low-lying valley. From the west side of the valley rose a high mountain wall, which had to be ascended in order to reach the plateau of Western Palestine. Various ravines or passes ran down from the plateau into the valley; at the top of one of these, a little to the north of Jericho, was Bethel, and farther down the pass, nearer the plain, the town or village of Ai. No remains of Ai are now visible, nor is there any tradition of the name, so that its exact position cannot be ascertained. It was an insignificant place, but necessary to be taken, in order to give

Joshua command of the pass, and enable him to reach the plateau above. The plan of Joshua seems to have been to gain command of the plateau about this point, and thereby, as it were, cut the country in two, so that he might be able to deal in succession with its southern and its northern sections. If once he could establish himself in the very centre of the country, keeping his communications open with the Jordan valley, he would be able to deal with his opponents in detail, and thus prevent those in the one section from coming to the assistance of the other. Neither Ai nor Bethel seemed likely to give him trouble; they were but insignificant places, and a very small force would be sufficient to deal with them.

Hitherto Joshua had been eminently successful, and his people too. Not a hitch had occurred in all the arrangements. The capture of Jericho had been an unqualified triumph. It seemed as if the people of Ai could hardly fail to be paralysed by its fate. After reconnoitring Ai, Joshua saw that there was no need for mustering the whole host against so poor a place— a detachment of two or three thousand would be enough. The three thousand went up against it as confidently as if success were already in their hands. It was probably a surprise to find its people making any attempt to drive them off. The men of Israel were not prepared for a vigorous onslaught, and when it came thus unexpectedly they were taken aback and fled in confusion. As the men of Ai pursued them down the pass, they had no power to rally or retrieve the battle; the rout was complete, some of the men were killed, while consternation was carried into the host, and their whole enterprise seemed doomed to failure.

And now for the first time Joshua appears in a somewhat humiliating light. He is not one of the men that never make a blunder. He rends his clothes, falls on his face with the elders before the ark of the Lord till even, and puts dust upon his head. There is something too abject in this prostration. And when he speaks to God, it is in the tone of complaint and in the language of unbelief. "Alas, O Lord God, wherefore hast Thou at all brought this people over Jordan, to deliver us into the hand of the Amorites, to destroy us? would to God we had been content, and dwelt on the other side Jordan! O Lord, what shall I say, when Israel turneth their backs before their enemies! For the Canaanites and all the inhabitants of the land shall hear of it, and shall environ us round, and cut off our name from the earth: and what wilt Thou do unto Thy great name?" Thus Joshua almost throws the blame on God. He seems to have no idea that it may lie in quite another quarter. And very strangely, he adopts the very tone and almost the language of the ten spies, against which he had protested so vehemently at the time: "Would God that we had died in the land of Egypt, or would God we had died in this wilderness! And wherefore hath the Lord brought us unto this land, to fall by the sword, that our wives and our children should be a prey?" What has become of all your courage, Joshua, on that memorable day? Is this the man to whom God said so lately, "Be strong, and of good courage; as I was with Moses, so I will be with thee. I will not fail thee nor forsake thee"? Like Peter on the waters, and like so many of ourselves, he begins to sink when the wind is contrary, and his cry is the querulous wail of a frightened child! After all he is but flesh and blood.

Now it is God's turn to speak. "Get thee up;

wherefore liest thou thus upon thy face?" Why do you turn on Me as if I had suddenly changed, and become forgetful of My promise? Alas, my friends how often is God slandered by our complaints! How often do we feel and even speak as if He had broken His word and forgotten His promise, as if He had induced us to trust in Him, and accept His service, only to humiliate us before the world, and forsake us in some great crisis! No wonder if God speak sharply to Joshua, and to us if we go in Joshua's steps. No wonder if He refuse to be pleased with our prostration, our wringing of our hands and sobbing, and calls us to change our attitude. "Get thee up; wherefore liest thou thus upon thy face?"

Then comes the true explanation—" Israel hath sinned." Might you not have divined that this was the real cause of your trouble? Is not sin directly or indirectly the cause of all trouble? What was it that broke up the joy and peace of Paradise? Sin. What brought the flood of waters over the face of the earth to destroy it? Sin. What caused the confusion of Babel and scattered the inhabitants over the earth in hostile races? Sin. What brought desolation on that very plain of Jordan, and buried its cities and its people under an avalanche of fire and brimstone? Sin. What caused the defeat of Israel at Hormah forty years ago, and doomed all the generation to perish in the wilderness? Sin. What threw down the walls of Jericho only a few days ago, gave its people to the sword of Israel, and reduced its homes and its bulwarks to the mass of ruins you see *there*? Again, sin. Can you not read the plainest lesson? Can you not divine that this trouble which has come on you is due to the same cause with all the rest? And if it be a first principle of Providence that all trouble is due to sin, would it not be more suitable that you and your elders should now be making diligent search for it, and trying to get it removed, than that you should be lying on your faces and howling to me, as if some sudden caprice or unworthy humour of mine had brought this distress upon you?

"Behold, the Lord's ear is not heavy that it cannot hear, nor His arm shortened that it cannot save. But your iniquities have separated between you and your God." What a curse that sin is, in ways and forms, too, which we do not suspect! And yet we are usually so very careless about it. How little pains we take to ascertain its presence, or to drive it away from among us! How little tenderness of conscience we show, how little burning desire to be kept from the accursed thing! And when we turn to our opponents and see sin in them, instead of being grieved, we fall on them savagely to upbraid them, and we hold them up to open scorn. How little we think if they are guilty, that their sin has intercepted the favour of God, and involved not them only, but probably the whole community in trouble! How unsatisfactory to God must seem the bearing even of the best of us in reference to sin! Do we really think of it as the object of God's abhorrence? As that which destroyed Paradise, as that which has covered the earth with lamentation and mourning and woe, kindled the flames of hell, and brought the Son of God to suffer on the cross? If only we had some adequate sense of sin, should we not be constantly making it our prayer—"Search me, O God, and know my heart; try me, and know my thoughts; and see if there be any wicked way in me, and lead me in the way everlasting"?

The peculiar covenant relation in which Israel stood

to God caused a method to be fallen on for detecting their sin that is not available for us. The whole people were to be assembled next morning, and inquiry was to be made for the delinquent in God's way, and when the individual was found condign punishment was to be inflicted. First the tribe was to be ascertained, then the family, then the man. For this is God's way of tracking sin. It might be more pleasant to us that He should deal with it more generally, and having ascertained, for example, that the wrong had been done by a particular tribe or community, inflict a fine or other penalty on that tribe in which we should willingly bear our share. For it does not grieve us very much to sin when every one sins along with us. Nay, we can even make merry over the fact that we are all sinners together, all in the same condemnation, in the same disgrace. But it is a different thing when we are dealt with one by one. The tribe is taken, the family is taken, but that is not all; the household that God shall take shall come MAN BY MAN! It is that individualizing of us that we dread; it is when it comes to that, that "conscience makes cowards of us all." When a sinner is dying, he becomes aware that this individualizing process is about to take place, and hence the fear which he often feels. He is no longer among the multitude, death is putting him by himself, and God is coming to deal with him by himself. If he could only be hid in the crowd it would not matter, but that searching eye of God—who can stand before it? What will all the excuses or disguises or glosses he can devise avail before Him who "sets our iniquities before Him, our secret sins in the light of His countenance"? "Neither is there any creature that is not manifest in His sight; for all things are naked, and opened unto the eyes of Him with whom we have to do." Happy, in that hour, they who have found the Divine covering for sin: "Blessed is he whose transgression is forgiven, whose sin is covered. Blessed is the man to whom the Lord imputeth not iniquity, and in whose spirit there is no guile."

But before passing on to the result of the scrutiny, we find ourselves face to face with a difficult question. If, as is here intimated, it was one man that sinned, why should the whole nation have been dealt with as guilty? Why should the historian, in the very first verse of this chapter, summarise the transaction by saying: "But the *children of Israel* committed a trespass in the devoted thing: for *Achan*, the son of Carmi, the son of Zabdi, the son of Zerah, of the tribe of Judah, took of the devoted thing; and the anger of the Lord was kindled against the children of Israel"? Why visit the offence of Achan on the whole congregation, causing a peculiarly humiliating defeat to take place before an insignificant enemy, demoralizing the whole host, driving Joshua to distraction, and causing the death of six-and-thirty men?

In dealing with a question of this sort, it is indispensable that we station ourselves at that period of the world's history; we must place before our minds some of the ideas that were prevalent at the time, and abstain from judging of what was done then by a standard which is applicable only to our own day.

And certain it is that, what we now call the *solidarity* of mankind, the tendency to look on men rather as the members of a community than as independent individuals, each with an inalienable standing of his own, had a hold of men's minds then such as it has not to-day, certainly among Western nations. To a certain extent, this principle of solidarity is inwoven in the very nature of things, and cannot be eliminated, however we may try. Absolute independence and isolation of individuals are impossible. In families, we suffer for one another's faults, even when we hold them in abhorrence. We benefit by one another's virtues, though we may have done our utmost to discourage and destroy them. In the Divine procedure toward us, the principle of our being a corporate body is often acted upon. The covenant of Adam was founded on it, and the fall of our first parents involved the fall of all their descendants. In the earlier stages of the Hebrew economy, wide scope was given to the principle. It operated in two forms: sometimes the individual suffered for the community, and sometimes the community for the individual. And the operation of the principle was not confined to the Hebrew or to other Oriental communities. Even among the Romans it had a great influence. Admirable though Roman law was in its regulation of property, it was very defective in its dealings with persons. "Its great blot was the domestic code. The son was the property of the father, without rights, without substantial being, in the eye of Roman law. . . . The wife again was the property of her husband, an ownership of which the moral result was most disastrous."[1]

We are to remember that practically the principle of solidarity was fully admitted in Joshua's time among his people. The sense of injustice and hardship to which it might give rise among us did not exist. Men recognised it as a law of wide influence in human affairs, to which they were bound to defer.

---

[1] See Mozley's "Ruling Ideas in the Early Ages," p. 40.

Hence it was that when it became known that one man's offence lay at the foundation of the defeat before Ai, and of the displeasure of God toward the people at large, there was no outcry, no remonstrance, no complaint of injustice. This could hardly take place if the same thing were to happen now. It is hard to reconcile the transaction with our sense of justice. And no doubt, if we view the matter apart and by itself, there may be some ground for this feeling. But the transaction will assume another aspect if we view it as but a part of a great whole, of a great scheme of instruction and discipline which God was developing in connection with Israel. In this light, instead of a hardship it will appear that in the end a very great benefit was conferred on the people.

Let us think of Achan's temptation. A large amount of valuable property fell into the hands of the Israelites at Jericho. By a rigorous law, all was devoted to the service of God. Now a covetous man like Achan might find many plausible reasons for evading this law. "What I take to myself (he might say) will never be missed. There are hundreds of Babylonish garments, there are many wedges of gold, and silver shekels without number, amply sufficient for the purpose for which they are devoted. If I were to deprive another man of his rightful share, I should be acting very wickedly; but I am really doing nothing of the kind. I am only diminishing imperceptibly what is to be used for a public purpose. Nobody will suffer a whit by what I do,—it cannot be very wrong."

Now the great lesson taught very solemnly and impressively to the whole nation was, that this was just awfully wrong. The moral benefit which the nation ultimately got from the transaction was, that this kind of sophistry, this flattering unction which leads so many persons ultimately to destruction, was exploded and blown to shivers. A most false mode of measuring the criminality of sin was stamped with deserved reprobation. Every man and woman in the nation got a solemn warning against a common but ruinous temptation. In so far as they laid to heart this warning during the rest of the campaign, they were saved from disastrous evil, and thus, in the long run, they profited by the case of Achan.

That sin is to be held sinful only when it hurts your fellow-creatures, and especially the poor among your fellow-creatures, is a very common impression, but surely it is a delusion of the devil. That it has such effects may be a gross aggravation of the wickedness, but it is not the heart and core of it. And how can you know that it will not hurt others? Not hurt your fellow-countrymen, Achan? Why, that secret sin of yours has caused the death of thirty-six men, and a humiliating defeat of the troops before Ai. More than that, it has separated between the nation and God. Many say, when they tell a lie, it was not a malignant lie, it was a lie told to screen some one, not to expose him, therefore it was harmless. But you cannot trace the consequences of that lie, any more than Achan could trace the consequences of his theft, otherwise you would not dare to make that excuse. Many that would not steal from a poor man, or waste a poor man's substance, have little scruple in wasting a rich man's substance, or in peculating from Government property. Who can measure the evil that flows from such ways of trifling with the inexorable law of right, the damage done to conscience, and the guilt contracted before God? Is there safety for man or woman except in the most rigid regard to right and truth, even in the smallest portions of them with which they have to do? Is there not something utterly fearful in the propagating power of sin, and in its way of involving others, who are perfectly innocent, in its awful doom? Happy they who from their earliest years have had a salutary dread of it, and of its infinite ramifications of misery and woe!

How well fitted for us, especially when we are exposed to temptation, is that prayer of the psalmist: "Who can understand his errors? cleanse Thou me from secret faults. Keep back Thy servant also from presumptuous sins; let them not have dominion over me: then shall I be perfect, and I shall be clear of great transgression."

CHAPTER XV.

ACHANS PUNISHMENT.

JOSHUA vii.

"BE sure your sin will find you out." It has an awful way of leaving its traces behind it, and confronting the sinner with his crime. "Though he hide himself in the top of Carmel, I will search and take him out thence; and though he be hid from My sight in the bottom of the sea, thence will I command the serpent, and he shall bite him" (Amos ix. 3). "For God shall bring every work into judgment, with every secret thing, whether it be good, or whether it be evil" (Eccles. xii. 14).

When Achan heard of the muster that was to take place next morning, in order to detect the offender, he must have spent a miserable night. Between the consciousness of guilt, the sense of the mischief he had done, the dread of detection, and the foreboding of retribution, his nerves were too much shaken to admit the possibility of sleep. Weariedly and anxiously he must have tossed about as the hours slowly revolved, unable to get rid of his miserable thoughts, which would ever keep swimming about him like the changing forms of a kaleidoscope, but with the same dark vision of coming doom.

At length the day dawns, the tribes muster, the

inquiry begins. It is by the sure, solemn, simple, process of the lot that the case is to be decided. First the lot is cast for the tribes, and the tribe of Judah is taken. That must have given the first pang to Achan. Then the tribe is divided into its families, and the family of the Zarhites is taken; then the Zarhite family is brought out man by man, and Zabdi, the father of Achan, is taken. May we not conceive the heart of Achan giving a fresh beat as each time the casting of the lot brought the charge nearer and nearer to himself? The coils are coming closer and closer about him; and now his father's family is brought out, man by man, and Achan is taken. He is quite a young man, for his father could only have been a lad when he left Egypt. Look at him, pale, trembling, stricken with shame and horror, unable to hide himself, feeling it would be such a relief if the earth would open its jaws and swallow him up, as it swallowed Korah. Look at his poor wife; look at his father; look at his children. What a load of misery he has brought on himself and on them! Yes, the way of transgressors *is* hard.

Joshua's heart is overcome, and he deals gently with the young man. "My son, give, I pray thee, glory to the Lord God of Israel, and make confession unto Him; and tell me now what thou hast done; hide it not from me." There was infinite kindness in that word "my son." It reminds us of that other Joshua, the Jesus of the New Testament, so tender to sinners, so full of love even for those who had been steeped in guilt. It brings before us the Great High Priest, who is touched with the feeling of our infirmities, seeing He was in all things tempted like as we are, yet without sin. A harsh word from Joshua might have set Achan in a defiant attitude, and drawn from him a denial that he had done anything amiss. How often do we see this! A child or a servant has done wrong; you are angry, you speak harshly, you get a flat denial. Or if the thing cannot be denied, you get only a sullen acknowledgment, which takes away all possibility of good arising out of the occurrence, and embitters the relation of the parties to each other.

But not only did Joshua speak kindly to Achan, he confronted him with God, and called on him to think how He was concerned in this matter. "Give glory to the Lord God of Israel." Vindicate Him from the charge which I and others have virtually been bringing against Him, of proving forgetful of His covenant. Clear Him of all blame, declare His glory, declare that He is unsullied in His perfections, and show that He has had good cause to leave us to the mercy of our enemies. No man as yet knew what Achan had done. He might have been guilty of some act of idolatry, or of some unhallowed sensuality like that which had lately taken place at Baal-peor; in order that the transaction might carry its lesson, it was necessary that the precise offence should be known. Joshua's kindly address and his solemn appeal to Achan to clear the character of God had the desired effect. " Achan answered Joshua, and said, Indeed I have sinned against the Lord God of Israel, and thus and thus have I done: when I saw among the spoils a goodly Babylonish garment, and two hundred shekels of silver, and a wedge of gold of fifty shekels weight, then I coveted them, and took them; and, behold, they are hid in the earth in the midst of my tent, and the silver under it."

The confession certainly was frank and full; but whether it was made in the spirit of true contrition, or whether it was uttered in the hope that it would mitigate the sentence to be inflicted, we cannot tell. It would be a comfort to us to think that Achan was sincerely penitent, and that the miserable doom which befell him and his family ended their troubles, and formed the dark introduction to a better life. Where there is even a possibility that such a view is correct we naturally draw to it, for it is more than our hearts can well bear to think of so awful a death being followed by eternal misery.

Certain it is that Joshua earnestly desired to lead Achan to deal with God in the matter. "Make confession," he said, "unto Him." He knew the virtue of confession to God. For "he that covereth his sins shall not prosper; but whoso confesseth and forsaketh them shall have mercy" (Prov. xxviii. 13). "When I kept silence, my bones waxed old through my roaring all the day. . . . I acknowledged my sin unto Thee, and mine iniquity have I not hid. I said, I will confess my transgressions unto the Lord; and Thou forgavest the iniquity of my sin" (Psalm xxxii. 3, 5). It is a hopeful circumstance in Achan's case that it was after this solemn call to deal with God in the matter that he made his confession. One hopes that the sudden appearance on the scene of the God whom he had so sadly forgotten, led him to see his sin in its true light, and drew out the acknowledgment,— "Against Thee, Thee only, have I sinned." For no moral effect can be greater than that arising from the difference between sin covered and sin confessed to God. Sin covered is the fruitful parent of excuses, and sophistries, and of all manner of attempts to disguise the harsh features of transgression, and to show that, after all, there was not much wrong in it.

Sin confessed to God shows a fitting sense of the evil, of the shame which it brings, and of the punishment which it deserves, and an earnest longing for that forgiveness and renewal which, the gospel now shows us so clearly, come from Jesus Christ. For nothing becomes a sinner before God so well as when he breaks down. It is the moment of a new birth when he sees what miserable abortions all the refuges of lies are, and, utterly despairing of being able to hide himself from God in his filthy rags, unbosoms everything to Him with whom "there is mercy and plenteous redemption, and who will redeem Israel from all his transgressions."

It is a further presumption that Achan was a true penitent, that he told so frankly where the various articles that he had appropriated were to be found. "Behold, they are hid in the midst of my tent." They were scalding his conscience so fearfully that he could not rest till they were taken away from the abode which they polluted and cursed. They seemed to be crying out against him and his with a voice which could not be silenced. To bring them away and expose them to public view might bring no relaxation of the doom which he expected, but it would be a relief to his feelings if they were dragged from the hiding hole to which he had so wickedly consigned them. For the articles were now as hateful to him as formerly they had been splendid and delightful. The curse of God was on them now, and on him too on their account. Is there anything darker or deadlier than the curse of God?

And now the consummation arrives. Messengers are sent to his tent, they find the stolen goods, they bring them to Joshua, and to all the children of Israel, and they lay them out before the Lord. We are not told how the judicial sentence was arrived at. But there seems to have been no hesitation or delay about it. "Joshua and all the children of Israel took Achan the son of Zerah, and the silver, and the garment, and the wedge of gold, and his sons, and his daughters, and his oxen, and his asses, and his sheep, and his tent, and all that he had: and they brought them unto the valley of Achor. And Joshua said, Why hast thou troubled us? the Lord shall trouble thee this day. And all Israel stoned him with stones, and they burned him with fire, after they had stoned them with stones. And they raised over him a great heap of stones unto this day. So the Lord turned from the fierceness of His anger. Therefore the name of that place was called, The valley of Achor, unto this day."

It seems a terrible punishment, but Achan had already brought defeat and disgrace on his countrymen, he had robbed God, and brought the whole community to the brink of ruin. It must have been a strong lust that led him to play with such consequences. What sin is there to which covetousness has not impelled men? And, strange to say, it is a sin which has received but little check from all the sad experience of the past. Is it not as daring as ever to-day? Is it not the parent of that gambling habit which is the terror of all good men, sapping our morality and our industry, and disposing tens of thousands to trust to the bare chance of an unlikely contingency, rather than to God's blessing on honest industry? Is it not sheer covetousness that turns the confidential clerk into a robber of his employer, and uses all the devices of cunning to discover how long he can carry on his infamous plot, till the inevitable day of detection arrive and he must fly, a fugitive and a vagabond, to a foreign land? Is it not covetousness that induces the blithe young maiden to ally herself to one whom she knows to be a moral leper, but who is high in rank and full of wealth? Is it not the same lust that induces the trader to send his noxious wares to savage countries and drive the miserable inhabitants to a deeper misery and degradation than ever? Catastrophes are always happening: the ruined gambler blows out his brains; the dishonest clerk becomes a convict, the unhappy young wife gets into the divorce court, the scandalous trader sinks into bankruptcy and misery. But there is no abatement of the lust which makes such havoc. If the old ways of indulging it are abandoned, new outlets are always being found. Education does not cripple it; civilization does not uproot it; even Christianity does not always overcome it. It goeth about, if not like a roaring lion, at least like a cunning serpent intent upon its prey. Within the Church, where the minister reads out " Thou shalt not covet," and where men say with apparent devoutness, " Lord, have mercy upon us, and incline our hearts to keep this law "—as soon as their backs are turned, they are scheming to break it. Still, as of old, " love of money is the root of all evil, which while some coveted after they erred from the faith, and pierced themselves through with many sorrows."

Achan's sin has found him out, and he suffers its bitter doom. All his visions of comfort and enjoyment to be derived from his unlawful gain are rudely shattered. The pictures he has been drawing of what he will do with the silver and the gold and the garment are for ever dispersed. He has brought disaster on the nation, and shame and ruin on himself and his house. In all coming time, he must stand in the pillory of history as the man who stole the forbidden spoil of Jericho. That disgraceful deed is the only thing that will ever be known of him. Further, he has sacrificed his life. Young though he is, his life will be cut short, and all that he has hoped for of enjoyment and honour will be exchanged for a horrible death and an execrable memory. O sin, thou art a hard master! Thou draggest thy slaves, often through a short and rapid career, to misery and to infamy!

Nevertheless, the hand of God is seen here. The punishment of sin is one of the inexorable conditions of His government. It may look dark and ugly to us, but it is there. It may create a very different feeling from the contemplation of His love and goodness, but in our present condition that feeling is wholesome and necessary. As we follow unpardoned sinners into the future world, it may be awful, it may be dismal to think of a state from which punishment will never be absent; but the awfulness and the dismalness will not change the fact. It is the mystery of God's character that He is at once infinite love and infinite righteousness. And if it be unlawful for us to exclude His love and dwell only on His justice, it is equally unlawful to exclude His justice and dwell only on His love. Now, as of old, His memorial is, "The Lord, the Lord God merciful and gracious, longsuffering and abundant in mercy and truth, forgiving iniquity and transgression and sin, and that will by no means clear the guilty."

But if it be awful to contemplate the death, and the mode of death of Achan, how much more when we think that his wife and his sons and his daughters were stoned to death along with him! Would that not have been a barbarous deed in any case, and was it not much more so if they were wholly innocent of his offence?

To mitigate the harshness of this deed, some have supposed that they were privy to his sin, if not instigators of it. But of this we have not a tittle of evidence, and the whole drift of the narrative seems to show that the household suffered in the same manner and on the same ground as that of Korah (Num. xvi. 31-33). As regards the mode of death, it was significant of a harsh and hard-tempered age. Neither death nor the sufferings of the dying made much impression on the spectators. This callousness is almost beyond our comprehension, the tone of feeling is so different now. But we must accept the fact as it was. And as to the punishment of the wife and children, we must fall back on that custom of the time which not only gave to the husband and father the sole power and responsibility of the household, but involved the wife and children in his doom if at any time he should expose himself to punishment. As has already been said, neither the wife nor the children had any rights as against the husband and father; as his will was the sole law, so his retribution was the common inheritance of all. With him they were held to sin, and with him they suffered. They were considered to belong to him just as his hands and his feet belonged to him. It may seem to us very hard, and when it enters, even in a modified form, into the Divine economy we may cry out against it. Many do still, and ever will cry out against original sin, and against all that has come upon our race in consequence of the sin of Adam.

But it is in vain to fight against so apparent a fact. Much wiser surely it is to take the view of the Apostle Paul, and rejoice that, under the economy of the gospel, the principle of imputation becomes the source of blessing infinitely greater than the evil which it brought at the fall. It is one of the greatest triumphs of the Apostle's mode of reasoning that, instead of shutting his eyes to the law of imputation, he scans it carefully, and compels it to yield a glorious tribute to the goodness of God. When his theme was the riches of the grace of God, one might have thought that he would desire to give a wide berth to that dark fact in the Divine economy—the imputation of Adam's sin. But instead of desiring to conceal it, he brings it forward in all its terribleness and universality of application; but with the skill of a great orator, he turns it round to his side by showing that the imputation of Christ's righteousness has secured results that outdo all the evil flowing from the imputation of Adam's sin. "Therefore as by the offence of one judgment came upon all men to condemnation; even so by the righteousness of one the free gift came upon all men unto justification of life. For as through the one man's disobedience the many were made sinners, even so through the obedience of the one shall the many be made righteous. Moreover the law entered that the offence might abound; but where sin abounded, grace did much more abound: that, as sin reigned in death, even so might grace reign through righteousness unto eternal life, through Jesus Christ our Lord" (Rom. v. 18-21).

Very special mention is made of the place where the execution of Achan and his family took place. "They brought them unto the valley of Achor, . . . and they raised over him a great heap of stones, . . . wherefore the name of that place is called, The valley of Achor, unto this day." Achor, which means *trouble*, seems to have been a small ravine near the lower part of the valley in which Ai was situated, and therefore near the scene of the disaster that befell the Israelites. It was not an old name, but a name given at the time, derived from the occurrence of which it had just been the scene. It seemed appropriate that poor Achan should suffer at the very place where others had suffered on his account. It is subsequently referred to three times in Scripture. Later in this book it is given as part of the northern boundary of the tribe of Judah (chap. xv. 7); in Isaiah (lxv. 10) it is referred to on account of its fertility; and in Hosea (ii. 15) it is introduced in the beautiful allegory of the restored wife, who has been brought into the wilderness, and made to feel her poverty and misery, but of whom God says, "I will give her vineyards from thence, and the valley of Achor for a door of hope." The reference seems to be to the evil repute into which that valley fell by the sin of Achan, when it became the valley of trouble. For, by Achan's sin, what had appeared likely to prove the door of access for Israel into the land was shut; a double trouble came on the people—partly because of their defeat, and partly because their entrance into the land appeared to be blocked. In Hosea's picture of Israel penitent and restored, the valley is again turned to its natural use, and instead of a scene of trouble it again becomes a door of hope, a door by which they may hope to enter their inheritance. It is a door of hope for the penitent wife, a door by which she may return to her lost happiness. The underlying truth is, that when we get into a right relation to God, what were formerly evils become blessings, hindrances are turned into helps. Sin deranges everything, and brings trouble everywhere. The ground was cursed on account of Adam: not literally, but indirectly, inasmuch as it needed hard and exhausting toil, it needed the sweat of his face to make it yield him a maintenance. "We know," says the Apostle, "that the whole creation groaneth and travaileth in pain together until now." "For the creation was subjected to vanity, not of its own will, but by reason of Him who subjected it, in hope that the creation itself also shall be delivered out of the bondage of corruption into the glorious liberty of the children of God."

No man can tell all the "trouble" that has come into the world by reason of sin. As little can we know the full extent of that deliverance that shall take place when sin comes to an end. If we would know anything of this we must go to those passages which picture to us the new heavens and the new earth: "In the midst of the street of it, and on either side of the river, was there the tree of life, which bare twelve manner of fruits, and yielded her fruit every month: and the leaves of the tree were for the healing of the nations. And there shall be no more curse: but the throne of God and of the Lamb shall be in it; and His servants shall serve Him: and they shall see His face; and His name shall be in their foreheads. And there shall be no night there; and they need no candle, neither light of the sun; for the Lord God giveth them light: and they shall reign for ever and ever."

CHAPTER XVI.

THE CAPTURE OF AI.

Joshua viii. 1—29.

JOSHUA, having dealt faithfully with the case of Achan, whose sin had intercepted the favour of God, is again encouraged, and directed to renew, but more carefully, his attack on Ai. That word is addressed to him which has always such significance when coming from the Divine lips—" Fear not." How much of our misery arises from fear! How many a beating heart, how many a shaking nerve, how many a sleepless night have come, not from evil experienced, but from evil apprehended! To save one from the apprehension of evil is sometimes more important, as it is usually far more difficult, than to save one from evil itself. An affectionate father finds that one of his most needed services to his children is to allay their fears. Never is he doing them a greater kindness than when he uses his larger experience of life to assure them, in some anxiety, that there is no cause for fear. Our heavenly Father finds much occasion for a similar course. He has indeed got a very timid family. It is most interesting to mark how the Bible is studded with " fear nots," from Genesis to Revelation; from that early word to Abraham—" Fear not, I am thy shield, and thy exceeding great reward"—to that most comforting assurance to the beloved disciple, "Fear not; I am the first and the last: I am He that liveth, and was dead; and, behold, I am alive for evermore, Amen; and have the keys of hades and of death." If only God's children could hear Him uttering that one word, from how much anxiety and misery would it set them free !

Virtually the command to Joshua is to "**try again.**" Success, though denied to the first effort, often comes to the next, or at least to a subsequent one. Even apart from spiritual considerations, it is those who try oftenest who succeed best. There is little good in a man who abandons an undertaking simply because he has tried once and failed. Who does not recall in this connection the story of Alfred the Great? Or of Robert the Bruce watching the spider in the barn that at last reached the roof after sixteen failures? Or, looking to what has a more immediate bearing on the kingdom of God, who has not admired the perseverance of Livingstone, undaunted by fever and famine, and the ferocity of savage chiefs; unmoved by his longings for home and dreams of plenty and comfort that mocked him when he awoke to physical wretchedness and want? Such perseverance gives a man the stamp of true nobility; we are almost tempted to fall down and worship. If failure be humiliating, it is redeemed by the very act and attitude of perseverance, and the self-denial and scorn of ease which it involves. In the Christian warfare no man is promised victory at the first. "Let us not be weary in welldoing, for in due season we shall reap if we faint not."

To Christian men especially, failure brings very valuable lessons. There is always something to be learned from it. In our first attempt we were too self-confident. We went too carelessly about the matter, and did not sufficiently realize the need of Divine support. Never was there a servant of God who learned more from his failures than St. Peter. Nothing could have been more humiliating than his thrice-repeated denial of his Lord. But when Peter came to himself, he saw on what a bruised reed he had been leaning when he said, "Though I should die with Thee yet will I not deny Thee." How miserably misplaced that self-confidence had been! But it had the effect of startling him, of showing him his danger, and of leading him to lift up his eyes to the hills from whence came his help. It might have seemed a risky, nay reckless thing for our Lord to commit the task of steering His infant Church over the stormy seas of her first voyage to a man who, six weeks before, had proved so weak and treacherous. But Peter was a genuine man, and it was that first failure that afterwards made him so strong. It is no longer Peter, but Christ in Peter that directs the movement. And thus it came to pass that, during the critical period of the Church's birth, no carnal drawback diminished his strength or diluted his faith; all his natural rapidity of movement, all his natural outspokenness, boldness, and directness were brought to bear without abatement on the advancement of the young cause. He conducted himself during this most delicate and vital period with a nobility beyond all praise. He took the ship out into the open sea amid raging storms without touching a single rock. And it was all owing to the fact that by God's grace he profited by his failure!

In the case of Joshua and his people, one of the chief lessons derived from their failure before Ai was the evil of covering sin. Alas, this policy is the cause of failures innumerable in the spiritual life! In numberless ways it interrupts Divine fellowship, withdraws the Divine blessing, and grieves the Holy Spirit. We have not courage to cut off a right hand and pluck out a right eye. We leave besetting sins in a corner of our hearts, instead of trying to exterminate them, and determining not to allow them a foothold there. The acknowledgment of sin, the giving up of all leniency towards it, the determination, by God's grace, to be done with it, always go before true revivals, before a true return of God to us in all His graciousness and power. Rather, we should say, they are the beginning of revival. In Israel of old the land had to be purged of every vestige of idolatry under Hezekiah and other godly kings, before the light of God's countenance was again lifted upon it. "To this man will I look, even to him that is poor and of a contrite spirit, and that trembleth at My word."

Joshua is instructed to go up again against Ai, but in order to interest and encourage the people, he resorts to a new plan of attack. A stratagem is to be put in operation. An ambuscade is to be stationed on the west side of the city, while the main body of the assaulting force is to approach it, as formerly, from the east. There is some obscurity and apparent confusion in the narrative, confined, however, to one point, the number composing the ambuscade and the main body respectively. Some error in the text appears to have crept in. From the statement in ver. 3 we might suppose that the men who were to lie in ambush amounted to thirty thousand; but in ver. 12 it is expressly stated that only five thousand were employed in this way. There can be little doubt (though it is not according to the letter of the narrative) that the whole force employed amounted to thirty thousand,

and that, of these, five thousand formed the ambush. Indeed, in such a valley, it would not have been possible for thirty thousand men to conceal themselves so as to be invisible from the city. It would appear (ver. 17) that the people of Bethel had left their own village and gone into Ai. Bethel, as we have said, was situated higher up; in fact, it was on the very ridge of the plateau of Western Palestine. It must have been but a little place, and its people seem to have deemed it better to join those of Ai, knowing that if the Israelites were repulsed from the lower city, the upper was safe.

The *ruse* was that the ambush should be concealed behind the city; that Ai, as before, should be attacked from the east by the main body of troops; that on receiving the onslaught from the city they should seem to be defeated as before; that Joshua, probably standing on some commanding height, should give a signal to the men in ambush by raising his spear; whereupon these men should rush down on the now deserted place and set it on fire. On seeing the flames, the pursuers would naturally turn and rush back to extinguish them; then the main body of Israel would turn likewise, and thus the enemy would be caught as in a trap from which there was no escape, and fall a victim to the two sections of Israel.

To plots of this kind, the main objection in a strategical sense lies in the risk of detection. For the five thousand who went to station themselves in the west it was a somewhat perilous thing to separate themselves from the host, and place themselves in the heart of enemies both in front and in rear. It needed strong faith to expose themselves in such a situation. Suppose they had been detected as they went stealing along past Ai in the darkness of the night; suppose they had come on some house or hamlet, and wakened the people, so that the alarm should have been carried to Ai, what would have been the result? It was well for Israel that no such mishap occurred, and that they were able in silence to reach a place where they might lie concealed. The ground is so broken by rocks and ravines that this would not have been very difficult; the people of Ai suspected nothing; probably the force on the east were at pains, by camp-fires and otherwise, to engage their attention, and whenever that force began to move, as if for the attack, every eye in the city would be fixed intently upon it.

The plot was entirely successful; everything fell out precisely as Joshua had desired. A terrible slaughter of the men of Ai took place, caught as they were on the east of the city between the two sections of Joshua's troops, for the Israelites gave no quarter either to age or sex. The whole number of the slain amounted to twelve thousand, and that probably included the people of Bethel too. We see from this what an insignificant place Ai must have been, and how very humiliating was the defeat it inflicted at first. With reference to the spoil of the city, the rigid law prescribed at Jericho was not repeated; the people got it for themselves. Jericho was an exceptional case; it was the firstfruits of the conquest, therefore holy to the Lord. If Achan had but waited a little, he would have had his share of the spoil of Ai or some other place. He would have got legitimately what he purloined unlawfully. In the slaughter, the king, or chief of the place, suffered a more ignominious doom than his soldiers; instead of being slain with the sword, he was hanged, and his body was exposed on a tree till sunset. Joshua did not want some drops of Oriental blood; he had the stern pleasure of the Eastern warrior in humbling those who were highest in honour. What remained of the city was burned; it continued thereafter a heap of ruins, with a great cairn of stones at its gate, erected over the dead body of the king.

We see that already light begins to be thrown on what at the time must have seemed the very severe and rigid order about the spoil of Jericho. Although Achan was the only offender, he was probably far from being the only complainer on that occasion. Many another Israelite with a covetous heart must have felt bitterly that it was very hard to be prevented from taking even an atom to oneself. "Were not our fathers allowed to spoil the Egyptians—why, then, should we be absolutely prevented from having a share of the spoil of Jericho?" It might have been enough to answer that God claimed the firstfruits of the land for Himself. Or to say that God designed at the very entrance of His people into Canaan to show that they were not a tumultuous rabble, rushing greedily on all they could lay their hands on, but a well-trained, well-mannered family, in whom self-restraint was one of the noblest virtues. But to all this it might have been added, that the people's day was not far off. It is not God's method to muzzle the ox that treadeth out the corn. And so to all who rush tumultuously upon the good things of this life, He says, "Seek first the kingdom of heaven and His righteousness, and all these things shall be added unto you." Let God arrange the order in which His gifts are distributed. Never hurry Providence, as Sarah did when she gave Hagar to Abraham. Sarah had good cause to repent of her impetuosity; it brought her many a bitter hour. Whereas God was really kinder to her than she had thought, and in due time He gave her Isaac, not the son of the bondwoman, but her own.

A question has been raised respecting the legitimacy of the stratagem employed by Joshua in order to capture Ai. Was it right to deceive the people; to pretend to be defeated while in reality he was only executing a *ruse*, and thus draw on the poor men of Ai to a terrible death? Calvin and other commentators make short work of this objection. If war is lawful, stratagem is lawful. Stratagem indeed, as war used to be conducted, was a principal part of it; and even now the term "strategic," derived from it, is often used to denote operations designed for a different purpose from that which at first appears. It is needless to discuss here the lawfulness of war, for the Israelites were waging war at the express command of the Almighty. And if it be said that when once you allow the principle that it is lawful in war to mislead the enemy, you virtually allow perfidy, inasmuch as it would be lawful for you, after pledging your word under a flag of truce, to disregard your promise, the answer to that is, that to mislead in such circumstances would be infamous. A distinction is to be drawn between acts where the enemy has no right to expect that you will make known your intention, and acts where they have such a right. In the ordinary run of strategic movements, you are under no obligation to tell the foe what you are about. It is part of their business to watch you, to scrutinize your every movement, and in spite of appearances to divine your real purpose. If they are too careless to watch, or too stupid to discern between a professed and a real plan, they must bear the consequences. But when a flag of truce is displayed, when a meeting takes place under its protection, and when conditions are agreed to on both sides, the case is very different. The enemy is entitled now to expect that you will not mislead them. Your word of honour has been passed to that effect. And to disregard that pledge, and deem it smart to mislead thereby, is a proceeding worthy only of the most barbarous, the most perfidious, the most shameless of men.

Thus far we may defend the usages of war; but at best it is a barbarous mode of operations. Very memorable was the observation of the Duke of Wellington, that next to the calamity of suffering a defeat was that of gaining a victory. To look over a great battlefield, fresh from the clash of arms; to survey the trampled crops, the ruined houses, the universal desolation ; to gaze on all the manly forms lying cold in death, and the many besides wounded, bleeding, groaning, perhaps dying; to think of the illimitable treasure that has been lavished on this work of destruction and the comforts of which it has robbed the countries engaged ; to remember in what a multitude of cases, death must carry desolation and anguish to the poor widow, and turn the remainder of life into a lonely pilgrimage, is enough surely to rob war of the glory associated with it, and to make good the position that on the part of civilized and Christian men it should only be the last desperate resort, after every other means of effecting its object has failed. We are not forgetful of the manly self-sacrifice of those who expose themselves so readily to the risk of mutilation and death, wherever the rulers of their country require it, for it is the redeeming feature of war that it brings out so much of this high patriotic devotion ; but surely they are right who deem arbitration the better method of settling national differences ; who call for a great disarmament of the European nations, and would put a stop to the attitude of every great country shaking its fist in the face of its neighbours. What has become of the prophecy " They shall beat their swords into ploughshares and their spears into pruning hooks " ? Or the beautiful vision of Milton on the birth of the Saviour ?—

> "No war, or battle's sound
>   Was heard the world around;
> The idle spear and shield were high uphung;
>   The hookèd chariot stood
>   Unstained with hostile blood,
> The trumpet spake not to the armèd throng;
> And kings sat still with awful eye
> As if they surely knew their sovran Lord was by."

One lesson comes to us with pre-eminent force from the operations of war. The activity displayed by every good commander is a splendid example for all of us in spiritual warfare. " Joshua arose " ; " Joshua lodged that night among the people " ; · " Joshua rose up early in the morning " ; " Joshua went that night into the middle of the valley " ; " Joshua drew not his hand back wherewith he stretched out the spear, until he had utterly destroyed all the inhabitants of Ai." Such expressions show how intensely in earnest he was, how unsparing of himself, how vigilant and indefatigable in all that bore upon his enterprise. And generally we still see that, wherever military expeditions are undertaken, they are pushed forward with untiring energy, and the sinews of war are supplied in unstinted abundance, whatever grumbling there may be afterwards when the bill comes to be paid. Has the Christian Church ever girded herself for the great enterprise of conquering the world for Christ with the same zeal and determination ? What are all the sums of money contributed for Christian missions, compared to those spent annually on military and naval forces, and multiplied indefinitely when active war goes on! Alas, this question brings out but one result of a painful comparison—the contrast between the ardour with which secular results are pursued by secular men, and spiritual results by spiritual men. Let the rumour spread that gold or diamonds have been found at some remote region of the globe, what multitudes flock to them in the hope of possessing themselves of a share of the spoil! Not even the prospect of spending many days and nights in barbarism, amid the misery of dirt and heat and insects, and with company so rude and rough and reckless that they have hardly the appearance of humanity, can overcome the impetuous desire to possess themselves of the precious material, and come home rich. What crowds rush in when the prospectus of a profitable brewery promises an abundant dividend, earned too often by the manufactory of drunkards! What eager eyes scan the advertisements that tell you that if persons bearing a certain name, or related to one of that name, would apply at a certain address, they would hear of something to their advantage! Once we knew of a young man who had not even seen such an advertisement, but had been told that it had appeared. There was a vague tradition in his family that in certain circumstances a property would fall to them. The mere rumour that an advertisement had appeared in which he was interested set him to institute a search for it. He procured a file of the *Times* newspaper, reaching over a series of years, and eagerly scanned its advertisements. Failing to find there what he was in search of, he procured sets of other daily newspapers and subjected them to the same process. And thus he went on and on in his unwearied search, till first he lost his situation, then he lost his reason, and then he lost his life. What will men not do to obtain a corruptible crown? Could it be supposed from *our* attitude and ardour that we are striving for the incorruptible? Could it be thought that the riches which we are striving to accumulate are not those which moth and rust do corrupt, but the treasures that endure for evermore? Surely "it is high time for us to awake out of sleep." Surely we ought to lay to heart that " the things which are seen are temporal, but the things which are not seen are eternal." Memorable are the poet's words respecting the great objects of human desire :—

> "The cloud-capt towers, the gorgeous palaces,
> The solemn temples, the great globe itself,
> Yea, all which it inherit, shall dissolve:
> And like this unsubstantial pageant faded,
> Leave not a rack behind."

CHAPTER XVII.

EBAL AND GERIZIM.

JOSHUA viii. 30—35.

COMMENTATORS on Joshua have been greatly perplexed by the place which this narrative has in our Bibles. No one can study the map, and take into account the circumstances of Joshua and the people, without sharing in this perplexity. It will be observed from the map that Ebal and Gerizim, rising from the plain of Shechem, are a long way distant from Ai and Bethel. If we suppose Joshua and not his army only, but the whole of his people (ver. 33), to have gone straight from Gilgal to Mount Ebal after the capture of Ai, the journey must have occupied several days each way, besides the time needed for the ceremony that took place there. It certainly would have needed an overwhelming reason to induce him at such a time, first to march a host like this all the way to Mount Ebal, and then to march them back to their encampment at Gilgal. Hence many have come to believe that, in some way which we cannot explain, this passage has been inserted out of its proper place. The most natural place for it would be at the end of chap. xi. or chap. xii., after the conquest of the whole country, and before its division among the tribes. Nearly all the manuscripts of the Septuagint insert it between

vv. 2 and 3 of the ninth chapter, but this does not go far to remove the difficulty. It has been thought by some that Joshua left the original Gilgal in the plain of Jordan, and fixed his camp at another Gilgal, transferring the name of his first encampment to the second. Mention is certainly made in Scripture of another Gilgal in the neighbourhood of Bethel (2 Kings ii. 2), but nothing is said to lead us to suppose that Joshua had removed his encampment thither.

Some have thought that no record has been preserved of one of Joshua's great campaigns, the campaign in which he subdued the central part of the country. A good deal may be said for this supposition. In the list of the thirty-one kings whom he subdued over the country (chap. xii.) we find several whose dominions were in this region. For instance, we know that Aphek, Taanach, and Megiddo were all situated in the central part of the country, and probably other cities too. Yet, while the fact is recorded that they were defeated, no mention is made of any expedition against them. They belonged neither to the confederacy of Adonizedec in the south nor to that of Jabin in the north, and they must have been subdued on some separate occasion. It is just possible that Joshua defeated them before encountering the confederacy of Adonizedec at Gibeon and Bethhoron. But it is far more likely that it was after that victory that he advanced to the central part of the country.

On the whole, while admitting the perplexity of the question, we incline to the belief that the passage has been transferred from its original place. This in no way invalidates the authority of the book, or of the passage, for in the most undoubtedly authentic books of Scripture we have instances beyond question—very notably in Jeremiah—of passages inserted out of their natural order.

It has been said that the passage in Deuteronomy (xxvii. 4-19) could not have been written by Moses, because he had never set foot in Canaan, and therefore could not have been acquainted with the names or the locality of Ebal and Gerizim. On the contrary, we believe that he had very good reason to be acquainted with both. For at the foot of Ebal lay the portion of ground which Jacob gave to his son Joseph, and where both Jacob's well and Joseph's tomb are pointed out at the present day. That piece of ground must have been familiar to Jacob, and carefully described to Joseph by its great natural features when he made it over to him. And as Joseph regarded it as his destined burial-place, the tradition of its situation must have been carefully transmitted to those that came after him, when he gave commandment concerning his bones. Joseph was not the oldest son of Jacob, any more than Rachel was his oldest wife, and for these reasons neither of them was buried in the cave of Machpelah. Moses therefore had good reasons for being acquainted with the locality. Probably it was at the time of the ceremony at Ebal that the bones of Joseph were buried, although the fact is not recorded till the very end of the book (Josh. xxiv. 32). But that passage, too, is evidently not in its natural place.

It was a most fitting thing that when he had completed the conquest of the country, Joshua should set about performing that great national ceremony, designed to rivet on the people's hearts the claims of God's law and covenant, which had been enjoined by Moses to be performed in the valley of Shechem. For though Joshua was neither priest nor prophet, yet as a warm believer and earnest servant of God, he felt it his duty on all suitable occasions to urge upon the people that there was no prosperity for them save on condition of loyalty to Him. He sought to mingle the thought of God and of God's claims with the very life of the nation; to make it run, as it were, in their very blood; to get them to think of the Divine covenant as their palladium, the very pledge of all their blessings, their one only guarantee of prosperity and peace.

When therefore Joshua conducted his people to the Mounts Ebal and Gerizim, in order that they might have the obligations of the law set before them in a form as impressive as it was picturesque, he was not merely fulfilling mechanically an injunction of Moses, but performing a transaction into which he himself entered heart and soul. And when the writer of the book records the transaction, it is not merely for the purpose of showing us how certain acts prescribed in a previous book were actually performed, but for the purpose of perpetuating an occurrence which in the whole future history of the nation would prove either a continual inspiration for good, or a testimony against them, so that out of their own life they should be condemned. Knowing Joshua as we do, we can easily believe that all along it was one of his most cherished projects to implement the legacy of Moses, and superintend this memorable covenanting act. It must have been a great relief from the bloody scenes and awful experiences of war to assemble his people among the mountains, and engage them in a service which was so much more in harmony with the beauty and sublimity of nature. No critic or writer who has any sense of the fitness of things can coolly remove this transaction from the sphere of history into that of fancy, or deprive

Joshua of his share in a transaction into which his heart was doubtless thrown as enthusiastically as that of David in after times when the ark was placed upon Mount Zion.

It could not be without thrilling hearts that Joshua and all of his people who were like-minded entered the beautiful valley of Shechem, which had been the first resting-place in Canaan of their father Abraham, the first place where God appeared to him, and the first place where "he builded an altar unto the Lord" (Gen. xii. 6, 7). By general consent the valley of Shechem holds the distinction of being one of the most beautiful in the country. "Its western side," says Stanley, "is bounded by the abutments of two mountain ranges, running from west to east. These ranges are Gerizim and Ebal; and up the opening between them, not seen from the plain, lies the modern town of Nablous [Neapolis = Shechem]. . . . A valley green with grass, grey with olives, gardens sloping down on each side, fresh springs running down in all directions; at the end a white town embosomed in all this verdure, lodged between the two high mountains which extend on each side of the valley—that on the south Gerizim, that on the north Ebal;—this is the aspect of Nablous, the most beautiful, perhaps it might be said the only very beautiful spot in Central Palestine."

If the host of Israel approached Ebal and Gerizim from the south, they would pass along the central ridge or plateau of the country till they reached the vale of Shechem, where the mountain range would appear as if it had been cleft from top to bottom by some great convulsion of nature. Then, as now, the country was studded thickly with villages, the plains clothed with grass and grain, and the rounded hills with orchards of fig, olive, pomegranate, and other trees. On either side of the fissure rose a hill of about eight hundred feet, about the height of Arthur Seat at Edinburgh, Ebal on the north and Gerizim on the south. It was not like the scene at Sinai, where the bare and desolate mountains towered up to heaven, their summits lost among the clouds. This was a more homely landscape, amid the fields and dwellings where the people were to spend their daily life. If the proclamation of the law from Sinai had something of an abstract and distant character, Ebal and Gerizim brought it home to the business and bosoms of men. It was now to be the rule for every day, and for every transaction of every day; the bride was now to be settled in her home, and if she was to enjoy the countenance and the company of her heavenly Bridegroom, the law of His house must be fully implemented, and its every requirement riveted on her heart.

The ceremony here under Joshua was twofold: first, the rearing of an altar; and second, the proclamation of the law.

1. The altar, as enjoined in Exod. xx. 24, was of whole, undressed stones. In its simple structure it was designed to show that the Most High dwelleth not in temples made with hands. In its open position it demonstrated that the most fitting place for His worship was not the secret recesses of the woods, but the open air and full light of heaven, seeing that He is light, and in Him is no darkness at all. On this altar were offered burnt offerings and peace offerings to the Lord. The sacrificial system had been little attended to amid the movements of the wilderness, and the warlike operations in which the people had been more or less engaged ever since their entrance on the land; but now was the beginning of a more regular worship.

The first transaction here performed was the sacrificial. Here sin was called to mind, and the need of propitiation. Here it was commemorated that God Himself had appointed a method of propitiation; that He had thereby signified His gracious desire to be at peace with His people; that He had not left them to sigh out, "Oh that we knew where we might find Him, that we might come even to His seat!"—but had opened to His people the gates of righteousness, that they might go in and praise the Lord.

Moreover, we read in Joshua, that "he wrote there upon the stones a copy of the law of Moses, which he wrote in the presence of the children of Israel." There is sufficient difference between the passages in Deuteronomy and Joshua to show that the one was not copied from the other. From Joshua we might suppose that it was on the stones of the altar that Joshua wrote, and there is no reference to the command given in Deuteronomy to plaister the stones with plaister. But from Deuteronomy it is plain that it was not the stones of the altar that were plaistered over, but memorial stones set up for the purpose. There has been no little controversy as to the manner in which this injunction was carried out. According to Dr. Thomson, in the "Land and the Book," the matter is very simple. The difficulty in the eyes of commentators has arisen from the idea that plaister is altogether too soft a substance to retain the impression of what is written on it. This Dr. Thomson wholly disputes: "A careful examination of Deut. xxvii. 4, 8 and Josh. viii. 30-32 will lead to the opinion that the law was written upon and in the plaister with which these pillars were coated. This could easily be done; and such writing was common in ancient times. I have seen numerous specimens of it certainly more than two thousand years old, and still as distinct as when they were first inscribed upon the plaister. . . . In this hot climate, where there is no frost to dissolve the cement, it will continue hard and unbroken for thousands of years,—which is certainly long enough. The cement on Solomon's pools remains in admirable preservation, though exposed to all the vicissitudes of the climate and with no protection. . . . What Joshua did therefore, when he erected those great stones on Mount Ebal, was merely to write *in* the still soft cement with a style, or more likely *on* the polished surface when dry, with red paint, as in ancient tombs. If properly sheltered, and not broken by violence, they would have remained to this day."

Joshua could not have written the whole of the law on his pillars; it was probably only the ten commandments. As we shall see, another arrangement was made for the rehearsal of the whole law; it was solemnly read out afterwards. But now the entire nation, with all the strangers and followers, took up their position in the valley between the two mountains. Half of the tribes separated from the rest to the slopes of Gerizim, and the other half to those of Ebal. From Deuteronomy we gather that those who were grouped on Gerizim were far the more important and numerous tribes. They embraced Simeon, Levi, Judah, Issachar, Joseph, and Benjamin. On Mount Ebal were stationed Reuben, Gad and Asher, Zebulun, Dan and Naphtali. The priests stood between, and read out blessings and curses. When blessings were read out the tribes on Gerizim shouted Amen. When curses were read out those on Ebal did the same. Let us imagine the scene. A mountain side covered with people is always a picturesque sight, and the effect is greatly heightened when the clothing of the multitude is of light, bright colours, as probably it was on this occasion. " It was," says Dr. Thomson, " beyond question or comparison the most august assembly the sun has ever shone upon ; and I never stand in the narrow plain, with Ebal and Gerizim rising on either hand to the sky, without involuntarily recalling and reproducing the scene. I have shouted to hear the echo, and then fancied how it must have been when the loud-voiced Levites proclaimed from the naked cliffs of Ebal, ' Cursed is the man that maketh any graven image, an abomination to Jehovah.' And then the tremendous AMEN ! tenfold louder from the united congregation, rising and swelling and re-echoing from Ebal to Gerizim, and from Gerizim to Ebal. AMEN ! Even so, let him be accursed. No, there never was an assembly to compare with this."

Very explicit mention is made of the fact that " there was not a word of all that Moses commanded which Joshua read not before all the congregation of the children of Israel, with the women and the little ones and the strangers that were conversant among them." This obviously implies that the law of Moses was in definite form, and that the reading of it took up a considerable portion of time.

The order of events had been very significant. First, a great work of destruction—the dispossession of the Canaanites. Next, the erection of an altar, and the offering up of sacrifices. And, lastly, the inscribing and proclamation of the law. " The surgeon has done his duty, and now nature will proceed to heal and comfort and bless. The enemy has been driven off the field. Now the altar is put up and the law is promulgated. Society without law is chaos. An altar without righteousness is evaporative sentiment. Prayer without duty may be a detachment of the wings from the bird they were designed to assist. . . . Having done the destructive work, do not imagine that the whole programme is complete; now begins the construction of the altar. And having made a place for prayer, do not imagine that the whole duty of man has been perfected; next put up the law; battle, prayer, law; law, prayer, battle."[1]

If the conjecture that this passage originally occupied a later place in the book be correct, the army was now about to be disbanded, and the people were about to be settled in homes of their own. It was a momentous crisis. They were about to lose, in a great degree, the influence of union, and the presence of men like Joshua and the godly elders, whose noble example and stirring words had ever been a power for what was good and true. Scattered over the land, they would now be more at the control of their own hearts, and often of what in them was least noble and least godly. On the part of Joshua, everything had been done, by this solemn gathering, to secure that they should separate with the remembrance of God's mighty works on their behalf filling their hearts, and the words of God's law ringing in their ears.

---

[1] "The People's Bible," by Joseph Parker, D.D.

CHAPTER XVIII.

THE STRATAGEM OF THE GIBEONITES.

JOSHUA ix.

WE now resume the thread of the story interrupted by the narrative of the transaction at Ebal and Gerizim. We learn from the testimony of Rahab of Jericho, as uttered to the spies (chap. ii. 9), that the terror of Israel had caused the hearts of the inhabitants of the country to faint, and that the fame of all that had been done for them by Jehovah had quite paralysed them. But when the host of Israel actually entered Western Palestine, and began their conquest by the destruction of Jericho and Ai, the inhabitants seem to have plucked up courage, and begun to consider what could be done in self-defence. It is very probable that they found considerable encouragement from what happened at Ai. There it had been seen that Israel was not invincible. Insignificant though Ai was, its people had been able to repel with great success the first attack of the Israelites. And though they had been destroyed in the second, this was achieved only by the combined influence of stratagem and an overwhelming force. The supernatural power under which Jericho had fallen had not been shown at Ai, and might not come into play in the future. There was therefore yet a chance for the Canaanites, if they should combine and act in concert. Steps were therefore taken for such a union. The kings or chiefs who occupied the hills, or central plateau of the country; those of the valleys, interspersed between the mountains; and those occupying the Shephelah, or maritime plains of Philistia, Sharon, and Phœnicia;—all the nations comprised under the well-known names Hittites, Amorites, Canaanites, Perizzites, Hivites, and Jebusites, entered into a league of defence, and prepared to confront Joshua and the Israelites with a determined resistance. The news of the confederacy would bring a tremor over some timid hearts in the camp of Israel, but would cause no serious anxiety to Joshua and all the men of faith, who, like him, felt assured that the Lord was with them.

There was one native community, however, that determined to follow another course. The Gibeonites were a branch of the Hivite race, inhabiting the town of Gibeon, and some other prominent towns in the great central plateau of the country. Gibeon is undoubtedly represented now by the village of El Jib, situated about half-way between Jerusalem and Bethel, four or five miles distant from each. Dr. Robertson describes El Jib as situated in a beautiful plain of considerable extent, on an oblong hill or ridge, composed of layers of limestone, rising as if by regular steps out of the plain. In the days of Joshua, it was a place of great importance, a royal city, and it had under its jurisdiction the towns of Beeroth, Chephirah, and Kirjath-jearim. Its inhabitants were in no humour to fight with Joshua. They had faith enough to understand what would be the inevitable result of that, and therein they were right, and the confederate kings were wrong. On the other hand, they were not prepared to make an honest and unconditional surrender. They probably knew that the orders under which Joshua was acting called on him to destroy all the people of the land, and they had no assurance that, being of the doomed nations, open submission would secure their lives. They resolved therefore to proceed by stratagem. A detachment was appointed to wait on Joshua at his camp at Gilgal, as if they were ambassadors from a distant country, and represent to him in pious tone that they had come from afar, "because of the name of the Lord his God, having heard the fame of Him, and all that He did in Egypt, and all that He did to the two kings of the Amorites that were beyond Jordan, to Sihon King of Heshbon, and to Og King of Bashan." They came with the desire to show respect to the people whose God was so powerful, and to be allowed, though far off, to live at peace with them. Then they presented their credentials, as it were; showing the old sacks, the shrivelled bottles, the musty bread they had brought with them, and the clouts upon their feet and ragged garments which attested the great length of their journey. "Those old Gibeonites," says the "Land and the Book," "did indeed 'work wilily' with Joshua. Nothing could be better calculated to deceive than their devices. I have often thought that their ambassadors, as described in the narrative, furnish one of the finest groups imaginable for a painter; with their old sacks on their poor asses; their wine bottles of goat skin, patched and shrivelled up in the sun, old, rent, and bound up; old shoes and clouted upon their feet; old garments, ragged and bedraggled, with bread dry and mouldy,—the very picture of an over-travelled and wearied caravan from a great distance. It is impossible to transfer to paper the ludicrous appearance of such a company. No wonder that, having tasted their mouldy victuals, and looked upon their soiled and travel-worn costume, Joshua and the elders were deceived, especially as they did not wait to ask counsel at the mouth of the Lord."

It was just the completeness of the disguise that threw Joshua and the men of Israel off their guard. For at first the idea did occur to them that the strangers might be neighbours, and therefore of the nations that they were called on to destroy. On closer inspection, however, that seemed out of the question; indeed, the supposition was so utterly preposterous that it was deemed hardly fitting to bring the matter before the Lord. It is as plain as day, Joshua and the elders would reason; the evidence of what they say is beyond question; theirs is no case of perplexity requiring us to go to God; we may surely exercise our common sense and make a league with these far-travelled men. In a short time they will be back in their own country, far beyond our boundaries, and the only effect of their visit and of our league will be a fresh tribute to the name and power of Jehovah, a fresh testimony to His presence with us, and a fresh pledge that He will bear us to success in the enterprise in which we are engaged. And when the confederate kings that are now leaguing against us hear that this distant people have come to us to propitiate our favour, they will be struck by a new terror and will be the more easily subdued.

We see in all this the simple, unsuspecting spirit of men who have spent their lives in the wilderness. As for the Gibeonites, there was a combination of good and bad in their spirit. They remind us in a measure of the woman with the issue of blood. In her there was certainly faith; but along with the faith, extraordinary superstition. In the Gibeonites there was faith—a belief that Israel was under the protection of a remarkable Divine power, under a Divine promise the truth of which even Balaam had very recently acknowledged —"I will bless them that bless thee, and curse him that curseth thee." Undoubtedly a religious feeling lay at the bottom of the proceeding. A great divine Being was seen to be involved, who was on Israel's side and against his enemies, and it would not do to trifle with Him. But in their way of securing exemption from the effects of His displeasure, the grossest superstition appeared. They were to gain their object by deceit. They were to get Him to favour them above their neighbours through an elaborate system of fraud, through a tissue of lies, through unmitigated falsehood. What a strange conception of God! What blindness to His highest attributes,—His holiness and His truth! What amazing infatuation to suppose that they could secure His blessing through acts fitted to provoke His utmost displeasure! What a miserable God men fashion to themselves when they simply invest Him with almighty power, or perhaps suppose Him to be moved by whims and prejudices and favouritisms like frail man, but omit to clothe Him with His highest glory—forget that "justice and judgment are the habitation of His throne, mercy and truth go before His face."

The conduct of the men was the more strange that it was impossible that they should not be speedily found out. And it was quite possible that, when found out, they would be dealt with more severely than ever. True, indeed, Joshua, when he did detect their plot, did not so act; he acted on a high, perhaps a mistaken sense of honour; but they had no right to count on that. Timidity is a poor adviser. All it can do is to turn the next corner. True faith, resting on eternal truth, acts for eternity. True faith is often blind, but in the deepest darkness it knows that it is on the right track, and under the guidance of the eternal light. Blind faith is very different from blind fear. Faith holds on in full expectation of deliverance; fear trembles and stumbles, in perpetual dread of exposure and humiliation.

"A lying tongue is but for a moment;" and the Gibeonite fraud lived just three days. Then it was discovered by Joshua that the Gibeonites lived in the immediate neighbourhood. But before that, he had made peace with them, and entered into a league to let them live, and the princes of the congregation had confirmed it by an oath. Nothing could have been more provoking than to discover that they had been duped and swindled. It is always a very bitter experience to find that our confidence has been misplaced. Men whom we thought trustworthy, and whom we commended to others as trustworthy, have turned out knaves. It is hard to bear, for we have committed ourselves to our friends in the matter. What would Joshua and his people think now of the supposed tribute to the God of Israel, and the impression expected to be made on the confederate kings? Before all the inhabitants of Canaan he and his people were befooled, humiliated. Not a man in all the country but would be making merry at their expense. Yet even that was not the worst of it. They had been guilty of over-confidence, and of neglect of means that were in their hands; they had neglected to get counsel of their God. They had trusted in their own hearts when they ought to have sought guidance from above. The trouble was their own creation; they were alone to blame.

We cannot but respect the way in which Joshua and

the princes acted when they discovered the fraud. It might have been competent to repudiate the league on the ground that it was agreed to by them under false pretences. It was made on the representation that the Gibeonites had come from a far country, and when that was seen to be utterly untrue there would have been an honourable ground for repudiating the transaction. But Joshua did not avail himself of this loophole. He and the princes had such respect for the sanctity of an oath that, even when they discovered that they had been grossly deceived, they would not resile from it. It seems to have been the princes that took up this ground, and they did so in opposition to the congregation (ver. 18). The fact that the name of the Lord God of Israel had been invoked in the oath sworn to the Gibeonites constrained them to abide by the transaction. It is a good sign of their spirit that they were so jealous of the honour of their God, and of the sanctity of their oath. They came out of the transaction with more honour than we should have expected. Personal interests were subordinated to higher considerations. They carried out that great canon of true religion —first and foremost giving "glory to God in the highest."

But though the lives of the Gibeonites were spared, that was all. They were to be reduced to a kind of slavery—to be " hewers of wood and drawers of water for the congregation and the altar of God." The expression has become a household word to denote a life of drudgery, but perhaps we fail to recognise the full significance of the terms. " I was forcibly reminded of this," says the author of " The Land and the Book," " by long files of women and children (near El Jib) carrying on their heads heavy bundles of wood. . . .

It is the severest kind of drudgery, and my compassion has often been enlisted in behalf of the poor women and children, who daily bring loads of wood to Jerusalem from these very mountains of the Gibeonites. To carry water, also, is very laborious and fatiguing. The fountains are far off, in deep wadies with steep banks, and a thousand times have I seen the feeble and the young staggering up long and weary ways with large jars of water on their heads. It is the work of slaves, and of the very poor, whose condition is still worse. Among the pathetic lamentations of Jeremiah there is nothing more affecting than this: 'They took the young men to grind, and the children fell under the wood' (i. 16). Grinding at the hand-mill is a low, menial work, assigned to female slaves, and therefore utterly humiliating to the young men of Israel. And the delicate children of Zion falling under the loads of hard, rough wood, along the mountain paths! Alas! 'for these things I weep; mine eye, mine eye runneth down with water, because the comforter that should relieve my soul is far from me: my children are desolate, because the enemy prevailed.'"

Respecting the after history of Gibeon and the Gibeonites we find some notices in the Old Testament, but none in the New. At one time there was a sanctuary at Gibeon, even after the ark had been removed to Mount Zion; for it was at Gibeon that Solomon offered his great sacrifice of a thousand burnt offerings, and had that remarkable dream in which, in reply to the Divine offer of a choice of gifts, he chose wisdom in preference to any other (1 Kings iii. 4 *sq.*). But the most remarkable reappearance of the Gibeonites in history is in the reigns of Saul and David. For some unknown reason, and probably quite unjustly, Saul had out some of them to death. And in the reign of David, probably the early part of it, when a succession of famines desolated the land, and inquiry was made as to the cause, the reply of the oracle was: "It is for Saul and his bloody house, because he slew the Gibeonites." And it was to avenge this unjust slaughter that seven descendants of Saul were put to death, on that occasion when Rizpah, the mother of two of them, showed such remarkable affection by guarding their dead bodies from the beasts and birds of prey. It is possible that even after the Babylonian captivity some Gibeonites survived under their old name, because it is said in Nehemiah that among the others who repaired the wall of Jerusalem were "Melatiah the Gibeonite, and Jadon the Meronothite, the men of Gibeon, and of Mizpah" (iii. 7). Only it is uncertain whether Melatiah was of the old Gibeonite stock, or an Israelite who had Gibeon for his city. While the old Gibeonites did survive they seem to have had a miserable lot, and the question might have been often asked by them—Did our fraud bring us any real good? Is life worth living?

Does anything resembling this fraud of the Gibeonites ever take place among ourselves? In answer, let us ask first of all, what is the meaning of pious frauds? Are they not transactions where fraud is resorted to in order to accomplish what are supposed to be religious ends? Granting that the fraud of the Gibeonites was not for a religious but for a secular object—their deliverance from the sword of Joshua—still they professed, in practising it, to be doing honour to God. It is the part of superstition at once to lower the intellectual and the moral attributes of God. It often represents that the most frivolous acts, the uttering of mysterious words, or the performance of senseless acts have such a power over God as to bring about certain desired results. More frequently it holds that cruelty, falsehood, injustice, and other crimes, if brought to bear on religious or ecclesiastical ends, are pleasing in God's sight. Is there anything more truly odious than this severance of religion from morality and humanity,—this representation that fraud and other immoral acts have value before God? How can anything be a real religious gain to a man, how can it be otherwise than disastrous in the last degree, if it develops a fraudulent spirit, if it perverts his moral nature, if it deepens and intensifies the moral disorder of his heart? If men saw "the beauty of holiness," "the beauty of the Lord," they could never bring their minds to such miserable distortions. It is pure blasphemy to suppose that God could thus demean Himself. It is self-degradation to imagine that anything that can be gained by oneself through such means, could make up for what is lost, or for the guilt incurred by such wickedness.

And this suggests a wider thought—the fearful miscalculation men make whensoever they resort to fraud in the hope of reaping benefit by means of it. Yet what practice is more common? The question is, Does it really pay? Does it pay, for instance, to cheat at cards? Have we not seen recently what swift and terrible retribution that may bring, making us feel for the culprit as we might have felt for Cain. Does it pay the merchant to cheat as to the quality of his goods? Does it not leak out that he is not to be trusted, and does not that suspicion lose more to him in the long run than it gains? Does it pay the preacher to preach another man's sermon as his own? Or, to vary the illustration. When one has entrapped a maiden under false promises, and then forsakes her; or when he conceals the fact that he is already married to another; or when he controls himself for a time, to conceal from her his ill temper, or his profligate habits, or his thirst for strong drink, does it pay in the end? The question is not, Does he succeed in his immediate object? but, How does the matter end? Is it a comfortable thought to any man that he has broken a trustful heart, that he has brought misery to a happy home, that he has filled some one's life with lamentation and mourning and woe? We are not thinking only of the future life, when so many wrongs will be brought to light, and so many men and women will have to curse the infatuation that made fraud their friend and evil their good. We think of the present happiness of those who live in an atmosphere of fraud, and worship daily at its shrine. Can such disordered souls know aught of real peace and solid joy? In the case of some of them, are there not occasional moments of sober feeling, when they think what their life was given them for, and contrast their selfish and heartless devices with the career of those who deal truly and live to do good? Bitter, very bitter is the feeling which the contrast raises. It is bitter to think how unfit one is for the society of honest men; how the master one is serving is the father of lies; and how, even when the master does grant one a momentary success, it is at the sacrifice of all self-respect and conscious purity, and with a dark foreboding of wrath in the life to come.

All Eastern nations get the character of being deceitful; but indeed the weed may be said to flourish in every soil where it has not been rooted out by living Christianity. But if it be peculiarly characteristic of Eastern nations, is it not remarkable how constantly it is rebuked in the Bible, even though that book sprang from an Eastern soil? No doubt the record of the Bible abounds with *instances* of deceit, but its voice is always against them. And its instances are always instructive. Satan gained nothing by deceiving our first parents. Jacob was well punished for deceiving Isaac. David's misleading of the high priest when he fled from Saul involved ultimately the slaughter of the whole priestly household. Ananias and Sapphira had an awful experience when they lied unto the Holy Ghost. All through the Bible it is seen that lying lips are an abomination to the Lord, but they that deal truly are His delight. And when our blessed Lord comes to show us the perfect life, how free He is from the slightest taint or vestige of deceit! How beautifully transparent is His whole life and character! No little child with his honest smile and open face was ever more guileless. In the light of that perfect example, who among us does not blush for our errors—for our many endeavours to conceal what we have done, to appear better than we were, to seem to be pleasing God when we were pleasing ourselves, or to be aiming at God's glory when we were really consulting for our own interests? Is it possible for us ever to be worthy of such a Lord? First, surely, we must go to His cross, and, bewailing all our unworthiness, seek acceptance through His finished work. And then draw from His fulness, even grace for grace; obtain through the indwelling of His Spirit that elixir of life which will send a purer life-blood through our souls, and assimilate us to Him of whom His faithful apostle wrote: " He did not sin, *neither was guile found in His mouth.*"

CHAPTER XIX.

THE BATTLE OF BETHHORON.

JOSHUA x.

OUT of the larger confederacy of the whole Canaanite chiefs against Joshua and his people recorded in the beginning of chap. ix., a smaller number, headed by Adonizedec, undertook the special task of chastising the Gibeonites, who had not only refused to join the confederacy, but, as it was thought, basely and treacherously surrendered to Joshua. It is interesting to find the King of Jerusalem, Adonizedec, bearing a name so similar to that of Melchizedek, King of Salem, in the days of Abraham. No doubt, since the days of Jerome, there have been some who have denied that the Salem of Melchizedek was Jerusalem. But the great mass of opinion is in favour of the identity of the two places. Melchizedek means King of Righteousness; Adonizedec, Lord of Righteousness; in substance the same. It was a striking name for a ruler, and it was remarkable that it should have been kept up so long, although in the time of Adonizedec its significance had probably been forgotten. Jerusalem was but five miles south of Gibeon; the other four capitals, whose chiefs joined in the expedition, were farther off. Hebron, eighteen miles south of Jerusalem, was memorable in patriarchal history as the dwelling-place of

Abraham and the burial-place of his family; Jarmuth, hardly mentioned in the subsequent history, is now represented by Yarmuk, six miles from Jerusalem; Lachish, of which we have frequent mention in Scripture, is probably represented by Um Lakis, about fifteen miles south-west of Jerusalem; and Eglon by Ajlan, a little farther west. The five little kingdoms embraced most of the territory afterwards known as the tribe of Judah, and they must have been far more than a match for Gibeon. Their chiefs are called "the five Amorite kings," but this does not imply that they were exclusively of the Amorite race, for "Amorite," like "Canaanite," is often used generically to denote the whole inhabitants (as in Gen. xv. 16). The five chiefs were so near Gibeon that it was quite natural for them to undertake this expedition. No doubt they reckoned that, by making a treaty with Joshua, the Gibeonites had strengthened his hands and weakened those of his opponents; they had made resistance to Joshua more difficult for the confederacy, and therefore they deserved to be chastised. To turn their arms against Gibeon, when they had Joshua to deal with, was probably an unwise proceeding; but to their resources it would seem a very easy task. Gibeon enjoyed nothing of that aid from a great unseen Power that made Joshua so formidable; little could they have dreamt that Joshua would come to the assistance of his new allies, and with God's help inflict on them a crushing defeat. "The Lord bringeth the counsel of the heathen to nought, He maketh the devices of the people of none effect. The counsel of the Lord standeth for ever, the thoughts of His heart to all generations."

The case was very serious for the Gibeonites. As Gibeon lay so near Jerusalem and the cities of the other confederates, it is likely that the appearance of the enemy before its walls was the first, or nearly the first, intimation of the coming attack. In their extremity they sent to Joshua imploring help, and the terms in which they besought him not to lose a moment, but come to them at his utmost speed, show the urgency of their danger. To appeal to Joshua at all after their shameful fraud was a piece of presumption, unless—and this is very unlikely—the treaty between them had promised protection from enemies. Had Joshua been of a mean nature he would have chuckled over their distress, and congratulated himself that now he would get rid of these Gibeonites without trouble on his part. But the same generosity that had refused to take advantage of their fraud when it was detected showed itself in this their time of need. Joshua was encamped at Gilgal on the banks of the Jordan; for the arguments that suppose him to have been at another Gilgal are not consistent with the terms used in the narrative (*e.g.*, ver. 9, "*went up* from Gilgal all night"). From Gilgal to Gibeon the distance is upwards of twenty miles, and a great part of the way is steep and difficult.

Encouraged by the assurance of Divine protection and favoured by the moonlight, Joshua, by a marvellous act of pluck and energy, went up by night, reached Gibeon in the morning, fell upon the army of the assembled kings, possibly while it was yet dark, and utterly discomfited them. It would have been natural for the routed armies to make for Jerusalem, only five miles off, by the south road, but either Joshua had occupied that road, or it was too difficult for a retreat. The way by which they did retreat, running west from Gibeon, is carefully described. First they took the way "that goeth up to Bethhoron." As soon as they had traversed the plain of Gibeon, they ascended a gentle slope leading towards Bethhoron the upper, then fled down the well-known pass, through the two Bethhorons, upper and nether, making for Jarmuth, Lachish, and other towns at the bottom of the hills. In the course of their descent a hailstorm overtook them, one of those terrific storms which seem hardly credible to us, but are abundantly authenticated both in ancient and modern times, and "they which died with hailstones were more than they whom the children of Israel slew with the sword." The Israelites, exhausted, no doubt, with their night march and morning exertions, seem to have been outstripped by the flying army, and in this way to have escaped the shower of hail. By the time the five kings, who had had to fly on foot, reached Makkedah at the foot of the mountains, they were unable to go farther and hid themselves in a cave. As Joshua passed he was informed of this, but, unwilling to stop the pursuit of the fugitives, he ordered large stones to be rolled to the door of the cave, locking the kings up as it were in a prison, and no doubt leaving a guard in charge. Then, when the pursuit had been carried to the very gates of the walled cities, he returned to the cave. The five kings were brought out, and the chiefs of the Israelite army put their feet upon their necks. The kings were slain, and their bodies hanged on trees till the evening.

Thereafter Joshua attacked the chief cities of the confederates, and took in succession Makkedah, Libnah, Lachish, Eglon, Hebron, and Debir. Nothing is said of his taking Jerusalem; indeed it appears from the after history that the stronghold of Jerusalem on Mount Zion remained in Jebusite hands up to the time of David. Many of the inhabitants were able to escape destruction, but substantially Joshua was now in possession of the whole southern division of the land, from the Jordan on the east to the borders of the Philistines on the west, and from Gibeon on the north to the wilderness on the south. It does not appear, however, that he retained full possession; while he was occupied in other parts of the country the people returned and occupied their cities. The clemency of Joshua in not destroying the inhabitants proved the source of much future trouble.

In all the subsequent history of the country, the victory of Gibeon was looked back on, and justly, as one of the most memorable that had ever been known. For promptitude, dash, and daring it was never eclipsed by any event of the kind; while the strength of the confederate army, the completeness of its defeat, and the picturesqueness of the whole situation constantly supplied materials for wonder and delight. Moreover, the hand of God had been conspicuously shown in more ways than one. The hailstorm that wrought such havoc was ascribed to His friendly hand, but a far more memorable token of His interest and support lay in the miracle that arrested the movements of the sun and the moon, in order that victorious Israel might have time to finish his work. And after the victory the capture of the fortified towns became comparatively easy. The remnant that had escaped could have no heart to defend them. Joshua must have smiled at the fate of the "cities walled up to heaven" that had so greatly distressed his brother spies when they came up to examine the land. And as he found them one by one yield to his army, as though their defence had really departed from them, he must have felt with fresh gratitude the faithfulness and lovingkindness of the Lord, and earnestly breathed the prayer that neither his faith nor that of his people might ever fail until the whole campaign was brought to an end.

In some respects this victory had a special significance. In the first place, it had a most important bearing on the success of the whole enterprise; its suddenness, its completeness, its manifold grandeur being admirably fitted to paralyse the enemy in other parts of the country, and open the whole region to Joshua. By some it has been compared to the battle of Marathon, not only on account of the suddenness with which the decisive blow was struck, but also on account of the importance of the interests involved. It was a battle for freedom, for purity, for true religion, in opposition to tyranny, idolatry, and abominable sensuality; for all that is wholesome in human life, in opposition to all that is corrupt; for all that makes for peaceful progress, in opposition to all that entails degradation and misery. The prospects of the whole world were brighter after that victory of Bethhoron. The relation of heaven to earth was more auspicious, and more full of promise for the days to come. Had any hitch occurred in the arrangements; had Israel halted half-way up the eastern slopes, and the troops of Adonizedec driven them back; had the tug of war in the plain of Gibeon proved too much for them after their toilsome night march; had no hailstorm broken out on the retreating enemy; had he been able to form again at the western foot of the hills and arrest the progress of Joshua in pursuit, the whole enterprise would have had a different complexion. No doubt the Divine arm might have been stretched out for Israel in some other way; but the remarkable thing was, that no such supplementary mode of achieving the desired result was required. At every point the success of Israel was complete, and every obstacle opposed to him by the enemy was swept away for the time being as smoke before the wind.

In the next place, the tokens of Divine aid were very impressive. After the experience which Joshua had had of the consequences of failing to ask God for direction when first the Gibeonites came to him, we may be very sure that on the present occasion he would be peculiarly careful to seek Divine counsel. And he was well rewarded. For "the sun stood still, and the moon stayed, until the people had avenged themselves upon their enemies." It does not need to be said that this miraculous incident has from first to last given birth to an immensity of perplexity and discussion. It will be observed that the record of it does not come in as part of the narrative, but as a quotation from a pre-existing book. Concerning that book we know very little. From its name, Jashar, "The upright," we may believe it to have been a record of memorable deeds of righteous men. In form it was poetical, the extract in the present case being of that rhythmical structure which was the mark of Hebrew poetry. The only other occasion on which it is mentioned is in connection with the song composed by David, after the death of Saul and Jonathan (2 Sam. i. 18). "David" (as the Revised Version puts it) "bade them teach the children of Israel the song of the bow; behold, it is written in the book of Jashar." As to the origin and nature of this book we can only conjecture. It may have been a public record, contributed to from time to time by various writers, under conditions and arrangements which at this distance of time, and under the obscurity of the whole subject, we cannot ascertain.

Then as to the miracle of the sun and the moon standing still. It is well known that this was one of the passages brought forward by the Church of Rome to condemn Galileo, when he affirmed that the earth and the moon revolved round the sun, and that it was not the motion of the sun round the earth, but the rotation of the earth on her own axis that produced the change of day and night. No one would dream now of making use of this passage for any such purpose. Whatever theory of inspiration men may hold, it is admitted universally that the inspired writers used the popular language of the day in matters of science, and did not anticipate discoveries which were not made till many centuries later. That expressions occur in Scripture which are not in accord with the best established conclusions of modern science would never be regarded by any intelligent person as an argument against the Scriptures as the inspired records of God's will, designed especially to reveal to us the way of life and salvation through Jesus Christ, and to be an infallible guide to us on all that "man is to believe concerning God, and the duty that God requires of man."

A far more serious question has been raised as to whether this miracle ever occurred, or could have occurred. To those who believe in the possibility of miracles, it can be no conclusive argument that it could not have occurred without producing injurious consequences the end of which can hardly be conceived. For if the rotation of the earth on its axis was suddenly arrested, all human beings on its surface, and all loose objects whatever must have been flung forward with prodigious violence; just as, on a small scale, on the sudden stoppage of a carriage, we find ourselves thrown forward, the motion of the carriage having been communicated to our bodies. But really this is a paltry objection ; for surely the Divine power that can control the rotation of the earth is abundantly able to obviate such effects as these. We can understand the objection that God, having adjusted all the forces of nature, leaves them to operate by themselves in a uniform way without disturbance or interference; but we can hardly comprehend the reasonableness of the position that if it is His pleasure miraculously to modify one arrangement, he is unable to adjust all relative arrangements, and make all conspire harmoniously to the end desired.

But was it a miracle ? The narrative, as we have it, implies not only that it was, but that there was something in it stupendous and unprecedented. It comes in as a part of that supernatural process in which God had been engaged ever since the deliverance of His people from Egypt, and which was to go on till they should be finally settled in the land. It naturally joins on to the miraculous division of the Jordan, and the miraculous fall of the walls of Jericho. We must remember that the work in which God was now engaged was one of peculiar spiritual importance and significance. He was not merely finding a home for His covenant people ; He was making arrangements for advancing the highest interests of humanity; He was guarding against the extinction on earth of the Divine light which alone could guide man in safety through the life that now is, and in preparation for that which is to come. He was taking steps to prevent a final and fatal severance of the relation between God and man, and He was even preparing the way for a far more complete and glorious development of that relation—to be seen in the person of His Incarnate Son, the spiritual Joshua, and made possible for men through that great work of propitiation which He was to accomplish on the cross. Who will take upon him to say that at an important crisis in the progress of the events which were to prepare the way for this grand consummation, it was not fitting for the Almighty to suspend for a time even the ordinances of heaven, in order that a day's work, carrying such vast consequences, might not be interrupted before its triumphant close?

There are commentators worthy of high respect who have thought that the fact of this incident being noticed in the form of a quotation from the Book of Jashar somewhat diminishes the credit due to it. It looks as if it had not formed part of the original narrative, but had been inserted by a subsequent editor from a book of poetry, expressed with poetic licence, and perhaps of later date. They are disposed to regard the words of Joshua, "Sun, stand thou still upon Gibeon; and thou, Moon, in the valley of Ajalon," as a mere expression of his desire that the light would last long enough to allow the decisive work of the day to be brought to a thorough conclusion. They look on it as akin to the prayer of Agamemnon ("Iliad," ii. 412 *sq*.) that the sun might not go down till he had sacked Troy; and the form of words they consider to be suited to poetical composition, like some of the expressions in the eighteenth psalm—"There went up a smoke out of His nostrils, and fire out of His mouth devoured: coals were kindled by it. He bowed the heavens also, and did come down: He rode upon a cherub, and did fly."

But whatever allowance we may make for poetical licence of speech, it is hardly possible not to perceive that the words as they stand imply a miracle of extraordinary sublimity; nor do we see any sufficient ground for resisting the common belief that in whatsoever way it was effected, there was a supernatural extension of the period of light, to allow Joshua to finish his work.[1]

One other notable feature in the transaction of this day was the completeness of the defeat inflicted by Joshua on the enemy. This defeat went on in successive stages from early morning till late at night. First, there was the slaughter in the plain of Gibeon. Then the havoc produced by the hail and by Joshua on the retreating army. Then the destruction caused as Joshua followed the enemy to their cities. And the work of the day was wound up by the execution of the five kings. Moreover, there followed a succession of similar scenes at the taking and sacking of their cities. When we try to realize all this in detail, we are confronted with a terrible scene of blood and death, and possibly we may find ourselves asking, Was there a particle of humanity in Joshua, that he was capable of such a series of transactions? Certainly Joshua was a great soldier, and a great religious soldier, but he was in many ways like his time. He had many of the qualities of Oriental commanders, and one of these qualities has ever been to carry slaughter to the utmost limit that the occasion allows. His treatment of the conquered kings, too, was marked by characteristic Oriental barbarity, for he caused his captains to put their feet upon their necks, needlessly embittering

---

[1] It seems hardly necessary to notice an explanation of the phenomenon that has been made lately—to the effect that it was in the morning, not the evening of the day, that Joshua expressed his wish. It was to prevent the allied kings about Gibeon knowing of his approach that he desired the sun to delay his rising in the east, a desire which was virtually fulfilled by that dark, cloudy condition of the sky which precedes a thunderstorm. The natural sense of the narrative admits neither of this explanation of the time nor of the miracle itself.

their dying moments, and he exposed their dead bodies to the needless humiliation of being hanged on a tree. But it must be said, and said firmly for Joshua, that there is no evidence of his acting on this or on other such occasions in order to gratify personal feelings; it was not done either to gratify a thirst for blood, or to gratify the pride of a conqueror. Joshua all through gives us the impression of a man carrying out the will of another; inflicting a judicial sentence, and inflicting it thoroughly at the first so that there might be no need for a constant series of petty executions afterwards. This certainly was his aim; but the enemy showed themselves more vital than he had supposed.

And when we turn to ourselves and think what we may learn from this transaction, we see a valuable application of his method to the spiritual warfare. God has enemies still, within and without, with whom we are called to contend. "For we wrestle not against flesh and blood, but against principalities and powers, against the rulers of the darkness of this world, against spiritual wickedness in high places." When we are fighting with the enemy within our own hearts leniency is our great temptation, but at the same time our greatest snare. What we need here is, courage to slay. We content ourselves with confessions and regrets, but the enemy lives, returns to the attack, and keeps us in perpetual discomfort. Oh that in this battle we resembled Joshua, aiming at killing the enemy outright, and leaving nothing belonging to him that breathes!

And in reference to the outside world, want of thoroughness in warfare is still our besetting sin. We play at missions; we trifle with the awful drunkenness and sensuality around us; we look on, and we see rural districts gradually depopulated; and we wring our hands at the mass of poverty, vice, and misery in our great crowded cities. How rare is it for any one to arise among us like General Booth, to face prevailing evils in all their magnitude, and even attempt to do battle with them along the whole line! Why should not such a spirit be universal in the Christian Church? Who can tell the evil done by want of faith, by languor, by unwillingness to be disturbed in our quiet, self-indulged life, by our fear of rousing against us the scorn and rage of the world? If only the Church had more faith, and, as the fruit of faith, more courage and more enterprise, what help from heaven might not come to her! True, she would not see the enemy crushed by hailstones, nor the sun standing in Gibeon, nor the moon in the valley of Ajalon; but she would see grander sights; she would see men of spiritual might raised up in her ranks; she would see tides of strong spiritual influence overwhelming her enemies. Jerichos dismantled, Ais captured, and the champions of evil falling like Lucifer from heaven to make way for the King of kings and Lord of lords.

Let us go to the cross of Jesus to revive our faith and recruit our energies. The Captain of our salvation has not only achieved salvation for us, but He has set us a blessed example of the spirit and life of true Christian warriors.

> "At the Name of Jesus
>   Satan's legions flee;
> On then, Christian soldiers,
>   On to victory.
> Hell's foundations quiver
>   At the shout of praise;
> Brothers, lift your voices,
>   Loud your anthems raise!

CHAPTER XX.

THE BATTLE OF MEROM.

JOSHUA xi., xii.

THERE is some appearance of confusion in the terms in which the great confederacy of native princes against Israel is brought in. In the beginning of the ninth chapter, a combination that embraced the whole country, north and south, east and west, is described as gathered together to fight with Joshua and with Israel. Nothing more is said till after the treaty with the Gibeonites, when five of these confederate kings residing in the south not far from Gibeon muster their forces to besiege that city. Of the utter rout and ruin of these five kings and of some of their neighbours we have just been reading. And now we read that, after these things, Jabin, King of Hazor, sent to his neighbours, and to all the princes in the northern part of the country, and organized a combined movement against Israel, for which the appointed rendezvous was at the waters of Merom, in the extreme north of the country. The statement at the beginning of the ninth chapter that the confederates "gathered themselves together," seems to be made proleptically ; the actual gathering together not having taken place till the occasions specified in the tenth and eleventh chapters respectively. The plan of the confederacy was no doubt formed soon after the fall of Jericho and Ai, and the arrangements for a vast united movement began to be made then. But it would necessarily consume a considerable time to bring so vast a host together. Meanwhile, another event had taken place. The Gibeonites had refused to join the confederacy and had made peace with Joshua. Their neighbours were intensely provoked, especially Adonizedec of Jerusalem, and without waiting for the general movement proceeded at once to chastise their treachery. As we have said already, they doubtless thought it would be an easy task. To the surprise of them all, Joshua, with an activity which they could not have looked for, hastened to the relief of Gibeon, and inflicted a defeat on the confederates which amounted to absolute ruin.

It has not been generally noticed how remarkably the Gibeonite fraud, and the honourable action of Joshua in connection with it, tended in the end to the good of Israel. Had Joshua, after the discovery of the fraud, repudiated his treaty and attacked and exterminated the Gibeonites, or had he disregarded their appeal to him for help and suffered them to be crushed by Adonizedec, there would have been nothing to hinder the southern kings from uniting with the northern, and thus presenting to Joshua the most formidable opposition that was ever mustered in defence of a country. The magnificent exploit of Joshua in the plain of Gibeon, down the pass of Bethhoron, and in the valley of Ajalon entirely frustrated any such arrangement. The armies of the southern kings were destroyed or demoralized. And though the united forces in the north, with their vast resources of war, still formed a most formidable opponent, the case would have been very different if the two had combined, or if one of them had hung on Joshua's rear while he was engaged in front with the other. Nothing could have fallen out more for the advantage of Israel than the procedure of the Gibeonites, which drew off so large and powerful a section of the confederates, and exposed them thus separate to the sword of Joshua.

Joshua was not allowed a long rest at Gilgal after his dealings with Adonizedec and his brethren. No doubt the news of that tremendous disaster would quicken the energies of the northern kings. The head of the new conspiracy was Jabin, King of Hazor. Jabin was evidently an official name borne by the chief ruler of Hazor, like Pharaoh in Egypt, for when, at a subsequent period, the place has recovered somewhat of its importance, and comes again into view as a Canaanite capital, Jabin is again the name of its chief ruler (Judg. iv. 2).

The situation of Hazor has been disputed by geographers, and Robinson, who is usually so accurate, differs from other authorities. He assigns it to a ruinous city on a hill called Tell Khuraibeh, overhanging the Lake Merom, for little other reason than that it seems to answer the conditions of the various narratives where Hazor is introduced. On the other hand, the author of "The Land and the Book" assigns it to a place still called Hazere, a little west of Merom, the remains of which lie in a large natural basin, and spread far up the hill, toward the south. "Heaps of hewn stone, old and rotten; open pits, deep wells, and vast cisterns cut in the solid rock—these are the unequivocal indications of an important city. . . . I inquired of an old sheikh what saint was honoured there. In a voice loud and bold, as if to make a doubtful point certain, he replied, Neby Hazûr, who fought with Yeshua Ibn Nun." The matter is of no great moment; all that it is important to know is that Hazor was situated near Lake Merom, and was the capital of a powerful kingdom.

The cities of some of the other confederates are named, but it is not easy to identify them all. The sites of Madon, Shimron, and Achshaph, are unknown, but they were apparently not far from Hazor. "The Arabah south of Chinneroth" (ver. 2, R.V.) denotes the plain of Jordan south of the lake of Galilee; the valley, or "lowland" (R.V.), denotes the maritime plain from the Philistines northward; "the heights of Dor on the west" (R.V.), or Highlands of Dor ("Speaker's Commentary"), the hills about a city on the sea coast, near the foot of Carmel, prominent in after history, but now reduced to a village with a few poor houses. The sacred historian, however, does not attempt to enumerate all the places from which the confederacy was drawn, and falls back on the old comprehensive formula—"Canaanites on the east and on the west, Amorites, Hittites, the Jebusites in the hill country, and the Hivite under Hermon in the land of Mizpeh." "The Canaanites on the west" embraced the people of Zidon, for Joshua is expressly stated to have followed a band of the fugitives to that city (ver. 8). The muster must have been an extraordinary one, as numerous "as the sand that is upon the sea shore in multitude." Josephus gives the numbers as 300,000 footmen, 10,000 horsemen, and 20,000 chariots; but we can hardly attach much value to his figures. "Horses and chariots" was an arm unknown to the Israelites, with which hitherto they had never contended. This vast host came together and pitched at the waters of

Merom. Merom, now called Huleh, is the little lake where, as already stated, the three streamlets that form the Jordan unite. It varies in size in summer and winter. To the north, a large plain spreads itself out, sufficient for the encampment of a great army. It was at or near this plain that Abraham overtook the five kings of Mesopotamia and defeated them, rescuing Lot, and all that had been taken from Sodom (Gen. xiv. 14, 15). Now again it is crowded with a mighty host: far as the eye can reach, the plain is darkened by the countless squadrons of the enemy. Probably, after mustering here, their intention was to bear down the Jordan valley, till they came on Joshua at Gilgal, or such other place as he might choose to meet them. But if this was their intention they were outwitted by the activity and, intrepidity of Joshua, who resolved, in spite of their overwhelming numbers, to take the aggressive; and, marching, as before, with extraordinary rapidity, to fall on them by surprise and throw them at once into confusion so that they should be unable to bring their chariots and horses into the action.

It was a very serious undertaking for Joshua, and before attempting it he stood much in need of the encouragement of Jehovah—"Be not afraid because of them: for to-morrow about this time will I deliver them up all slain before Israel: thou shalt hough their horses, and burn all their chariots with fire." Not on the number nor on the bravery of his own people, though they had stood by him most nobly, was he to place his reliance, but on the power of God. "Rule thou in the midst of thine enemies" was his *mot d'ordre*, as it was afterwards of that other Joshua, whose battles were not with confused noise nor with garments rolled in blood, but were triumphs of truth and love. Where else should the true warrior be found but in the midst of his enemies ? Joshua knew it, and with the promised help of God, did not flinch from the position, though his opponents were like the sand of the seaside, with a corresponding multitude of chariots and horses. Jesus, too, knew it, and resting on the same promise did not shrink from the conflict in His own person ; nor did He hesitate to send His apostles into all the world to preach the gospel to every creature, and look forward to a victory not less complete than that of Joshua, when the hordes of the Canaanites were scattered before him.

"To-morrow about this time will I deliver them up all slain before Israel." When he got that assurance, Joshua must already have left Gilgal some days before, and was now within a moderate distance of Merom. There was to be no delay in the completing of the enterprise. "To-morrow about this time." Though, as a rule, the mills of God grind slowly, there are times when their velocity is wonderfully accelerated. He has sometimes wonderful to-morrows. When Hezekiah was gazing appalled on the hosts of Sennacherib as they lay coiled round Jerusalem, God had a "to-morrow about this time" when the terror would be exchanged for a glorious relief. When the apostles met in the upper chamber, and were wondering how they were ever to conquer the world for their Master, there was a "to-morrow" at hand, when the Spirit was to "come down like rain on the mown grass, and like showers that water the earth." When, at the end of the world, iniquity abounds and faith is low, and scoffers are asking, "Where is the promise of His coming?" there will come a "to-morrow about this time" when the heavens will pass away with a great noise, and the elements shall melt with fervent heat, the earth also and all that is therein shall be destroyed. Hold on, brave Joshua, for a little longer; hold on too, ye soldiers of the Lord Jesus, though all the powers of darkness are leagued against you; hold on, ye suffering saints, whose days of pain and nights of waking are such a weariness to your flesh; the glorious "to-morrow" may be at hand which is to end your troubles and bring you the victory!

> "We expect a bright to-morrow,
> All will be well."

And all was well with Joshua. Arriving suddenly at the waters of Merom, he fell on the mighty host of the enemy, who, taken by surprise, seem not to have struck one blow, but to have been seized at once with that panic which so thoroughly demoralizes Eastern hordes, and to have fled in consternation. In three great streams the fugitives sought their homes. One portion made for Misrephothmaim in the south-west, now, it is thought, represented by Musheirifeh on the north border of the plain of Acre; another struck in a north-easterly direction through the valley of the upper Jordan, or east of Hermon to the valley of Mizpeh; a third, passing through the gorge of the Litany, made for great Zidon, in the distant north. Joshua himself would seem to have pursued this column of fugitives, and, passing over a rough path of more than forty miles, not to have abandoned them till they took refuge within the walls of Zidon. If he had attacked and destroyed that stronghold, it might have changed for the better much of the future history of his country; for the Jezebels and Athaliahs of after days were among the worst enemies of Israel. But he did not deem himself called to that duty It seemed more urgent that he should demolish Hazor, the capital of the confederacy that he had just scattered. So "he turned back and took Hazor, and smote the king thereof with the sword; for Hazor beforetime was the head of all those kingdoms." For this reason Hazor was treated like Jericho, utterly destroyed, as were also the other cities of the confederate kings. One class of cities was spared, called in our version "the cities that stood still in their strength," but better in the Revised—"the cities that stood on their mounds." The custom referred to is that of building cities on mounds or hills for the sake of protection. With the exception of Hazor, none of these were destroyed. The reason probably was, that it would have cost too much time. But it was in such places that the old inhabitants rallied and entrenched themselves, and from them they were able in after years to inflict much loss and give great trouble to Israel. Joshua, however, had not received instructions to destroy them; they were left to serve a purpose in God's plan of discipline (Judg. ii. 3), and while Israel was often humbled under them their attacks proved occasions of rallying, bringing them back to God, whose worship they were so ready to neglect.

The conquest of Western Palestine was thus virtually completed. First, by taking Jericho, Joshua had possessed himself of the Jordan valley, and established a clear communication with Bashan and Gilead, which the two and a half tribes had received for their inheritance. By the conquest of Ai and Bethel, he had made a way to the great plateau of Western Palestine, and by his treaty with the Gibeonites he had extended his hold a considerable way farther to the south and the west. Then, by the great victory of Bethhoron, he had crushed the southern chiefs and possessed himself, for the time at least, of all that quarter. As to the inhabitants of the central part, we know not (as we have already said) how they were dealt with, but most probably they were too frightened to resist him. (See p. 202).

The northern section had been subdued at Merom, and much crippled through the pursuit of Joshua after the battle there. The only important parts of the country of which he did not gain possession were the land of the Philistines, the strip of sea coast held by Tyre and Zidon, and some small kingdoms on the north-east. It would seem that in the instructions received by him from Moses, these were not included, for it is expressly said of him that "he left nothing undone of all that the Lord commanded Moses." Emphasis is laid on the fact that his conquests were not confined to one section or denomination of territory, but embraced the whole. "Joshua took all that land, the hill country, and all the South, and all the land of Goshen, and the lowland, and the Arabah, and the hill country of Israel, and the lowland of the same; from Mount Halak (or, the bare mountain) [on the south], that goeth up to Seir [the land of Edom], even unto Baalgad in the valley of Lebanon under Mount Hermon [in the north] : and all their kings he took, and smote them, and put them to death" (R.V.). The "Goshen" here spoken of cannot, of course, be the Egyptian Goshen, for this city was in the neighbourhood of Gibeon (chap. x. 41); but its site has not been identified.

We are told that the wars of Joshua occupied a long time. Probably from five to seven years were consumed by them, for though the pitched battles of Bethhoron and Merom virtually decided the mastership of the country, there must have been a large amount of guerilla warfare, and the sieges of the various cities may have required much time. The list of kings subdued, as given in chap. xii., is a remarkable document. Granting that though called kings they were mostly but little chieftains, still they were formidable enough to a pastoral people unused to the pursuits of war; and it was very striking that not one of them by himself, nor all of them combined, were equal to Joshua. If Joshua was not divinely aided, the conquest of all these chieftains and the capture of their cities is the most inexplicable event in history.

Two additional statements are made towards the close of the eleventh chapter. One is, that with the single exception of Gibeon, no attempt was made by any of the chiefs or cities to make peace with Joshua. "For it was of the Lord to harden their hearts that they should come against Israel in battle, that he might destroy them utterly, and that they might have no favour, but that he might destroy them, as the Lord commanded Moses." It would have been very embarrassing to Joshua if they had submitted spontaneously, and cast themselves on his generosity, for his orders were to destroy them. But this difficulty did not arise. None of the cities seem to have shared the conviction of the Gibeonites that opposition was needless, that Israel was sure to prevail, and get possession of the country. When men's backs are up, to use a common phrase, they will do wonders in the way of facing danger and enduring suffering. Even the resistance of the martyrs cannot be wholly ascribed to holy faith and loyalty to God; in many cases, no doubt, something was due to that dogged spirit that won't submit, that won't be beat, that will endure incredible privation rather than give in. The effect of this resistance by the Canaanites was, that while Joshua's task was increased in one way, it was simplified in another. Ages before, God had given the country to the fathers of the Hebrew nation. That people now came and demanded in God's name possession of the land which He had given them. Had the nations submitted voluntarily they must have left the country to seek new settlements elsewhere. By resisting, they compelled Joshua to meet them with the sword; and having resisted Israel with all their might, nothing remained but that they should encounter the doom which they had so fiercely provoked.

That some of the Canaanites did leave the country seems very probable, although little importance is to be attached to the statement of Procopius that after trying Egypt they settled in Libya, and overspread Africa as far as the Pillars of Hercules: At a fortress in Numidia called Tigisis or Tingis he says that so late as the sixth century after Christ there were discovered near a great wall two pillars of white stone bearing, in Phœnician, the inscription, "We are those who fled before the robber Jeshus, son of Nane." Ewald and others by whom this tradition is noticed are not disposed, owing to its late date, to attach to it any weight.

The other statement relates to the Anakim. Sometime, not precisely defined, while engaged in his conflicts Joshua "cut off the Anakims from the mountains, from Hebron, from Debir, from Anab, and from all the mountains of Judah, and from all the mountains of Israel," leaving none of them except in Gaza, in Gath, and in Ashdod (xi. 21). Afterwards it is said (xv. 14) that it was Caleb that drove from Hebron the three sons of Anak, Sheshai, Ahiman, and Talmai; but this cannot be counted a contradiction inasmuch as "Joshua," being the leader of the army, must be held to represent and include all who fought in connection with his enterprise. These Anakim were the men that had so terrified the ten spies. "And there we saw the giants, the sons of Anak, which come of the giants: and we were in our own sight as grasshoppers, and so we were in their sight" (Num. xiii. 33). To men of little faith, giants, whether physical or moral, are always formidable. Kings, with the resources of an empire at their back; generals, at the head of mighty battalions; intellectual chiefs, with all their talent and brilliancy, their wit, their irony, their power to make the worse appear the better reason, are more than a match for the obscure handfuls to whom the battles of the faith are often left. But if the obscure handfuls are allied with the Lord of hosts, their victory is sure; the triumphant experience of the forty-sixth psalm awaits them: "God is in the midst of her, she shall not be moved; God shall help her, and that right early."

We are weary of the din of arms, and come at last to the refreshing statement: "And the land rested from war." The annals of peace are always more brief than the records of war; and when we reach this short but welcome clause we might wish that it were so expanded as to fill our eyes and our hearts with the blessings which peace scatters with her kindly hand. For that impression we need only to turn to another page of our Bible, and read of the campaigns of another Joshua. "And Jesus went about all Galilee, teaching in their synagogues, and preaching the gospel of the kingdom, and healing all manner of sickness, and all manner of disease among the people." The contrast is very glorious. In His Galilee journeys, Jesus traversed the very region where Joshua had drawn his sword against the confederate kings. Joshua had pursued them as far as Zidon, leaving marks of bloodshed along the whole way; Jesus, when "He departed to the coasts of Tyre and Sidon," went to reward faith, to dispossess devils, and to kindle in a desolate heart thanksgiving and joy. Everywhere, throughout all Galilee and the regions beyond, His advent was accompanied with benedictions, and blessings were scattered by Him in His path.

But let us not indulge in too complete a contrast between the two conquerors. Joshua's rough ploughshare prepared the way for Jesus' words of mercy and deeds of love. God's message to man is not all in honeyed words. Even Jesus, as He went through Galilee, proclaimed, "Repent, for the kingdom of heaven is at hand." And it was those only who gave heed to the call to repent that became possessors of the kingdom.

CHAPTER XXI.

JOSHUA'S OLD AGE—DIVISION FOR THE EASTERN TRIBES.

JOSHUA xiii., xiv. 1—5.

"THE Lord said unto Joshua, Thou art old and stricken in years." To many men and women this would not be a welcome announcement. They do not like to think that they are old. They do not like to think that the bright, joyous, playful part of life is over, and that they are arrived at the sombre years when they must say, "There is no pleasure in them." Then, again, there are some who really find it hard to believe that they are old. Life has flown past so swiftly that before they thought it was well begun it has gone. It seems so short a time since they were in the full play of their youthful energies, that it is hardly credible that they are now in the sere and yellow leaf. Perhaps, too, they have been able to keep their hearts young all the time, and still retain that buoyant sensation which seems to indicate the presence of youth. And are there not some who have verified the psalm—"They that are planted in the house of the Lord shall flourish in the courts of our God. They shall still bring forth fruit in old age, they shall be fat and flourishing"?

But however much men may like to be young, and however much some may retain in old age of the feeling of youth, it is certain that the period of strength has its limit, and the period of life also. To the halest and heartiest, if he be not cut off prematurely, the time must come when God will say to him, "Thou art old." It is a solemn word to hear from the lips of God. God tells me my life is past; what use have I made of it? And what does God think of the use I have made of it? And what account of it shall I be able to give when I stand at His bar?

Let the young think well of this, before it is too late to learn how to live.

To Joshua the announcement that he was old and stricken in years does not appear to have brought any painful or regretful feeling. Perhaps he had aged somewhat suddenly; his energies may have failed consciously and rapidly, after his long course of active and anxious military service. He may have been glad to hear God utter the word; he may have been feeling it himself, and wondering how he should be able to go through the campaigns yet necessary to put the children of Israel in full possession of the land. That word may have fallen on his ear with the happy feeling—how considerate God is! He will not burden my old age with a load not suited for it. Though *His* years have no end, and He knows nothing of failing strength, "He knoweth *our* frame, He remembereth that we are dust." He will not "cast me off in the time of old age, nor forsake me when my strength faileth." Happy confidence, especially for the aged poor! It is the want of trust in the heavenly Father that makes so many miserable in old age. When you will not believe that He is considerate and kind, you are left to your own resources, and often to destitution and misery. But when between Him and you there is the happy relation of father and child; when through Jesus Christ you realize His fatherly love and pity, and in real trust cast yourselves on Him who clothes the lilies and feeds the ravens, your trust is sure to be rewarded, for your heavenly Father knoweth what things you have need of before you ask them.

So Joshua finds that he is now to be relieved by his considerate Master of laborious and anxious service. Not of all service, but of exhausting service, unsuited to his advancing years. Joshua had been a right faithful servant; few men have ever done their work so well. From that day when he stood against Amalek from morning to night, while the rod of Moses was stretched out over him on the hill; thereafter, during all his companionship with Moses on the mount; next in that search-expedition when Caleb and he stood so firm, and did not flinch in the face of the congregation, though every one was for stoning them; and now, from the siege of Jericho to the victory of Merom, and all through the trying and perilous sieges of city after city, year after year, Joshua has proved himself the faithful servant of God and the devoted friend of Israel. During these last years he has enjoyed supreme power, apparently without a rival and without a foe; yet, strange to say, there is no sign of his having been corrupted by power, or made giddy by elevation. He has led a most useful and loyal life, which there is some satisfaction in looking back on. No doubt he is well aware of unnumbered failings: "Who can understand his errors?" But he has the rare satisfaction—oh! who would not wish to share it?—of looking back on a well-spent life, habitually and earnestly regulated amid many infirmities by regard to the will of God. Neither he, nor St. Paul after him, had any trust in their own good works, as a basis of salvation; yet Paul could say, and Joshua might have said it in spirit: "I have fought the good fight, I have finished my course, I have kept the faith: henceforth there is laid up for me a crown of righteousness."

Yet Joshua was not to complete that work to which he had contributed so much: "there remaineth yet very much land to be possessed." At one time, no doubt, he thought otherwise, and he desired otherwise. When the tide of victory was setting in for him so steadily, and region after region of the land was falling into his hands, it was natural to expect that before he ended he would sweep all the enemies of Israel before him, and open every door for them throughout the land, even to its utmost borders. Why not make hay when the sun shone? When God had found so apt an instrument for His great design, why did He not employ him to the end? If the natural term of Joshua's strength had come, why did not that God who had supernaturally lengthened out the day for completing the victory of Bethhoron, lengthen out Joshua's day that the whole land of Canaan might be secured?

Here comes in a great mystery of Providence. Instead of lengthening out the period of Joshua's strength, God seems to have cut it short. We can easily understand the lesson for Joshua himself. It is the lesson which so many of God's servants have had to learn. They start with the idea they are to do everything; they are to reform every abuse, overthrow every stronghold of evil, reduce chaos to order and beauty; as if each were

> "the only man on earth
> Responsible for all the thistles blown
> And tigers couchant, struggling in amaze

Against disease and winter, snarling on
For ever, that the world's not paradise."

Sooner or later they find that they must be satisfied with a much humbler *rôle*. They must learn to

"be content in work,
To do the thing we can, and not presume
To fret because it's little. 'Twill employ
Seven men, they say, to make a perfect pin, . . .
Seven men to a pin, and not a man too much!
Seven generations, haply to this world,
To right it visibly a finger's breadth,
And mend its rents a little."

Joshua must be made to feel—perhaps he needs this— that this enterprise is not his, but God's. And God is not limited to one instrument, or to one age, or to one plan. Never does Providence appear to us so strange, as when a noble worker is cut down in the very midst of his work. A young missionary has just shown his splendid capacity for service, when fever strikes him low, and in a few days all that remains of him is rotting in the ground. What can God mean? we sometimes ask impatiently. Does He not know the rare value and the extreme scarcity of such men, that He sets them up apparently just to throw them down? But "God reigneth, let the people tremble." All that bears on the Christian good of the world is in God's plan, and it is very dear to God, and " precious in the sight of the Lord is the death of His saints." But He is not limited to single agents. When Stephen died, He raised up Saul. For Wicliffe He gave Luther. When George Wishart was burnt He raised up John Knox. Kings, it is said, die, but the king never. The herald that announces "The king is dead," proclaims in the same breath, "God save the king!" God's workers die, but His work goes on. Joshua is superannuated, so far as the work of conquest is concerned, and that work for a time is suspended. But the reason is that, at the present moment, God desires to develop the courage and energy of each particular tribe. And when the time comes to extend still farther the dominion of Israel, an agent will be found well equipped for the service. From the hills of Bethlehem, a godly youth of dauntless bearing will one day emerge, under whom every foe to Israel shall be brought low, and from the river of Egypt to the great river, the river Euphrates, the entire Promised Land shall come under Israel's dominion. And the conquests of David will shine with a brighter lustre than Joshua's, and will be set, as it were, to music of a higher strain. Associated with David's holy songs and holy experience, and with his early life of sadness and humiliation, crowned at last with glory and honour, they will more fitly symbolize the work of the great Joshua, and there will then be diffused over the world a more holy aroma than that of Joshua's conquests,—a fragrance sweet and refreshing to souls innumerable, and fostering the hope of glory,—the rest that remaineth for the people of God, the inheritance incorruptible, and undefiled, and that fadeth not away.

So Joshua must be content to have done his part, and done it well, although he did not conquer all the land, and there yet remained much to be possessed. Without entering in detail into all the geographical notices of this chapter, it will be well to note briefly what parts of the country were still unsubdued.

First, there were all the borders of the Philistines, and all Geshuri; the five lords of the Philistines, dwelling in Gaza, Ashdod, Ascalon, Gath, and Ekron; and also the Avites. This well defined country consisted mainly of a plain "remarkable in all ages for the extreme riches of its soil; its fields of standing corn, its vineyards and oliveyards, are incidentally mentioned in Scripture (Judg. xv. 5); and in the time of famine the land of the Philistines was the hope of Palestine (2 Kings viii. 2). . . . It was also adapted to the growth of military power; for while the plain itself permitted the use of war chariots, which were the chief arm of offence, the occasional elevations which rise out of it offered secure sites for towns and strongholds. It was, moreover, a commercial country; the great thoroughfare between Phœnicia and Syria on the north and Egypt and Arabia on the south. Ashdod and Gaza were the keys of Egypt, and commanded the transit trade, and the stores of frankincense and myrrh which Alexander captured in the latter place prove it to have been a depôt of Arabian produce."[1]

Geshuri lay between Philistia and the desert, and the Avites were probably some remainder of the Avims, from whom the Philistines conquered the land (Deut. ii. 23).

In many respects it would have been a great boon for the Israelites if Joshua had conquered a people that were so troublesome to them as the Philistines were for many a day. What Joshua left undone, Saul began, but failed to achieve, and at last David accomplished. The Geshurites were subdued with the Amalekites while he was dwelling at Ziklag as an ally of the Philistines (1 Sam. xxvii. 8), and the Philistines themselves were brought into subjection, and had to yield to Israel many of their cities (1 Sam. vii. 14; 2 Sam. viii. 1, 12).

---

[1] Smith's "Bible Dictionary."

Another important section of the country unsubdued was the Phœnician territory—the land of the Sidonians (vv. 4, 6). Also the hilly country across Lebanon, embracing the valley of Cœle-Syria, and apparently the region of Mount Carmel ("from Lebanon unto Misrephothmaim," ver. 6, and comp. chap. xi. 8). No doubt much of this district was recovered in the time of the Judges, and still more in the time of David; but David made peace with the King of Tyre, who still retained the rocky strip of territory that was so useful to a commercial nation, but would have been almost useless to an agricultural people like the Israelites.

Joshua was not called on to conquer these territories in the sense of driving out all the old inhabitants; but he was instructed to divide the whole land among his people—a task involving, no doubt, its own difficulties, but not the physical labour which war entailed. And in this division he was called first to recognise what had already been done by Moses with the part of the country east of the Jordan. That part had been allotted to Reuben, Gad, and half the tribe of Manasseh; and the allotment was still to hold good.

It is remarkable with what fulness the places are described. First, we have the boundaries of that part of the country generally (vv. 9-12); then of the allotments of each of the two and a half tribes (vv. 15-31). With regard to the district as a whole, the conquest under Moses was manifestly complete, from the river Arnon on the south, to the borders of the Geshurites and Maachathites on the north. The only part not subdued were the territories of these Geshurites and Maachathites. The Geshurites here are not to be confounded with the people of the same name mentioned in ver. 2, who were at the opposite extreme—the south-west instead of, as here, the north-east of the land. But no doubt the Syrian Geshurites and Maachathites were brought into subjection by David, with all the other tribes in that region, in his great Syrian war, " when he went to recover his border at the river Euphrates" (2 Sam. viii. 3). But instead of expelling or exterminating them, David seems to have allowed them to remain in a tributary condition, for Geshur had its king in the days of Absalom (2 Sam. xiii. 37), to whom that prince fled after the murder of Amnon. With the Maachathites also David had a family connection (2 Sam. iii. 3).

But though the subjugation and occupation of the eastern part of the land was thus tolerably complete (with the exceptions just mentioned), it remained in the undisturbed possession of Israel for the shortest time of any. From Moabites and Ammonites on the south, Canaanites and Syrians on the north and the east, as well as the Midianites, Amalekites, and other tribes of the desert, it was subject to continual invasions. In fact, it was the least settled and least comfortable part of all the country; and doubtless it became soon apparent that though the two tribes and a half had seemed to be very fortunate in having their wish granted to settle in this rich and beautiful region, yet on the whole they had been penny-wise and pound-foolish. Not only were they incessantly assailed and worried by their neighbours, but they were the first to be carried into captivity, when the King of Assyria directed his eyes to Palestine. They had shown somewhat of the spirit of Lot, and they suffered somewhat of his punishment. It is worthy of remark that even at this day this eastern province is the most disturbed part of Palestine. The Bedouins are ever liable to make their attacks wherever there are crops or cattle to tempt their avarice. People will not sow where they have no chance of reaping; and thus it is that much of that productive region lies waste. The moral is not far to seek: in securing wealth, look not merely at the apparent productiveness of the investment, but give heed to its security, its stability. It is not all gold that glitters either on the stock-exchange or anywhere else. And even that which is real gold partakes of the current instability. We must come back to our Saviour's advice to investors, if we would really be safe: "Lay not up for yourselves treasures on earth, where moth and rust do corrupt, and where thieves break through and steal. But lay up for yourselves treasures in heaven, where moth and rust do not corrupt, and where thieves do not break through nor steal."

The specification of the allotments need not detain us long. Reuben's was the farthest south. His southern and eastern flanks were covered by the Moabites, who greatly annoyed him. "Unstable as water, he did not excel." Gad settled north of Reuben. In his lot was the southern part of Gilead; Mahanaim, and Peniel, celebrated in the history of Jacob, and Ramoth-gilead, conspicuous in after times. East of Gad were the Ammonites, who proved as troublesome to that tribe as Moab did to Reuben. To the half-tribe of Manasseh the kingdom of Og fell, and the northern half of Gilead. Jabesh-gilead, where Saul routed the Ammonites, was in this tribe (1 Sam. xi.). Here also were some of the places on the lake of Galilee mentioned in the gospel history; here the "desert place" across the sea to which our Lord used to retire for rest; here He fed the multitude; here He cured the demoniac; and here were some of the mountains where He would spend the night in prayer.

In our Lord's time this portion of Palestine was called Perea. Under the dominion of the Romans, it was comparatively tranquil, and our Lord would sometimes select it, on account of its quiet, as his route to Jerusalem. And many of His gifts of love and mercy were doubtless scattered over its surface.

Two statements are introduced parenthetically in this chapter which hardly belong to the substance of it. One of these, occurring twice, respects the inheritance of the Levites (vv. 14, 33). No territorial possessions were allotted to them corresponding to those of the other tribes. In the one place it is said that "the sacrifices of the Lord God of Israel made by fire were their inheritance"; in the other, that "the Lord God of Israel was their inheritance." We shall afterwards find the arrangements for the Levites more fully detailed (chaps. xx., xxi.). This early allusion to the subject, even before the allotments in Western Palestine begin to be described, shows that their case had been carefully considered, and that it was not by oversight but deliberately that the country was divided without any section being reserved for them.

The other parenthetical statement respects the death of Balaam. "Balaam also, the soothsayer, did the children of Israel slay with the sword among them that were slain by them" (ver. 22). It appears from Numb. xxxi. 8 that the slaughter of Balaam took place in the days of Moses, by the hands of the expedition sent by him to chastise the Midianites for drawing the Israelites into idolatry. That the fact should be again noticed here is probably due to the circumstance that the death of Balaam occurred at the place which had just been noted—the boundary line between Reuben and Gad. It was a fact well worthy of being again noted. It was a fact never to be forgotten that the man who had been sent for to curse was constrained to bless. As far as Balaam's public conduct was concerned, he behaved well to Israel. He emphasized their Divine election and their glorious privileges. He laid especial stress upon the fact that they were not a Bedouin horde, rushing about in search of plunder, but a sacramental host, executing the judgments of a righteous God—" The Lord his God is with him, and the shout of a king is among them." This was a valuable testimony, for which Israel might well be grateful. It was when Balaam took part in that disgraceful plot to entice Israel into sensuality and idolatry that he came out in his real colours. It seemed to him very clever, no doubt, to obey the Divine command in the letter by absolutely refusing to curse Israel, while at the same time he accomplished the object he was sent for by seducing them into sins which brought down on them the judgments of God. Nevertheless, he reckoned without his host. Possibly he gained his reward, but he did not live to enjoy it ; and " what shall a man be profited if he gain the whole world and forfeit his own life ? " (Matt. xvi. 26, R.V.).

The two and a half tribes were well taught by the fate of Balaam that, in the end, however cunningly a man may act, his sin will find him out. They were emphatically reminded that the sins of sensuality and idolatry are exceedingly hateful in the sight of God, and certain to be punished. They were assured by the testimony of Balaam, that Israel, if only faithful, would never cease to enjoy the Divine protection and blessing. But they were reminded that God is not mocked ; that whatsoever a man soweth, that shall he also reap. Balaam had sown to the flesh ; of the flesh it behoved him to reap corruption. And so must it ever be ; however ingeniously you may disguise sin, however you may conceal it from yourself, and persuade yourself to believe that you are not doing wrong, sin must show itself ultimately in its true colours, and your ingenious disguises will not shield it from its doom :—" The wages of sin is DEATH."

CHAPTER XXII.

THE INHERITANCE OF CALEB.[1]

JOSHUA xiv. 6—15.

CALEB is one of those men whom we meet with seldom in Bible history, but whenever we do meet them we are the better for the meeting. Bright and brave, strong, modest and cheerful, there is honesty in his face, courage and decision in the very pose of his body, and the calm confidence of faith in his very look and attitude. It is singular that there should be cause to doubt whether his family were *originally* of the promised seed. When introduced to us in the present passage he is emphatically called "Caleb, the son of

---

[1] There is some difficulty in adjusting the three passages in which the settlement of Caleb is referred to. From this first passage of the three, we are led to think that it was before the tribe of Judah obtained its portion. Again, from chap. xv. 13 we might suppose that it was simultaneously with the rest of the tribe. From Judg. i. 10, again, it might be thought that the subduing of the natives in Hebron was effected, not by Caleb alone, but by the tribe of Judah, and that it took place "after the death of Joshua" (Judg. i. 1). Putting all these together, it would appear that Hebron was assigned to Caleb before the tribe of Judah was settled; that this allocation was ratified at the general settlement; that as Caleb was a member of the tribe, his services against the Canaanites, and especially the Anakim, were ascribed to his tribe; and that the process of dispossessing the Canaanites went on for some time after the death of Joshua. The repetitions in the narrative concerning Caleb form one of the considerations that favour the idea of more sources than one having been made use of in the composition of this book.

Jephunneh the Kenezite" (R.V., Kenizzite, rightly, same as Kenizzite in Gen. xv. 19), as if he had been a descendant of Kenaz, a son of Esau (Gen. xxxvi. 11 and 15), and a member of the Kenizzite tribe. It was not customary to distinguish Israelites in this way, but only those who had come among them from other tribes, like "Heber the Kenite," "Jael, the wife of Heber the Kenite" (Judg. iv. 11, 17), Uriah the Hittite, Hushai the Archite, etc. Moreover, Othniel, Caleb's younger brother, is called the son of Kenaz (Josh. xv. 17); and further, when it is recorded in the fourteenth verse of this chapter that Hebron became the possession of Caleb, the reason assigned is that he "wholly followed the Lord God *of Israel.*" On the other hand, in the genealogical list of 1 Chron. iv. 13, 15, Othniel and Caleb occur as if they were regular members of the tribe; but that list shows obvious signs of imperfection. On the whole, the preponderance of evidence is in favour of the opinion that Caleb's family were originally outside the covenant, but had become proselytes, like Hobab, Rahab, Ruth, and Heber. Their faith was pre-eminently the fruit of conviction, and not the accident of heredity. It had a firmer basis than that of most Israelites. It was woven more closely into the texture of their being, and swayed their lives more powerfully. It is pleasing to think that there may have been many such proselytes; that the promise to Abraham may have attracted souls from the east, and the west, and the north, and the south; that even beyond the limits of the twelve tribes many hearts may have been cheered, and many lives elevated and purified by the promise to him, "In thee and in thy seed shall all the families of the earth be blessed."

Caleb and Joshua had believed and acted alike, in

opposition to the other ten spies; but Caleb occupies the more prominent place in the story of their heroism and faith. It was he that "stilled the people before Moses, and said, Let us go up at once, and possess it; for we are well able to overcome it" (Numb. xiii. 30); and at first his name occurs alone, as exempted from the sentence of exclusion against the rest of his generation : " But my servant Caleb, because he had another spirit with him, and hath followed Me fully, him will I bring into the land whereinto he went: and his seed shall possess it" (Numb. xiv. 24). As we have said before, it is probable that Caleb was the readier speaker, and it is possible that he was the firmer man. Joshua seems to have wanted that power of initiation which Caleb had. It was because he had always been a good follower that Joshua in his old age was fitted to be a leader. Because he had been a good servant he became a good master. As long as Moses lived, Joshua was his servant. After Moses died, Joshua set himself simply to carry out his instructions. It was a happy thing for him on the return of the ten spies that Caleb was one of them, otherwise he might have found himself in a condition of embarrassment. Caleb was evidently the man who led the opposition to the ten, not only asserting the course of duty, but manifesting the spirit of contempt and defiance toward the faithless cowards that forgot that God was with them. In his inmost heart Joshua was quite of his mind, but probably he wanted the energetic manner, the ringing voice, the fearless attitude of his more demonstrative companion. Certain it is that Caleb reaped the chief honour of that day.[1]

---

[1] Some readers may no doubt prefer the explanation that when Caleb is mentioned alone one document was followed, and when Caleb and Joshua are coupled, another.

It is beautiful to see that there was no rivalry between them. Not only did Caleb interpose no remonstrance when Joshua was called to succeed Moses, but he seems all through the wars to have yielded to him the most loyal and hearty submission. God had set His seal on Joshua, and the people had ratified the appointment, and Caleb was too magnanimous to allow any poor ambition of his, if he had any, to come in the way of the Divine will and the public good. His affectionate and cordial bearing on the present occasion seems to show that not even in the corner of his heart did there linger a trace of jealousy toward the old friend and companion whom on that occasion he had surpassed, but who had been set so much higher than himself. He came to him as the recognised leader of the people—as the man whose voice was to decide the question he now submitted, as the judge and arbiter in a matter which very closely concerned him and his house.

And yet there are indications of tact on the part of Caleb, of a thorough understanding of the character of Joshua, and of the sort of considerations by which he might be expected to be swayed. There were two grounds on which he might reasonably look for the conceding of his request—his personal services, and the promise of Moses. Caleb knows well that the promise of Moses will influence Joshua much more than any other consideration; therefore he puts it in the foreground. "Thou knowest the thing that the Lord said unto Moses, the man of God, concerning me and thee in Kadesh-barnea." "Moses, the man of God." Why does Caleb select that remarkable epithet? Why add anything to the usual name, Moses? The use of the epithet was honouring to all the three.

That which constituted the highest glory of Moses was that he was so much at one with God. God's will was ever his law, and he was in such close sympathy with God that whatever instructions he gave on any subject might be assumed to be in accordance with God's will. Moreover, in calling him "the man of God" when addressing Joshua, Caleb assumed that Joshua would be impressed by this consideration, and would be disposed to agree to a request which was not only sanctioned by the will of Moses, but by that higher will which Moses constantly recognised. In short, when Joshua considered that the particular wish of Moses which Caleb now recalled was only the expression of the Divine will, Caleb felt assured that he could not withhold his consent. The three men were indeed a noble trio, worthy descendants of their father Abraham, even if one of the three was no son of Jacob. Long before our Lord taught the petition "Thy will be done on earth as it is in heaven," it had become habitual to them all. Moses was indeed "the man of God,"—pre-eminently in fellowship with Him; in a lower sphere both Caleb and Joshua were of the same order, men who tried to live their lives, and every part of them, only in God.

Having fortified his plea with this strong reference at once to Moses and to God, Caleb proceeds to rehearse the service which had led to the promise of Moses. The facts could not but be well known to Joshua. "Forty years old was I when Moses, the servant of the Lord, sent me from Kadesh-barnea to spy out the land, and I brought him word again as it was in my heart. Nevertheless, my brethren that went up with me made the heart of the people melt; but I wholly followed the Lord my God." Why does Caleb put the matter in this way? Why does he not couple Joshua with himself as having been faithful on that never-to-be-forgotten occasion? The only explanation that seems feasible is, that from the pre-eminent position of Joshua this was unnecessary, perhaps it might have appeared even unbecoming. A soldier making a request of the Duke of Wellington, and recalling some service he had done at the battle of Waterloo, would hardly think it necessary, or even becoming, to say how the Duke, too, had been there, and what surpassing service he had rendered on that day. A soldier like the Duke occupying a position of unrivalled pre-eminence on account of long and brilliant service, does not need to be told what he has done. Joshua was now the leader of Israel, and the last few years had crowned him with such manifold glory that his whole life was transfigured, and individual acts of service did not need to be spoken of. Caleb was comparatively an obscure individual, whose fame rested on a single service now nearly half a century old, which could not, indeed, be quite forgotten, but amid the brilliant events of later times might easily pass out of sight and out of mind. There was no disparagement of Joshua, therefore, in his not being mentioned by Caleb, but, on the contrary, a silent tribute to his exalted office as chief ruler of Israel, and to his all but unparalleled services, especially during these later years.

"I brought him word again, *as it was in my heart.*" The statement is made in no boasting spirit, and yet what a rare virtue it denotes! Caleb, as we now say, had the courage of his convictions. He had both an honest heart and an honest tongue. We can have but little idea what temptations he lay under *not* to speak what was in his heart. For six weeks these ten men had been his close companions. They had eaten together, slept under the same canvas, walked by the same paths, beguiled the long way by story and anecdote, and no doubt by joke and play of humour, and done kind offices to each other as circumstances required. To break away from your own set, from the comrades of your campaign, to upset their plans, and counsel those in power to a course diametrically opposed to theirs, is one of the most difficult of social duties. And in these days of ours there is no duty more commonly set aside. Moral cowardice has been well said to be one of the most common vices of our age.

What more common in Parliament, for example, than for men to differ strongly from some of the measures of their party, and yet, because it is their party, support them by their votes? And in the ranks of the Church and of its various sections the same tendency prevails, though it may be in a less degree. Of the many able and seemingly honest prelates of the Roman Church who dissented, often with vehemence, from the Vatican decree of the pope's infallibility, what became finally of their opposition? Were there more than one or two who did not surrender in the end, and agree to profess what they did not believe? And to come to more ordinary matters, when our opinions on religious subjects are at a discount, when they are met with ridicule, how often do we conceal them, or trim and modify them in order that we may not share in the current condemnation? The men that have the courage of their convictions are often social martyrs, shut out from the fellowship of their brethren, shut out from every berth of honour or emolument, and yet, for their courage and honesty, worthy of infinitely higher regard than whole hundreds of the time-servers that "get on" in the world by humouring its errors and its follies.

Nevertheless, though most of us show ourselves miserably weak by *not* speaking out all that is "in our hearts," especially when the honour of our Lord and Master is concerned, we are able to appreciate and cannot fail to admire the noble exhibitions of courage that we sometimes meet with. That beautiful creation of Milton's, the Seraph Abdiel, "faithful found among the faithless, faithful only he," is the type and ideal of the class. Shadrach, Meshach, and Abednego resisting the enthusiasm of myriads and calmly defying the fiery furnace; the Apostle Paul clinging to his views of the law and the gospel when even his brother Peter had begun to waver; Martin Luther, with his foot on the Bible confronting the whole world; John Knox defying sovereign and nobles and priests alike, determined that the gospel should be freely preached; Carey, going out as a missionary to India amid the derision of the world, because he could not get the words out of his head, "Go ye into all the world, and preach the gospel unto every creature,"—have all exemplified the Caleb spirit that must utter what is in the heart; nor has any new idea commonly laid hold of mankind till the struggles of some great hero or the ashes of some noble martyr have gone to sanctify the cause.

"He that believeth shall not make haste." Caleb believed, and therefore he was patient. Five-and-forty long years had elapsed since Moses, the man of God, speaking in the Spirit of God, had promised him a particular inheritance in the land. It was a long time for faith to live on a promise, but, like a tree in the face of a cliff that seems to grow out of the solid rock, it derived nourishment from unseen sources. It was a long time to be looking forward; but Caleb, though he did not receive the promise during all that time, was persuaded of it and embraced it, and believed that at last it would come true. He did not anticipate the proper time, though he might have had as plausible reasons for doing so as the two tribes and a half had for asking leave to settle on the east side of the river. He bore his share of warlike work, bore the burden and heat of the day, waited till the proper time for dividing the land. Nor did he rush forward selfishly by himself, disregarding the interests of the rest of his tribe; for the children of Judah, recognising his claim, draw near to Joshua along with him. Nor was it a portion of the land which any tribe might be eager to enter upon that he asked; for it was still so harassed by the Anakim, that there would be no peace till that formidable body of giants were driven out.

It seems that when acting as one of the twelve spies, Caleb had in some emphatic way taken his stand on Hebron. "The land *on which thy foot hath trodden* will be an inheritance to thee." Perhaps the spies were too terrified to approach Hebron, for the sons of the Anakim were there, and, in the confidence of faith, Caleb, or Caleb and Joshua, had gone into it alone. Moses had promised him Hebron, and now he came to claim it. But he came to claim it under circumstances that would have induced most men to let it alone. The driving out of the Anakim was a formidable duty, and the task might have seemed more suitable for one who had the strength and enthusiasm of youth on his side. But Caleb, though eighty-five, was yet young. Age is not best measured by years. He was a remarkable instance of prolonged vigour and youthful energy. "As yet I am as strong this day as I was in the day that Moses sent me; as my strength was then, even so is my strength now, for war, and to go out and to come in." Faith, and temperance, and cheerfulness are wonderful aids to longevity. As one reads these words of Caleb, one recalls the saying of a well-known physician, Dr. Richardson, that the human frame might last for a hundred years if it were only treated aright.

There is something singularly touching in Caleb's asking as a favour what was really a most hazardous but important service to the nation. Rough though these Hebrew soldiers were, they were capable of the most gentlemanly and chivalrous acts. There can be no higher act of courtesy than to treat as a favour to yourself what is really a great service to another. Well done, Caleb! You do not ask for a berth which there will be no trouble in taking or in keeping. You are not like Issachar, the strong ass couching between the sheepfolds: "and he saw a resting-place that it was good, and the land that it was pleasant; and he bowed his shoulder to bear, and became a servant under task-work." The dew of youth is yet upon you, the stirring of lofty purpose and noble endeavour; you are like the warhorse of Job—" he paweth in the valley and rejoiceth in his strength; he mocketh at fear, and is not dismayed; he smelleth the battle afar off, the thunder of the captains and the shouting."

There is nothing we admire more in military annals than a soldier volunteering for the most hazardous and difficult of posts,—showing

> "That stern joy which warriors feel
> In foemen worthy of their steel."

In the spiritual warfare, too, we do not want instances

of the same spirit. We recall Captain Allan Gardiner choosing Tierra del Fuego as his mission sphere just because the people were so ferocious, the climate so repulsive, and the work so difficult that no one else was likely to take it up. We think of the second band who went out after Gardiner and his companions had been starved to death; and still more after these were massacred by the natives, of the third detachment who were moved simply by the consideration that the case was seemingly so desperate. Or we think of Livingstone begging the directors of the London Missionary Society, wherever they sent him, to be sure that it was " Forward"; turning aside from all previous mission stations, and the comparative ease they afforded, to grapple with the barbarian where he had never begun to be tamed; his eyes thirsting for unknown scenes and untried dangers, because he scorned to build on the foundation of others, and thirsted for " fresh woods and pastures new." We think of him persevering in his task from year to year in the same lofty spirit; disregarding the misery of protracted pain, the intense longings of his weary heart for home, the repulsive society of savages and cannibals, the vexations, disappointments, and obstacles that seemed to multiply every day, the treachery of so-called friends whom he had helped to raise, the indifference of a careless world, and of a languid Church; but ever girding himself with fresh energy for the task which he had undertaken, and of which the difficulties and trials had never been absent from his thoughts. We think of many a young missionary turning away from the comfortable life which he might lead at home and which many of his companions will lead, that he may go where the need is greatest and the fight is hottest, and so render to his

Master the greatest possible service. A crowd of noble names comes to our recollection—Williams, and Judson, and Morrison, and Burns, and Patteson, and Keith-Falconer, and Hannington, and Mackay—men for whom even the Anakim had no terrors, but rather an attraction; but who, serving under another Joshua, differed from Caleb in this, that what they desired was not to destroy these ferocious Anakim, but to conquer them by love, and to demonstrate the power of the gospel of Jesus Christ to change the vilest reprobates into sons of God.

And even now there are other Anakim among us for whom the fate of the Canaanite giants ought to be reserved. Anakim within us—greed, selfishness, love of ease, lust, passion, cruelty—all, if we are faithful, to be put to the edge of the sword. And there are Anakim, tremendous Anakim, around us—drunkenness, and all that fosters it, despite the paltry excuses we so often hear; sensuality, that vile murderer of soul and body together ; avarice, so cruelly unjust, and content to gather its hoard from the thews and sinews of men and women to whom life has become worse than slavery; luxurious living, that mocks the struggles of thousands to whom one crumb from the table or one rag from the wardrobe would bring such a blessed relief. With giants like these we need to wage incessant war, and for the necessary spirit we need constant supplies of the faith and courage that were so remarkable in Caleb. He followed the Lord *fully*; believing that if the Lord deserved to be followed at all, He deserved to be followed in full. What was there to gain by following Him one half, and surrendering the other half to the world? Could he count on God helping him if he went with but half his heart into His service, and, like Lot's wife, looked back even when flying from Sodom? "Thou shalt love the Lord thy God with all thy heart, and with all thy soul, and with all thy strength, and with all thy might."

The tendency to compromise is one of the besetting sins of the day. In the army or the navy, if one is to serve God at all, one must serve Him wholly. Decision is eminently requisite there, and Christians there are commonly more whole-hearted and consistent than in many circles nominally Christian. Decision is manly, is noble; it brings rest within, and in the end it conciliates the respect of the bitterest foes. Courage is the ornament of Christianity, and the crown of the Christian youth. "FEAR NOT" is one of the brightest gems of the Bible.

CHAPTER XXIII.

THE DISTRIBUTION OF THE LAND.

JOSHUA xv.--xix.

WE come now in earnest to the distribution of the land. The two and a half tribes have already got their settlements on the other side of Jordan; but the other side of Jordan, though included in the land of promise, was outside the part specially consecrated as the theatre of Divine manifestation and dealing. From Dan to Beersheba and from Jordan to the sea was *par excellence* the land of Israel; it was here the patriarchs had dwelt; it was here that most of the promises had been given; it was here that Abraham, Isaac, and Jacob had been buried; and here also, though in another tomb, that the bones of Joseph had been laid. This portion was the kernel of the inheritance, surrounded by a wide penumbra of more feeble light and fewer privileges. In due time there arose a holy of holies within this consecrated region, when Jerusalem became the capital, the focus of blessing and holy influence.

Now that the distribution of this part of the country begins, we must give special attention to the operation. The narrative looks very bare, but important principles and lessons underlie it. These lists of unfamiliar names look like the *débris* of a quarry—hard, meaningless, and to us useless. But nothing is inserted in the Bible without a purpose,—a purpose that in some sense bears on the edification of the successive generations and the various races of men. We are not to pass the distribution over because it looks unpromising, but rather to inquire with all the greater care what the bearing of it is on ourselves.

Now, in the first place, there is something to be learned from the maintenance of the distinction of the twelve tribes, and the distribution of the country into portions corresponding to each. In some degree this was in accordance with Oriental usage; for the country had already been occupied by various races, dwelling in a kind of unity—the Canaanites, Amorites, Hittites, Hivites, Jebusites, Perizzites, and Girgashites. What was peculiar to Israel was, that each of the tribes was descended from one of Jacob's sons, and that their relation to each other was conspicuously maintained, though their dwelling-places were apart. It was an arrangement capable of becoming a great benefit under a right spirit, or a great evil under the opposite. As in the case of the separate states of North America, or the separate cantons of Switzerland, it provided for variety in unity; it gave a measure of local freedom and independence, while it maintained united action; it contributed to the life and vigour of the commonwealth, without destroying its oneness of character or impairing its common purpose and aim. It promoted that picturesque variety often found in little countries, where each district has a dialect, or a pronunciation, or traditions, or a character of its own; as Yorkshire differs from Devon, or Lancashire from Cornwall; Aberdeenshire from Berwick, or Fife from Ayr. As in a garden, variety of species enlivens and enriches the effect, so in a community, variety of type enriches and enlivens the common life. A regiment of soldiers clothed in the same uniform, measuring the same stature, marching to the same step, may look very well as a contrast to the promiscuous crowd; but when a painter would paint a striking picture it is from the promiscuous crowd in all their variety of costume and stature and attitude that his figures are drawn. In the case of the Hebrew commonwealth, the distinction of tribes became smaller as time went on, and in New Testament times the three great districts Judæa, Samaria, and Galilee showed only the survival of the fittest. A larger individuality and a wider variety would undoubtedly have prevailed if a good spirit had continued to exist among the tribes, and if all of them had shown the energy and the enterprise of some.

But the wrong spirit came in, and came in with a witness, and mischief ensued. For distinctions in race and family are apt to breed rivalry and enmity, and not only to destroy all the good which may come of variety, but to introduce interminable mischief. For many a long day the Scottish clans were like Ishmael, their hand against every man, and every man's hand against them ; or at least one clan was at interminable feud with another, and the country was wretched and desolate. Among the twelve tribes of Israel the spirit of rivalry soon showed itself, leading to disastrous consequences. In the time of the judges, the men of Ephraim exhibited their temper by envying Gideon when he subdued the Midianites, and Jephthah when he subdued the Ammonites ; and under Jephthah a prodigious slaughter of Ephraimites resulted from their unreasonable spirit. In the time of the kings, a permanent schism was caused by the revolt of the ten tribes from the house of David. Thus it is that the sin of man often perverts arrangements designed for good, and so perverts them that they become sources of grievous evil. The family order is a thing of heaven; but let a bad spirit creep into a family, the result is fearful. Let husband and wife become alienated; let father and son begin to quarrel; let brother set himself against brother, and let them begin to scheme not for mutual benefit but for mutual injury, no limits can be set to the resulting mischief and misery.

Many arrangements of our modern civilization that conduce to our comfort when in good order, become sources of unexampled evil when they go wrong. The drainage of houses conduces much to comfort while it works smoothly; but let the drains become choked, and send back into our houses the poisonous gases bred of decomposition, the consequences are appalling. The sanitary inspector must be on the alert to detect mischief in its very beginnings, and apply the remedy before we have well become conscious of the evil. And so a vigilant eye needs ever to be kept on those arrangements of providence that are so beneficial when duly carried out, and so pernicious when thoughtlessly perverted. What a wonderful thing is a little forbearance at the beginning of a threatened strife! What a priceless blessing is the soft answer that turneth away wrath! There is a pithy tract bearing the title "The Oiled Feather." The oiled feather has a remarkable power of smoothing surfaces that would otherwise grate and grind upon each other, and so of averting evil. Among Christians it should be always at hand; for surely, if the forbearance and love that avert quarrels ought to be found anywhere, it is among those who have received the fulness of Divine love and grace in Jesus Christ. Surely among them there should be no perversion of Divine arrangements; in their homes no quarrels, and in their hearts no rivalry. They ought, instead, to be the peacemakers of the world, not only because they have received the peace that passeth understanding, but because their Master has said, "Blessed are the peacemakers, for they shall be called the children of God."

2. Again, in the allocation of the tribes in their various territories we have an instance of a great natural law, the law of distribution, a law that, on the whole, operates very beneficially throughout the world. In society there is both a centripetal and a centrifugal force; the centripetal chiefly human, the centrifugal chiefly Divine. Men are prone to cluster together; God promotes dispersion. Through the Divine law of marriage, a man leaves his father's house and cleaves to his wife; a new home is established, a new centre of activity, a new source of population. In the early ages they clustered about the plain of Shinar; the confusion of tongues scattered them abroad. And generally, in any fertile and desirable spot, men have been prone to multiply till food has failed them, and either starvation at home or emigration abroad becomes inevitable. And so it is that, in spite of their cohesive tendency, men are now pretty well scattered over the globe. And when once they are settled in new homes, they acquire adaptation to their locality, and begin to love it. The Esquimaux is not only adapted to his icy home, but is fond of it. The naked negro has no quarrel with the burning sun, but enjoys his sunny life. We of the temperate zone can hardly endure the heat of the tropics, and we shiver at the very thought of Lapland. It is a proof of Divine wisdom that a

world that presents such a variety of climates and conditions has, in all parts of it, inhabitants that enjoy their life.

The same law operates in the vegetable world. Everywhere plants seem to discover the localities where they thrive best. Even in the same country you have one flora for the valley and another for the mountain. The lichen spreads itself along the surface of rocks, or the hard bark of ancient trees; the fungus tarries in damp, unventilated corners; the primrose settles on open banks; the fern in shady groves. There is always a place for the plant, and a plant for the place. And it is so with animals too. The elephant in the spreading forest, the rabbit in the sandy down, the beaver beside the stream, the caterpillar in the leafy garden. If we could explore the ocean we should find the law of distribution in full activity there. There is one great order of fishes for fresh water, another for salt; one great class of insects in hot climates, another in temperate; birds of the air, from the eagle to the humming-bird, from the ostrich to the bat, in localities adapted to their habits. We ask not whether this result was due to creation or to evolution. There it is, and its effect is to cover the earth. All its localities, desirable and undesirable, are more or less occupied with inhabitants. Some of the great deserts that our imagination used to create in Africa or elsewhere do not exist. Barren spots there are, and "miry places and marshes given to salt," but they are not many. The earth has been replenished, and the purpose of God so far fulfilled.

And then there is a distribution of talents. We are not all created alike, with equal dividends of the gifts and faculties that minister in some way to the purposes of our life. We depend more or less on one another;

women on men, and men on women; the young on the old, and sometimes the old on the young; persons of one talent on those of another talent, those with strong sinews on those with clear heads, and those with clear heads on those with strong sinews; in short, society is so constituted that what each has he has for all, and what all have they have for each. The principle of the division of labour is brought in; and in a well-ordered community the general wealth and well-being of the whole are better promoted by the interchange of offices, than if each person within himself had a little stock of all that he required.

The same law of distribution prevails in the Church of Christ. It was exemplified in an interesting way in the case of our Lord's apostles. No one of these was a duplicate of another. Four of them, taking in Paul, were types of varieties which have been found in all ages of the Church. In a remarkable paper in the *Contemporary Review*, Professor Godet of Neuchâtel, after delineating the characteristics of Peter, James, John, and Paul, remarked what an interesting thing it was, that four men of such various temperaments should all have found supreme satisfaction in Jesus of Nazareth, and should have yielded up to Him the homage and service of their lives. And throughout the history of the Church, the distribution of gifts has been equally marked. Chrysostom and Augustine, Jerome and Ambrose, Bernard and Anselm, were all of the same stock, but not of the same type. At the Reformation men of marked individuality were provided for every country. Germany had Luther and Melancthon; France, Calvin and Coligny; Switzerland, Zwingle and Farel, Viret and Œcolampadius; Poland, À-Lasco; Scotland, Knox; England, Cranmer, Latimer, and Hooper. The missionary field has in like manner been provided for. India has had her Schwartz, her Carey, her Duff, and a host of others; China her Morrison, Burmah her Judson, Polynesia her Williams, Africa her Livingstone. The most unattractive and inhospitable spots have been supplied. Greenland was not too cold for the Moravians, nor the leper-stricken communities of India or Africa too repulsive. And never were Christian men more disposed than to-day to honour that great Christian law of distribution—"Go ye into all the world, and preach the gospel to every creature."

It was a great providential law, therefore, that was recognised in the partition of the land of Canaan among the tribes. Provision was thus made for so scattering the people that they should occupy the whole country, and become adapted to the places where they settled, and to the pursuits proper to them. Even where there seems to us to have been a mere random distribution of places, there may have been underlying adaptations for them, or possibilities of adaptation known only to God; at all events the law of adaptation would take effect, by which a man becomes adapted and attached to the place that not only gives him a home but the means of living, and by which, too, he becomes a greater adept in the methods of work which ensure success.

3. Still further, in the allocation of the tribes in their various territories we have an instance of the way in which God designed the earth to minister most effectually to the wants of man. We do not say that the method now adopted in Canaan was the only plan of distributing land that God ever sanctioned; very probably it was the same method as had prevailed among the Canaanites; but it is beyond doubt that,

such as it was, it was sanctioned by God for His chosen people.

It was a system of peasant proprietorship. The whole landed property of the country was divided among the citizens. Each freeborn Israelite was a landowner, possessing his estate by a tenure, which, so long as the constitution was observed, rendered its permanent alienation from his family impossible. At the fiftieth year, the year of jubilee, every inheritance returned, free of all encumbrance, to the representatives of the original proprietor. The arrangement was equally opposed to the accumulation of overgrown properties in the hands of the few, and to the loss of all property on the part of the many. The extremes of wealth and poverty were alike checked and discouraged, and the lot eulogised by Agur—a moderate competency, neither poverty nor riches, became the general condition of the citizens.

It is difficult to tell what extent of land fell to each family. The portion of the land divided by Joshua has been computed at twenty-five million acres.[1] Dividing this by 600,000, the probable number of *families* at the time of the settlement, we get forty-two acres as the average size of each property. For a Roman citizen, seven acres was counted enough to yield a moderate maintenance, so that even in a country of ordinary productiveness the extent of the Hebrew farms would, before further subdivision became necessary, have been ample. When the population increased the inheritance would of course have to be subdivided. But for several generations this, so far from an inconvenience, would be a positive benefit. It would bring

---

[1] See Wines on the "Laws of the Ancient Hebrews," p. 388.

about a more complete development of the resources of the soil. The great rule of the Divine economy was thus honoured—nothing was lost.

There is no reason to suppose that the peasant proprietorship of the Israelites induced a stationary and stagnant condition of society, or reduced it to one uniform level—a mere conglomeration of men of uniform wealth, resources, and influence. Though the land was divided equally at first, it could not remain so divided long. In the course of providence, when the direct heirs failed, or when a man married a female proprietor, two or more properties would belong to a single family. Increased capital, skill and industry, or unusual success in driving out the remaining Canaanites, would tend further to the enlargement of properties. Accordingly we meet with "men of great possessions," like Jair the Gileadite, Boaz of Bethlehem, Nabal of Carmel, or Barzillai the Gileadite, even in the earlier periods of Jewish history.[1] There was a sufficient number of men of wealth to give a pleasing variety and healthful impulse to society, without producing the evils of enormous accumulation on the one hand, or frightful indigence on the other.[2]

We in this country, after reaching the extreme on the opposite side, are now trying to get back in the direction of this ancient system. All parties seem now agreed that something of the nature of peasant proprietorship is necessary to solve the agrarian problem in Ireland and in Great Britain too. It is only the fact that in Britain commercial enterprise and emigration afford so many outlets for the energies of our landless

---

[1] Judg. x. 4; Ruth ii. 1; 1 Sam. xxv. 2; 2 Sam. xvii. 27.

[2] See the author's essay "An Old Key to our Social Problems" in "Counsel and Cheer for the Battle of Life."

countrymen that has tolerated the abuses of property so long among us,—the laws of entail and primogeniture, the accumulation of property far beyond the power of the proprietor to oversee or to manage, the employment of land agents acting solely for the proprietor, and without that sense of responsibility or that interest in the welfare of the people which is natural to the proprietor himself. It is little wonder that theories of land-possession have risen up which are as impracticable in fact as they are wild and lawless in principle. Such desperate imaginations are the fruit of despair—absolute hopelessness of getting back in any other way to a true land law,—to a state of things in which the land would yield the greatest benefit to the whole nation. Not only ought it to supply food and promote health, but also a familiarity with nature, and a sense of freedom, and thus produce contentment and happiness, and a more kindly feeling among all classes. It seems to us one of the most interesting features of the land law recently brought in for Ireland that it tends towards an arrangement of the land in the direction of God's early designs regarding it. If it be feasible for Ireland, why not have it for England and Scotland? Some may scout such matters as purely secular, and not only unworthy of the interference of religious men, but when advocated by them as fitted to prejudice spiritual religion. It is a narrow view. All that is right is religious; all that is according to the will of God is spiritual. Whatever tends to realize the prayer of Agur is good for rich and poor alike: "Give me neither poverty nor riches; feed me with food convenient for me."

4. Lastly, in the arrangements for the distribution of the land among the twelve tribes we may note a

proof of God's interest in the temporal comfort and prosperity of men. It is not God that has created the antithesis of secular and spiritual, as if the two interests were like a see-saw, so that whenever the one went up the other must go down. Things in this world are made to be enjoyed, and the enjoyment of them is agreeable to the will of God, provided we use them as not abusing them. If Scripture condemns indulgence in the pleasures of life, it is when these pleasures are preferred to the higher joys of the Spirit, or when they are allowed to stand in the way of a nobler life and a higher reward. In ordinary circumstances God intends men to be fairly comfortable; He does not desire life to be a perpetual struggle, or a dismal march to the grave. The very words in which Christ counsels us to consider the lilies and the ravens, instead of worrying ourselves about food and clothing, show this; for, under the Divine plan, the ravens are comfortably fed, and the lilies are handsomely clothed.

This is the Divine plan; and if those who enjoy a large share of the comforts of life are often selfish and worldly, it is only another proof how much a wrong spirit may pervert the gifts of God and turn them to evil. The characteristic of a good man, when he enjoys a share of worldly prosperity, is, that he does not let the world become his idol,—it is his servant, it is under his feet; he jealously guards against its becoming his master. His effort is to make a friend of the mammon of unrighteousness, and to turn every portion of it with which he may be entrusted to such a use for the good of others, that when at last he gives in his account, as steward to his Divine Master, he may do so with joy, and not with grief.

CHAPTER XXIV.

THE INHERITANCE OF JUDAH.[1]

Joshua xv.

JUDAH was the imperial tribe, **and it was fitting** that he should be planted in a conspicuous territory. Even if the republic had not been destined to give place to the monarchy, some pre-eminence was due to the tribe which had inherited the patriarchal blessing, and from which He was to come in whom all the families of the earth were to be blessed. Judah and the sons of Joseph seem to have obtained their settle-

---

[1] We do not encumber our exposition with a discussion of the extraordinary theory of Wellhausen, to the effect that Judah and Simeon, with Levi, were the first to cross the Jordan and attack the Canaanites; that Simeon and Levi were all but annihilated; that Joshua, who belonged to the tribe of Ephraim, did little more than settle that tribe; and that there was hardly such a thing as united action by the tribes, most of them having acted and fought at their own hand. This theory rests professedly on the ground that Judges i. is a more true and trustworthy account of the settlement than the narrative of Joshua. It is a strange proof of the greater truthfulness of Judges that, according to this theory, its very first statement should be a lie—"It came to pass *after the death of Joshua!*" The narrative of Judges naturally follows that of Joshua because it is plain that while Joshua secured for his people standing ground in the country, he did not secure undisturbed possession. Joshua set them an example of faith and courage which, if followed up by them, would have secured undisturbed possession; but with few exceptions they preferred to tolerate the Canaanites at their side, instead of making a vigorous effort to dispossess them wholly.

ments not only before the other tribes, but in a different manner. They did not obtain them by lot, but apparently by their own choice and by early possession. Judah was not planted in the heart of the country. That position was gained by Ephraim and Manasseh, the children of Joseph, while Judah obtained the southern section. In this position his influence was not so commanding at first as it would have been had he occupied the centre. The portion taken possession of by Judah had belonged to the first batch of kings that Joshua subdued,—the kings that came up to take vengeance on the Gibeonites. What was first assigned to Judah was too large, and the tribe of Simeon got accommodation within his lot (chap. xix. 9). Dan also obtained several cities that had first been given to Judah (comp. chaps. xv. 21-62 and xix. 40-46). In point of fact, Judah ere long swallowed up a great part of Simeon and Dan, and Benjamin was so hemmed in between him and Ephraim that, while Jerusalem was situated within the limits of Benjamin, it was, for all practical purposes, a city of Judah.

The territory of Judah was not pre-eminently fruitful; it was not equal in this respect to that of Ephraim and Manasseh. It had some fertile tracts, but a considerable part of it was mountainous and barren. It was of four descriptions—the hill country, the valley or low country, the south, and the wilderness. "The hill country," says Dean Stanley, "is the part of Palestine which best exemplifies its characteristic scenery; the rounded hills, the broad valleys, the scanty vegetation, the villages and fortresses sometimes standing, more frequently in ruins, on the hill tops; the wells in every valley, the vestiges of terraces whether for corn or wine."
Here the lion of the tribe of Judah entrenched himself,

to guard the southern frontier of the Chosen Land, with Simeon, Dan, and Benjamin nestled around him. Well might he be so named in this wild country, more than half a wilderness, the lair of savage beasts, of which the traces gradually disappear as we advance into the interior. Fixed there, and never dislodged, except by the ruin of the whole nation, "he lay down, he couched as a lion, and as an old lion; who shall rouse him up?"

Many parts of Judah were adapted for the growth of corn: witness Bethlehem, "the house of bread." But the cultivation of the vine was pre-eminently the feature of the tribe. "Here more than elsewhere in Palestine are to be seen on the sides of the hills the vineyards, marked by their watch-towers and walls, seated on their ancient terraces, the earliest and latest symbol of Judah. The elevation of the hills and table-lands of Judah is the true climate of the vine. He 'bound his foal unto the vine, and his ass's colt unto the choice vine; he washed his garments in wine, and his clothes in the blood of grapes.' It was from the Judæan valley of Eshcol, 'the torrent of the cluster,' that the spies cut down the gigantic cluster of grapes. 'A vineyard on a "hill of olives"' with the 'fence,' and 'the stones gathered out,' and the tower in 'the midst of it,' is the natural figure which both in the prophetical and evangelical records represents the kingdom of Judah. The 'vine' was the emblem of the nation on the coins of the Maccabees, and in the colossal cluster of golden grapes which overhung the porch of the second Temple; and the grapes of Judah still mark the tombstones of the Hebrew race in the oldest of their European cemeteries at Prague."[1]

---

[1] Stanley's "Sinai and Palestine."

The chapter now before us has a particularly barren look; but if we examine it with care we shall find it not deficient in elements of interest.

1. First, we have an elaborate delineation of the boundaries of the territory allotted to Judah. It is not difficult to follow the boundary line in the main, though some of the names cannot be identified now. The southern border began at the wilderness of Zin, where the host had been encamped more than forty years before, when the twelve spies returned with their report of the land. The line moved in a south-westerly course till it reached "the river of Egypt" and the sea shore. What this "river of Egypt" was is far from clear. Naturally one thinks of the Nile, the only stream that seems to be entitled to such an appellation. On the other hand, the term translated "river" is commonly though not always, applied to brooks or shallow torrents, and hence it has been thought to denote a brook, now called El Arish, about midway in the desert between Gaza and the Pelusiac mouth of the Nile. While we incline to the former view, we own that practically the question is of little consequence; the only difference being that if the boundary reached to the Nile, it included a larger share of the desert than if it had a more northerly limit. The Dead Sea was the chief part of the eastern frontier. The northern boundary began near Gilgal, and stretched westwards to the Mediterranean by a line that passed just south of Jerusalem.

The position of Judah was peculiar, in respect of the enemies by whom he was surrounded. On his eastern frontier, close to the Dead Sea, he was in contact with Moab, and on the south with Edom, the descendants of Esau. On the south-west were the Amalekites of the desert; and on the west the Philistines, and pre-eminent among them, until Caleb subdued them, the sons of Anak, the giants. On his extreme north, but within the tribe of Benjamin, was the great fortress of the Jebusites. It was no bed of roses that was thus prepared for the lion of the tribe of Judah. If he should rule at all, he must rule in the midst of his enemies. Hemmed in by fierce foes on every side, he needed to show his prowess if he was to prevail against them. It was the necessity of contending with these and other enemies that developed the military genius of David (1 Sam. xvii. 50, xviii. 5, 17, 27, xxvii. 8), and made him the fitting type of the heavenly warrior who goes forth "conquering and to conquer." The vigilance that was needed to keep these enemies at bay was one means of preserving the vigour and independence of the tribe. Living thus in the very heart of foes, Judah was the better fitted to symbolize the Church of Christ, as she is usually found when faithful to her high calling. " Behold, I send you forth as sheep in the midst of wolves." "We wrestle not against flesh and blood, but against principalities and powers, against the rulers of the darkness of this world, against spiritual wickedness in high places." As long as the Church is militant, it cannot be otherwise; and it little becomes her either to complain on the one hand, or be despondent on the other, however strong and bitter the opposition or even the persecution of her foes.

2. Next, a little episode comes into our narrative (vv. 13-19), in connection with a special allocation of territory within the tribe. The incident of Caleb is rehearsed, as an introduction to the narrative that follows. Caleb, on the strength of his promise to drive

out the Anakim, had got Hebron for his inheritance, and a portion of the country around. Near to Hebron, but on a site now unknown, stood Debir, or Kirjath-sepher, apparently a stronghold of the Anakim. We do not know the circumstances that induced Caleb to put this place up, as it were, to public competition. Whoever should capture it was promised his daughter Achsah in marriage. Othniel, who is called his younger brother, which may perhaps mean his brother's son, took the place, and, according to the bargain, got Achsah for his wife. The capture of Debir is recorded twice, here and in Judges i. 14, 15, and in the latter case with the addition of an incident that followed the marriage, as if in both cases it had been copied from an older record. Achsah was evidently a woman who could look well after her interests. She was not satisfied with the portion of land that fell to Othniel. There was a certain field besides, on which she had set her affection, and which she induced her husband to ask of Caleb. This he appears to have obtained. Then she herself turned supplicant, and having gone to Caleb and lighted down from off her ass,[1] and Caleb having said to her, "What wouldest thou?" she said unto her father, "Give me a blessing; for thou hast given me a south land; give me also springs of water." ["And she said, Give me a blessing (*margin*, present); for thou hast set me in the land of the south; give me also springs of water," R.V.] Her request was

---

[1] Founding on the expression, "having lighted off her ass," some have thought that she feigned to fall off, and that her father coming to help her in the compassionate spirit one shows in a case of accident, she took the opportunity to ask and obtain this gift. The explanation is far-fetched if not foolish. Her dismounting is explained by the universal custom when one met a person of superior rank. Comp. Gen. xxiv. 64. See Kitto's "Pictorial Commentary."

granted :—" he gave her the upper springs and the nether springs."

The incident, though picturesque, is somewhat strange, and we naturally ask, why should it have a place in the dry narrative of the settlement? Possibly for the very reason that what concerns the settlement was very dry, and that an incident like this gave it something of living interest. Those who lived at the time must have had a special interest in the matter, for in Judges i. 14 it is said that Achsah moved Othniel to ask of her father "*the* field" (*Heb.*), implying that it was a particular field, well known to the public. The moral interest of the narrative is the light it throws on the generosity of Caleb. His son-in-law asked of him a field, a field apparently of special value; he got it: his daughter asked springs of water, and she too gained her request. We contrast Caleb with Saul, as we afterwards read of him. In no such fashion was David treated by his father-in-law, after his brilliant victories over the Philistines. So far was he from acquiring field or fountain, that he did not even acquire his wife:—"It came to pass at the time when Merab, Saul's daughter, should have been given to David, that she was given unto Adriel the Meholathite to wife" (1 Sam. xviii. 19). Caleb had another spirit with him. He had the heart of a father, he had a genuine interest in his daughter and son-in-law, and desired to see them comfortable and happy. Kindly and large-hearted, he at once transferred to them valuable possessions that a greedier man would have kept for himself. Evidently he was one of those godlike men that enjoy giving, that have more pleasure in making others happy than in multiplying their own store. "The liberal man deviseth liberal things, and by liberal things shall he stand." "There is that scattereth, and yet increaseth; and there is that withholdeth more than is meet, and it tendeth to poverty."

It is no great wonder that an incident which reveals the flowing generosity of a godlike heart, should sometimes be turned to account as a symbol of the liberality of God. All human generosity is but a drop from the ocean of the Divine bounty, a faint shadow of the inexhaustible substance. "If ye that are evil know how to give good gifts to your children, how much more shall your Father in heaven give good things to them that ask Him?" If in the earthly father's bosom there be that interest in the welfare of his children which is eager to help them where help is needed and it is in his power to give it, how much more in the bosom of the Father in heaven? Why should any be backward to apply to Him—to say to Him, like Achsah, "Give me a blessing"? It pleases Him to see His children reposing trust in Him, believing in His infinite love. All that He asks of us is to come to Him through Jesus Christ, acknowledging our unworthiness, and pleading the merit of His sacrifice and intercession, as our only ground of acceptance in His sight. After His revelation of His grace in Christ our requests cannot be restricted to mere temporal things; when we ask a blessing it must be one of higher scope and quality. Yet such is His bounty that nothing can be withheld that is really for our good. "No good thing will the Lord withhold from them that walk uprightly." "Prove me now herewith, saith the Lord; if I will not open to you the windows of heaven, and pour you out a blessing that there shall not be room enough to receive it."

3. We leave this picturesque incident to re-enter

the wilderness of unfamiliar names. We find a list of no fewer than a hundred and fifteen cities which lay within the confines of the tribe of Judah (vv. 21-32). They fall into four divisions. First, twenty-nine cities belonged to "the south"—the "Negeb" of the Hebrews, the part of the country which bordered on the desert, and to some degree partook of its character. Cities they are called, but few of them were more than villages, and hardly any were important enough to leave their mark on the history. There are two, however, having memorable associations with men of mark, the one carrying us back to a glorious past, the other forward to a disgraceful future. Strange association—Abraham and Judas Iscariot! With Beersheba the name of Abraham is imperishably associated, as well as the name of Isaac. And to this day the very name Beersheba seems to emit a holy fragrance. With Kerioth (ver. 25) we connect the traitor Judas—the Is-cariot of the New Testament being equivalent to Ish-Kerioth, a man of Kerioth, of the Old. Our heart fills with a sense of nausea as we recall the association. The traitor was doubly connected with the tribe of Judah, —by his name and by his birthplace. What mockery of a noble name! "Judah, thou art he whom thy brethren shall praise." What contrast could be greater than that between the Judah who surrendered himself to slavery to set his brother free, and the Judah who sold his Lord for thirty pieces of silver! What extremes of character may we find under the same name, and often in the same family! Strange that so few are drawn by the example of the noble, and so many follow the course of the vile!

The next division, "the valley," the lowland, or Shephelah, embraced three subdivisions—the north-eastern Shephelah with her fourteen towns (vv. 33-36), the middle, with sixteen (vv. 37-41), and the southern, with nine (vv. 42-44); to which are added three of the cities of the Philistines,—Ekron, Ashdod, and Gaza (vv. 45-47). Many of the places in this list became famous in the history. Eshtaol and Zorah were of note in the history of Samson, but in his time they were Danite settlements. Jarmuth, Lachish, Eglon, and Makkedah had been conspicuous in Joshua's great battle of Bethhoron. Adullam and Keilah figured afterwards in David's outlaw history, and Ashdod and Ekron were two of the Philistine cities to which the ark was taken after the battle of Ebenezer and Aphek (1 Sam. iv. 1, v. 1, 10). In later years Lachish and Libnah were among the places attacked by Sennacherib, King of Assyria, in his great raid upon the country (Isa. xxxvii. 8).

The third great group of cities were those of "the mountain," or highlands. These were mostly in the central part of the territory, on the plateau or ridge that runs along it, rising up from the valley of the Dead Sea on the east, and the Shephelah, or "valley," on the west. Here there were four groups of cities: eleven on the south-west (vv. 48-51), nine farther north (vv. 52-54), ten to the east (vv. 55-57), and six to the north (vv. 58, 59), along with Kirjath-baal and Rabbah in the same neighbourhood. This group included Hebron, of which we hear so much; also Carmel, Maon, and Ziph, conspicuous in the outlaw life of David. It is remarkable that there is no mention of Bethlehem, which lay in "the mountain": it probably had not yet attained to the rank of a town. But its very omission may be regarded as a proof of the contemporaneous date of the book; for soon after Bethlehem was a well-known place (Ruth i.—iv.), and if the Book of Joshua had been written at the late date sometimes assigned to it, that city could not have failed to have a place in the enumeration.

A fourth group of cities were in "the wilderness" or Migdar. This was a wild rocky region extending between the Dead Sea and the mountains of Hebron. "It is a plateau of white chalk, terminated on the east by cliffs which rise vertically from the Dead Sea shore to a height of about two thousand feet. The scenery is barren and wild beyond all description. The chalky ridges are scored by innumerable torrents, and their narrow crests are separated by broad, flat valleys. Peaks and knolls of fantastic forms rise suddenly from the swelling downs, and magnificent precipices of rugged limestone stand up like fortress walls above the sea. Not a tree nor a spring is visible in the waste; and only the desert partridge and the ibex are found ranging the solitude."[1] This district was in large measure the scene of David's wanderings, and well might he call it "a dry and thirsty land where there is no water" (Psalm lxiii. 1). It was also the scene of the preaching of John the Baptist, at least at the beginning (Matt. iii. 1); for when the administration of baptism became common, it was necessary for him to remove to a better-watered region (John iii. 23). There is some reason to believe that it was also the scene of our Lord's temptation (Matt. iv. 1), the more especially because one of the Evangelists has said that "He was there with the wild beasts" (Mark i. 12).

Only six cities are enumerated as "in the wilderness" (vv. 61, 62), so that its population must have been very small. And of those mentioned some are wholly unknown. The most interesting of the six is

---

[1] Conder's "Handbook to the Bible," pp. 213, 214.

Engedi, which derived its name from a celebrated fountain, meaning "fountain of the kid." It is noted as one of the hiding-places of David; Saul pursued him to it, and it was there that David spared his life when he found him in a cave (1 Sam. xxiv.). Solomon extols its vineyards and its camphire (Song of Solomon i. 14) [henna-flowers, R.V.], Josephus its balsam (Ant., ix. 1, § 2), and Pliny its palms (v. 17). In ancient times it was the site of a town, and in the fourth century, in Jerome's time, there was still a considerable village; now, however, there is no trace of anything of the kind. Sir Walter Scott, in the "Talisman," makes it the abode of a Christian hermit— Theodoric of Engaddi. It is situated near the middle of the western shore of the Dead Sea. A rich plain, half a mile square, slopes gently from the base of the mountains to the sea; and about a mile up the western acclivity, four hundred feet above the plain, is the fountain of Ain Jiddy, from which the place gets its name.

Such, then, was the distribution of the cities of Judah over the four sections of the territory, the south, the Shephelah, the highlands, and the wilderness. It was an ample and varied domain, and after Caleb expelled the Anakim, there seems to have been little or no opposition to the occupation of the whole by the tribe. But "the crook in the lot" was not wanting. The great Jebusite fortress, Jerusalem, was on the very edge of the northern boundary of Judah. Nominally, as we have said, Jerusalem was in the territory of Benjamin, but really it was a city of Judah. For it is said (ver. 63), "As for the Jebusites, the children of Judah could not drive them out; but the Jebusites dwell with the children of Judah at Jerusalem unto this day."[1] For some reason Joshua had omitted to take possession of this stronghold after the battle of Beth-horon. The stream of pursuit had gone westward, and the opportunity of taking Jerusalem when the king had been slain and his army cut to pieces, was lost. And just as in modern history, when the opportunity of taking Sebastopol was lost after the battle of the Alma, and a long, harassing and most disastrous siege had to be resorted to, so it was with Jerusalem; the Jebusites, recovering their spirits after the defeat, were able to hold it, and to defy the tribe of Judah, and all the tribes, for many a long year. While the fortress was held by the Jebusites, Jew and Jebusite dwelt together in the city, leading no doubt a comfortless life, neither the one nor the other feeling truly at home.

The moral is not far to seek. There is a crisis in some men's lives, when they come under the power of religion, and feel the obligation to live to God. If they had decision and courage enough at this crisis to break off all sinful habits and connections, to renounce all unchristian ways of life, to declare with Joshua, " As for me and my house, we will serve the Lord,"— they would no doubt experience a sharp opposition, but it would pass over, and peace would come. But often they hesitate, and shrink, and cower; they cannot endure opposition and ridicule; they retain religion enough to appease their consciences, but not to give them satisfaction and joy. It is another case of the men of Judah dwelling with the Jebusites, and with the same result; they are not happy, they are not at rest; they bring little or no honour to their Master, and they have little influence on the world for good.

---

[1] A proof that Joshua was written before the time of David.

CHAPTER XXV.

THE INHERITANCE OF JOSEPH.

JOSHUA xvi., xvii.

NEXT to Judah, the most important tribe was Joseph; that is, the double tribe to which his two sons gave names, Ephraim and Manasseh. In perpetual acknowledgment of the service rendered by Joseph to the family, by keeping them alive in the famine, it was ordained by Jacob that his two sons should rank with their uncles as founders of tribes (Gen. xlviii. 5). It was also prophetically ordained by Jacob that Ephraim, the younger son, should take rank before Manasseh (Gen. xlviii. 19). The privilege of the double portion, however, remained to Manasseh as the elder son. Hence, in addition to his lot in Gilead and Bashan, he had also a portion in Western Palestine. But Ephraim was otherwise the more important tribe; and when the separation of the two kingdoms took place, Ephraim often gave his name to the larger division. And in the beautiful prophetic vision of Ezekiel, when the coming re-union of the nation is symbolized, it is on this wise: "Son of man, take thou one stick and write upon it, For Judah, and for the children of Israel his companions; then take another stick and write upon it, For Joseph, the stick of Ephraim, and for all the house of Israel his companions, and join them for thee one to another into one stick, that they may become one in thine hand" (xxxvii. 16, 17). The superiority allotted to Ephraim was not followed by very happy results; it raised an arrogant spirit in that tribe, of which we find some indications in the present chapter, but more pronounced and mischievous manifestations further on.

The delimitation of the tribes of Ephraim and Manasseh is not easy to follow, particularly in the Authorized Version, which not only does not translate very accurately, but uses some English expressions of uncertain meaning. The Revised Version is much more helpful, correcting both classes of defects in its predecessor. Yet even the Revised Version sometimes leaves us at a loss. It has been supposed, indeed, that some words have dropped out of the text. Moreover, it has not been found possible to ascertain the position of all the places mentioned. Uncertainty as to the precise boundaries cannot but prevail, and differences of opinion among commentators. But the uncertainty applies only to the minuter features of the description, it bears chiefly on the points at which one tribe adjoined another. The portion of the land occupied by Ephraim and Manasseh is, on the whole, very clearly known, just as their influence on the history of the country is very distinctly marked.

In point of fact, the lot of Joseph in Western Palestine was, in many respects, the most desirable of any. It was a fertile and beautiful district. It embraced the valley of Shechem, the first place of Abraham's sojourn, and reckoned by travellers to be one of the most beautiful spots, some say the most beautiful spot, in Palestine. Samaria, at the head of another valley celebrated for its "glorious beauty," and for its "fatness" or fertility (Isa. xxviii. 1), was at no great distance. Tirzah, a symbol of beauty, in the

Song of Solomon (vi. 4) was another of its cities, as was also Jezreel, "a lovely position for a capital city" (*Tristram*). On the other hand, this portion of the country laboured under the disadvantage of not having been well cleared of its original inhabitants. The men of Ephraim did not exert themselves as much as the men of Judah. This is apparent from what is said in chap. xvi. 10, "They drove not out the Canaanites that dwelt in Gezer"; and also from Joshua's answer to the request of Ephraim for more land (xvii. 15-18).

As we have said already, we have no information regarding Joshua's conquest of this part of the country. It seems to have been run over more superficially than the north and the south. Consequently the ancient inhabitants were still very numerous, and they were formidable likewise, because they had chariots of iron.

In the definition of boundaries we have first a notice applicable to Joseph as a whole, then specifications applicable to Ephraim and Manasseh respectively. The southern border is delineated twice with considerable minuteness, and its general course, extending from near the Jordan at Jericho, past Bethel and Luz, and down the pass of Bethhoron to the Mediterranean, is clear enough. The border between Ephraim and Manasseh is not so clear, nor the northern border of Manasseh. It is further to be remarked that, while we have an elaborate statement of boundaries, we have no list of towns in Ephraim and Manasseh such as we have for the tribe of Judah. This gives countenance to the supposition that part of the ancient record has somehow dropped out. We find, however, another statement about towns which is of no small significance. At chap. xvi. 9 we find that several cities were appropriated to Ephraim that were situated in the territory of Manasseh. And in like manner several cities were given to Manasseh which were situated in the tribes of Issachar and Asher. Of these last the names are given. They were Bethshean, Ibleam, Dor, Endor, Taanach, and Megiddo. Some of them were famous in after history. Bethshean was the city to whose wall the bodies of Saul and his sons were fixed after the fatal battle of Gilboa; Ibleam was in the neighbourhood of Naboth's vineyard (2 Kings ix. 25, 27); Endor was the place of abode of the woman with a familiar spirit whom Saul went to consult; Taanach was the battle-field of the kings of Canaan whom Barak defeated, and of whom Deborah sung,—

> "The kings came and fought;
> Then fought the kings of Canaan,
> In Taanach by the waters of Megiddo:
> They took no gain of money" (Judg. v. 19).

As for Megiddo, many a battle was fought in its plain. So early as the days of Thotmes III. of Egypt (about 1600 B.C.) it was famous in battle, for in an inscription on the temple of Karnak, containing a record of his conquests in Syria, Megiddo flourishes as the scene of a great conflict. The saddest and most notable of its battles was that between King Josiah and the Egyptians, in which that good young king was killed. In fact, Megiddo obtained such notoriety as a battle-field that in the Apocalypse (xvi. 16) Ar-Mageddon (Har-magedon, R.V.) is the symbol of another kind of battle-ground—the meeting-place for "the war of the great day of God the Almighty."

We can only conjecture why these cities, most of which were in Issachar, were given to Manasseh. They were strongholds in the great plain of Esdraelon, where most of the great battles of Canaan were fought.

For the defence of the plain it seemed important that these places should be held by a stronger tribe than Issachar. Hence they appear to have been given to Manasseh. But, like Ephraim, Manasseh was not able to hold them at first. "The children of Manasseh could not drive out the inhabitants of those cities; but the Canaanites would dwell in that land. And it came to pass, when the children of Israel were waxen strong that they put the Canaanites to task-work, and did not utterly drive them out" (R.V.). This last verse appears to have been inserted at a later date, and it agrees with 1 Chron. vii. 29, where several of the same towns are enumerated, and it is added, "In these dwelt the children of Joseph, the son of Israel."

Undoubtedly these sons of Joseph occupied a position which gave them unrivalled opportunities of benefiting their country. But with the exception of the splendid exploit of Gideon, a man of Manasseh, and his little band, we hear of little in the history that redounded to the credit of Joseph's descendants. Nobility of character is not hereditary. Sometimes nature appears to spend all her intellectual and moral wealth on the father, and almost to impoverish the sons. And sometimes the sons live on the virtues of their fathers, and cannot be roused to the exertion or the sacrifice needed to continue their work and maintain their reputation. A humorous saying is recorded of an eminent pastor of the Waldensian Church who found his people much disposed to live on the reputation of their fathers, and tried in vain to get them to do as their fathers did; he said that they were like the potato—the best part of them was under the ground. If you say, "We have Abraham for our father," take care that you say it in the proper sense. Be sure that you are following hard in his footsteps, and using his example as a spur to move your languid energies, and not as a screen to conceal your miserable defects. If you think of Abraham or of any forefather or body of forefathers as a cover for your nakedness, or a compensation for your defects, you are resorting to a device which has never proved successful in past ages, and is not likely to change its character with you.

After the division, the vain, self-important spirit of Ephraim broke out in a characteristic way. "Why," said he to Joshua, "hast thou given me but one lot and one part for an inheritance, seeing I am a great people, forasmuch as hitherto the Lord hath blessed me?" A grumbling reference seems to be made here to his brother Manasseh, who had received two lots, one on each side of the Jordan. At first it appears that there was some reason in the complaint of Ephraim. The *free* part of his lot seems to have been small, that is, the part not occupied by Canaanites. But we cannot think that the whole inheritance of Ephraim was so small as we find represented in the map of Major Conder, of the Palestine Exploration Fund, in his "Handbook to the Bible," because it is said, both in the Authorized and in the Revised Version, that his western boundary extended to the sea, while Major Conder makes it cease much sooner. But, looking at the whole circumstances, it is probable that Ephraim's complaint was dictated by jealousy of Manasseh, who certainly had received the double inheritance.

Alas, how apt is the spirit of discontent still to crop up when we compare our lot with that of others! Were we quite alone, or were there no case for comparison, we might be content enough; it is when we think how much more our brother has than we, that we are most liable to murmur. And, bad though murmuring and grieving at the good of our brother may be, it is by no means certain that the evil spirit will stop there. At the very dawn of history we find Cain the murderer of his brother because the one had the favour of God and not the other. What an evil feeling it is that grudges to our brother a larger share of God's blessing; if at the beginning it be not kept under it may carry us on to deeds that may well make us shudder.

Joshua dealt very wisely and fearlessly with the complaint of Ephraim, though it was his own tribe. You say you are a great people—be it so; but if you are a great people, you must be capable of great deeds. Two great undertakings are before you now. There are great woodlands in your lot that have not been cleared—direct your energies to them, and they will afford you more room for settlements. Moreover, the Canaanites are still in possession of a large portion of your lot; up and attack them and drive them out, and you will be furnished with another area for possession. Joshua accepted their estimate of their importance, but gave it a very different practical turn. What they had wished him to do was to take away a portion from some other tribe and give it as an extra allotment to them, so that it would be theirs without labour or trouble. What Joshua did was to spur them to courageous and self-denying exertion, in order that their object might be gained through the instrumentality of their own labour. For the sickly sentiment that desires a mine of gold to start into being and scatter its untold treasure at our feet, he substituted the manly sentiment of the proverb, "No gains without pains." "The soul of the sluggard desireth and hath nothing; but the hand of the diligent maketh rich." If they wished more land they must work for it; they must not take idleness for their patron-saint.

We have all heard of the dying father who informed his sons that there was a valuable treasure in a certain field, and counselled them to set to work to find it. With great care they turned up every morsel of the soil; but no treasure appeared, till, observing in autumn what a rich crop covered the field, they came to understand that the fruit of persevering labour was the treasure which their father meant. We have heard, too, of a physician who was consulted by a rich man suffering cruelly from gout, and asked if he had any cure for it. "Yes," said the doctor, "live on sixpence a day, and work for it." The same principle underlay the counsel of Joshua. Of course it gratifies a certain part of our nature to get a mass of wealth without working for it. But this is not the best part of our nature. Probably in no class has the great object of life been so much lost, and the habit of indolence and self-indulgence become so predominant as in that of young men born to the possession of a great fortune, and never requiring to turn a hand for anything they desired. After all, the necessity of work is a great blessing. We speak of the curse of toil, but except when the labour is excessive, or unhealthy in its conditions, or when it has to be prosecuted in sickness or failing strength, it is not a curse but a blessing. Instead of being ashamed of labour, we have cause rather to be proud of it. It guards from numberless temptations; it promotes a healthy body and a healthy mind; it increases the zest of life; it promotes cheerfulness and flowing spirits; it makes rest and healthy recreation far sweeter when they come, and it gives us affinity to the great Heavenly Worker, by whom, and through whom, and for whom are all things.

This great principle of ordinary life has its place too in the spiritual economy. The age is now past that had for its favourite notion, that seclusion from the world and exemption from all secular employment was the most desirable condition for a servant of God. The experiment of the hermits was tried, but it was a failure. Seclusion from the world and the consecration of the whole being to private acts of devotion and piety were no success. He who moves about among his fellows, and day by day knows the strain of labour, is more likely to prosper spiritually than he who shuts himself up in a cell, and looks on all secular work as pollution. It is not the spiritual invalid who is for ever feeling his pulse and whom every whiff of wind throws into a fever of alarm, that grows up to the full stature of the Christian; but the man who, like Paul, has his hands and his heart for ever full, and whose every spiritual fibre gains strength and vitality from his desires and labours for the good of others. And it is with churches as with individuals. An idle church is a stagnant church, prone to strife, and to all morbid experiences. A church that throws itself into the work of faith and labour of love is far more in the way to be spiritually healthy and strong. It was not for the good of the world merely, but of the church herself likewise, that our Lord gave out that magnificent *mot d'ordre*,—" Go ye into all the world, and preach the gospel to every creature."

Before we pass from the inheritance of the sons of Joseph, it is proper that we should direct attention to an incident which may seem trifling to us, but which was evidently regarded as of no little moment at the time. What we refer to is the petition presented by the five daughters of Zelophehad, a member of the tribe of Manasseh, for an inheritance in their tribe. Their father had no son, so that the family was represented wholly by daughters. No fewer than four times the incident is referred to, and the names of the five girls given in full (Numb. xxvi. 33, xxvii. 1-11, xxxvi. 11; Josh. xvii. 3). We know not if there be another case in Scripture of such prominence given to names for no moral or spiritual quality, but simply in connection with a law of property.

The question decided by their case was the right of females to inherit property in land when there were no heirs male in the family. We find that the young women themselves had to be champions of their own cause. Evidently possessed of more than ordinary spirit, they had already presented themselves before Moses, Eleazar the priest, and the princes of the congregation, at the door of the tabernacle, and formally made a claim to the inheritance that would have fallen to their father had he been alive. The case was deemed of sufficient importance to be laid before the Lord, because the decision on it would settle similar cases for the whole nation and for all time. The decision was, that in such cases the women should inherit, but under the condition that they should not marry out of their own tribe, so that the property should not be transferred to another tribe. In point of fact, the five sisters married their cousins, and thus kept the property in the tribe of Manasseh.

The incident is interesting, because it shows a larger regard to the rights of women than was usually conceded at the time. Some have, indeed, found fault with the decision as not going far enough. Why, they have asked, was the right of women to inherit land limited to cases in which there were no men in the family? The decision implied that if there had been one brother, he would have got all the land; the sisters would have been entitled to nothing. The answer to this objection is, that had the rights of women been recognised to this extent, it would have been too great an advance on the public opinion of the time. It was not God's method to enjoin laws absolutely perfect, but to enjoin what the conscience and public opinion of the time might be fairly expected to recognise and support. It may be that under a perfect system women ought to inherit property on equal terms with men. But the Jewish nation was not sufficiently advanced for such a law. The benefit of the enactment was that, when propounded, it met with general approval.

Certainly it was a considerable advance on the ordinary practice of the nations. It established the principle that woman was not a mere chattel, an inferior creature, subject to the control of the man, with no rights of her own. But it was far from being the first time when this principle obtained recognition. The wives of the patriarchs—Sarah, Rebekah, Rachel—were neither chattels, nor drudges, nor concubines. They were ladies, exerting the influence and enjoying the respect due to cultivated, companionable women. And though the law of succession did not give the females of the family equal rights with the males, it recognised them in another way. While the eldest son succeeded to the family home and a double portion of the land, he was expected to make some provision for his widowed mother and unmarried sisters. In most cases the sisters came to be provided for by marriage.

It is the circumstance that among us so many women remain unmarried that has drawn so keen attention to their rights, and already caused so much to be done, as no doubt more will be done speedily, for enlarging their sphere and protecting their interests.

No doubt these spirited daughters of Zelophehad conferred a great benefit on their sex in Israel. Their names are entitled to grateful remembrance, as the names of all are who bring about beneficial arrangements that operate in many directions and to all time. Yet one would be sorry to think that this was the only service which they rendered in their day. One would like to think of them as shedding over their households and friends the lustre of those gentle, womanly qualities which are the glory of the sex. Advocacy of public rights may be a high duty, for the faithful discharge of which the highest praise is due ; but such a career emits little of the fragrance which radiates from a female life of faithful love, domestic activity, and sacred devotion. What blessed ideals of life Christianity furnishes for women even of middling talent and ordinary education ! It is beautiful to see distinguished talents, high gifts, and persuasive elements directed to the advocacy of neglected claims. "And yet I show unto you a more excellent way."

CHAPTER XXVI.

THE DISTRIBUTION COMPLETED.

JOSHUA xviii., xix.

AN event of great importance now occurs; the civil arrangements of the country are in a measure provided for, and it is time to set in order the ecclesiastical establishment. First, a place has to be found as the centre of the religious life; next, the tabernacle has to be erected at that place—and this is to be done in the presence of all the congregation. It is well that a godly man like Joshua is at the head of the nation; a less earnest servant of God might have left this great work unheeded. How often, in the emigrations of men, drawn far from their native land in search of a new home, have arrangements for Divine service been forgotten! In such cases the degeneracy into rough manners, uncouth ways of life, perhaps into profanity, debauchery, and lawlessness, has usually been awfully rapid. On the other hand, when the rule of the old puritan has been followed, " Wherever I have a house, there God shall have an altar "; when the modest spire of the wooden church in the prairie indicates that regard has been had to the gospel precept—" Seek ye first the kingdom of God and His righteousness, and all these things shall be added unto you,"—a touch of heaven is imparted to the rude and primitive settlement, we may believe that the spirit of Christ is not unknown; the angels of virtue and piety are surely hovering around it.

The narrative is very brief, and no reason is given why Shiloh was selected as the religious centre of the nation. We should have thought that the preference would be given to Shechem, a few miles north, in the neighbourhood of Ebal and Gerizim, which had already been consecrated in a sense to God. That Shiloh was chosen by Divine direction we can hardly doubt, although there may have been reasons of various kinds that commended it to Joshua. Josephus says it was selected for the beauty of the situation; but if the present Seilûn denotes its position, as is generally believed, there is not much to corroborate the assertion of Josephus. Its locality is carefully defined in the Book of Judges (xxi. 19),—" on the north side of Bethel, on the east side of the highway that goeth up from Bethel to Shechem, and on the south of Lebonah." As for its appearance, Dean Stanley says, "Shiloh is so utterly featureless that had it not been for the preservation of its name, Seilûn, and for the extreme precision with which its situation is described in the Book of Judges, the spot could never have been identified; and, indeed, from the time of Jerome till the year 1838 [when Robinson identified it], its real site was completely forgotten." Robinson does not think so poorly of it as Stanley, describing it as "surrounded by hills, and looking out into a beautiful oval basin" ("Biblical Researches," ii. 268).

From the days of Joshua, all through the period of the Judges, and on to the last days of Eli the high priest, Shiloh continued to be the abode of the tabernacle, and the great national sanctuary of Israel.

Situated about half-way between Bethel and Shechem, in the tribe of Ephraim, it was close to the centre of the country, and, moreover, not difficult of access for the eastern tribes. Here for many generations the annual assemblies of the nation took place. Here came Hannah from her home in Mount Ephraim to pray for a son; and here little Samuel, "lent to the Lord," spent his beautiful childhood. Through that opening in the mountains, old Eli saw the ark carried by the rash hands of his sons into the battle with the Philistines, and there he sat on his stool watching for the messenger that was to bring tidings of the battle. After the ark was taken by the Philistines, the city that had grown up around the tabernacle appears to have been taken and sacked and the inhabitants massacred (Psalm lxxviii. 60-64). We hear of it in later history as the abode of Ahijah the prophet (1 Kings xi. 29); afterwards it sinks into obscurity. It is to be noted that its name occurs nowhere among the towns of the Canaanites; it is likely that it was a new place, founded by Joshua, and that it derived its name, Shiloh, "rest," from the sacred purpose to which it was now devoted.

Here, then, assembled the whole congregation of the children of Israel, to set up the tabernacle, probably with some such rites as David performed when it was transferred from the house of Obed-Edom to Mount Zion. Hitherto it had remained at Gilgal, the headquarters and depôt of the nation. The "whole congregation" that now assembled does not necessarily mean the whole community, but only selected representatives, not only of the part that had been engaged in warfare, but also of the rest of the nation.

If we try to form a picture of the state of Israel

while Joshua was carrying on his warlike campaigns, it will appear that his army being but a part of the whole, the rest of the people were occupied in a somewhat random manner, here and there, in providing food for the community, in sowing and reaping the fields, pasturing their flocks, and gathering in the fruits. And from the tone of Joshua it would appear that many of them were content to lead this somewhat irregular life. In a somewhat sharp and reproachful tone he says to them, "How long are ye slack to go to possess the land which the Lord God of your fathers has given you?" One of Joshua's great difficulties was to organize the vast mass of people over whom he presided, to prevent them from falling into careless, slatternly ways, and to keep them up to the mark of absolute regularity and order. Many of them would have been content to jog on carelessly as they had been doing in the desert, in a sort of confused jumble, and to forage about, here and there, as the case might be, in pursuit of the necessaries of life. Their listlessness was provoking. They knew that the Divine plan was quite different, that each tribe was to have a territory of its own, and that measures ought to be taken at once to settle the boundaries of each tribe. But they were taking no steps for this purpose; they were content with social hugger-mugger.

Joshua is old, but his impatience with laziness and irregularity still gives sharpness to his remonstrance, "How long are ye slack to possess the land?" The ring of authority is still in his voice; it still commands obedience. More than that, the organizing faculty is still active—the faculty that decides how a thing is to be done. "Give out from among you three men for each tribe; and I will send them, and they shall rise and go through the land and describe it according to the inheritance of them."

The men are chosen, three from each of the seven tribes that are not yet settled ; and they go through and make a survey of the land. Judah and Joseph are not to be disturbed in the settlements that have already been given to them ; but the men are to divide the rest of the country into seven parts, and thereafter it is to be determined by lot to which tribe each part shall belong. It would appear that special note was to be taken of the cities, for when the surveyors returned and gave in their report they "described the land by cities into seven parts in a book." Each city had a certain portion of land connected with it, and the land always went with the city. The art of writing was sufficiently practised to enable them to compose what has been called the " Domesday Book " of Canaan, and the record being in writing was a great safeguard against the disputes that might have arisen had so large a report consisted of mere oral statement. When the seven portions had been balloted for, there was no excuse for any of the tribes clinging any longer to that nomad life, for which, while in the wilderness, they seem to have acquired a real love.

And now we come to the actual division. The most interesting of the tribes yet unsupplied was Benjamin, and the region that fell to him was interesting too. It may be remarked as an unusual arrangement, that when portions were allotted to Judah and to Ephraim, a space was allowed to remain between them, so that the northern border of Judah was at some distance from the southern border of Ephraim. As Judah and Ephraim were the two leading tribes, and in some respects rivals, the benefit of this intervening space between them is apparent. But for this, whenever their relations became strained, hostilities might have taken place.

Now it was this intervening space that constituted the inheritance of the tribe of Benjamin. For the most part it consisted of deep ravines running from west to east, from the central table-land down to the valley of the Jordan, with mountains between. Many of its cities were perched high in the mountains, as is shown by the commonness of the names Gibeon, Gibeah, Geba, or Gaba, all of which signify "hill"; while Ramah is a "high place," and Mizpeh a "tower." In the wilderness, Benjamin had marched along with Ephraim and Manasseh, all the descendants of Joseph forming a united company; and after the settlement Benjamin naturally inclined towards fellowship with these tribes. But, as events went on, he came more into fellowship with the tribe of Judah, and though Saul, Shimei, and Sheba, the bitterest enemies of the house of David, were all Benjamites, yet, when the separation of the two kingdoms took place under Rehoboam, Benjamin took the side of Judah (1 Kings xii. 21). On the return from the captivity it was the tribes of Judah and Benjamin that took the lead (Ezra i. 5), and throughout the Book of Ezra the returned patriots are usually spoken of as "the men of Judah and Benjamin."

The cities of Benjamin included several of the most famous. Among them was Jericho, the rebuilding of which as a fortified place had been forbidden, but which was still in some degree inhabited; Bethel, which was already very famous in the history, but which, after the separation of the kingdoms, was taken possession of by Jeroboam, and made the shrine of his calves; Gibeon, the capital of the Gibeonites, and afterwards a shrine frequented by Solomon (1 Kings iii. 5); Ramah, afterwards the dwelling-place of Samuel (1 Sam. vii. 17); Mizpeh, one of the three places where he judged Israel (1 Sam. vii. 16); Gibeath, or Gibeah, where Saul had his palace (1 Sam. x. 26); and last, not least, Jerusalem. As to Jerusalem, some have thought that it lay partly in the territory of Judah, and partly in that of Benjamin. When certain terms in the description of the boundaries are studied there are difficulties that might suggest this solution. But we have seen that in practice there was a considerable amount of giving and taking among the tribes with reference to particular cities, and that sometimes a city, locally within one tribe, belonged to the people of another. So it was with Jerusalem; locally within the inheritance of Benjamin, it was practically occupied by the men of Judah (see chap. xv. 63).

Benjamin was counted the least of the tribes (1 Sam. ix. 31), and when, with other tribes, it was represented by its chief magistrate, it was rather disparagingly distinguished as "little Benjamin with their ruler" (Psalm lxviii. 27). Yet it was strong enough, on one occasion, to set at defiance for a time the combined forces of the other tribes (Judg. xx. 12, etc.). It was distinguished for the singular skill of its slingers; seven hundred, who were left-handed, "could every one sling stones at an hair-breadth and not miss" (Judg. xx. 16). The character of its territory, abounding in rocky mountains, and probably in game, for the capture of which the sling was adapted, might, in some degree, account for this peculiarity.

Many famous battles were fought on the soil of Benjamin. The battle of Ai; that of Gibeon, followed by the pursuit through Bethhoron, both under Joshua; Jonathan's battle with the Philistines at Michmash (1 Sam. xiv.); and the duel at Gibeon between twelve men of Saul and twelve of David (2 Sam. ii. 15, 16); were all fought within the territory of Benjamin. And when Sennacherib approached Jerusalem from the north, the places which were thrown into panic as he came near were in this tribe. "He is come to Aiath, he is passed through Migron; at Michmash he layeth up his baggage: they are gone over the pass; they have taken up their lodging at Geba: Ramah trembleth; Gibeah of Saul is fled. Cry aloud with thy voice, O daughter of Gallim! hearken, O Laishah! O thou poor Anathoth! Madmenah is a fugitive; the inhabitants of Gebim gather themselves to flee. This very day shall he halt at Nob: he shaketh his hand at the mount of the daughter of Zion, the hill of Jerusalem" (Isa. x. 28-32, R.V.). In later times Judas Maccabeus gained a victory over the Syrian forces at Bethhoron; and, again, Cestius and his Roman troops were defeated by the Jews; and, once more, centuries later, Richard Cœur de Lion and the flower of English chivalry, when they pushed up through Bethhoron in the hope of reaching Jerusalem, were compelled to retire.

Even down to New Testament times, as Dean Stanley remarks, the influence of Benjamin remained, for the name of Saul, the king whom Benjamin gave to the nation, was preserved in Hebrew families; and when a far greater of that name appeals to his descent, or to the past history of his nation, a glow of satisfaction is visible in the marked emphasis with which he alludes to "the stock of Israel, the tribe of Benjamin" (Phil. iii. 5), and to God's gift of "Saul the son of Kish, a man of the tribe of Benjamin" (Acts xiii. 21).

There is little to be said of Simeon, the second of the seven that drew his lot. It is admitted that his portion was taken out of the first allotment to Judah (ver. 9), which was found to be larger than that tribe required, and many of his cities are contained in Judah's list. One act of valour is recorded of Simeon in the first chapter of Judges; after the first settlement, he responded to the appeal of Judah and accompanied him against the Canaanites. But the history of this tribe as a whole might be written in the words of Jacob's prophecy—"I will divide them in Jacob, and scatter them in Israel." There is no historical reason for the supposition of Wellhausen that Simeon and Levi were all but annihilated on occasion of their attack on the Canaanites. If Simeon had been virtually extinguished, it would not have had a territory assigned to it in the ideal division of the country by Ezekiel (xlviii. 24), nor would it have afforded the twelve thousand of the "sealed" in the symbolical vision of St. John (Rev. vii. 7). While the tribe was scattered, the name of its founder survived, and both as Simeon and Simon it was crowned with honour. It was the name of one of the family of Maccabean patriots; it was borne by the just and devout man that waited in the temple for the consolation of Israel; and it was the Hebrew name of the great Apostle whose honour it was to lay the foundation of the Christian Church.

Next came the tribe of Zebulun, the boundaries of which are given with much precision; but as most of the names are now unknown, and there are also appearances of imperfection in the text, the delineation cannot be followed. "The brook that is before Jokneam" is supposed to be the Kishon, and Chisloth-Tabor, or the flanks of Tabor, points to the mountain which is the traditional, though probably not the real scene of our Lord's transfiguration. Gittah-hepher, or Gath-hepher, was the birthplace of the prophet Jonah. Bethlehem, now Beit-Lahm, is a miserable village, not to be confounded with the Bethlehem of Judah. As no mention is made either of the sea or the lake of Galilee as a boundary, it is probable that Zebulun was wholly an inland tribe. Strange to say, there is no mention, either here or in any part of the Old Testament, of by far the most famous place in the tribe,—Nazareth, the early residence of our Lord. Yet its situation would indicate that it must have been a very ancient place. Nor is it likely to have escaped the notice of the surveyors when they went through the land. The omission of this name has given rise to the opinion that the list is incomplete.

Issachar occupied an interesting and important site. Jezreel, the first name in the definition of its boundaries, is also the most famous. Jezreel, now represented by Zerin, was situated on a lofty height, and gave name to the whole valley around. Here Ahab had his palace in the days of Elijah. By its association with the worship of Baal, Jezreel got a bad reputation, and in the prophet Hosea degenerate Israel is called Jezreel, a name somewhat similar, but with very different associations (chap. i. 4). Shunem was the place of encampment of the Philistine army before the battle of Gilboa, and also the residence of the woman whose son Elisha restored to life. Bethshemesh must not be confounded with the town of the same name in Judah, nor with that in the tribe of Naphtali Signifying " house of the sun," it was a very common name among the Canaanites, as being noted for the worship of the heavenly bodies. As we have already remarked in connection with Megiddo which belonged to Manasseh, the valley of Jezreel, now usually called the plain of Esdraelon, was noted as the great battle-field of Palestine.

Asher also had an interesting territory. Theoretically it extended from Carmel to Sidon, embracing the whole of the Phœnician strip; but practically it did not reach so far. Naphtali was adjacent to Asher, and had the Jordan and the lakes of Merom and Galilee for its eastern boundary. It is in the New Testament that Naphtali enjoys its greatest distinction, the lake of Galilee and the towns on its banks, so conspicuous in the gospel history, having been situated there.

These northern tribes, as is well known, constituted the district of Galilee. The contrast between its early insignificance and its later glory is well brought out in the Revised Version of Isa. ix. 1, 2: "But there shall be no gloom to her that was in anguish. In the former time He brought into contempt the land of Zebulun and the land of Naphtali, but in the latter time hath He made it glorious, by the way of the sea, beyond Jordan, Galilee of the nations. The people that walked in darkness have seen a great light: they that dwelt in the land of the shadow of death, upon them hath the light shined."

Dan was the last tribe whose lot was drawn. And it really seemed as if the least desirable of all the portions fell to him. He was hemmed in between Judah on the one hand and the Philistines on the other, and the Philistines were anything but comfortable neighbours. The best part of the level land was no doubt in their hands, and Dan was limited to what lay at the base of the mountains (see Judg. i. 34, 35).

Very early, therefore, in the history, a colony of Dan went out in search of further possessions, and, having dispossessed some Sidonians at Laish in the extreme north, gave their name to that city, which proverbially denoted the most northerly city in the country, as Beersheba, in like manner, denoted the most southerly.

The division of the country was now completed, save that one individual was still unprovided for. And that was Joshua himself. As in a shipwreck, the captain is the last to leave the doomed vessel, so here the leader of the nation was the last to receive a portion. With rare self-denial he waited till every one else was provided for. Here we have a glimpse of his noble spirit. That there would be much grumbling over the division of the country, he no doubt counted inevitable, and that the people would be disposed to come with their complaints to him followed as matter of course. See how he circumvents them! Whoever might be disposed to go to him complaining of his lot, knew the ready answer he would get—you are not worse off than I am, for as yet I have got none! Joshua was content to see the fairest inheritances disposed of to others, while as yet none had been allotted to him. When, last of all, his turn did come, his request was a modest one—" They gave him the city that he asked, even Timnath-serah in the hill country of Ephraim." He might have asked for an inheritance in the fertile and beautiful vale of Shechem, consecrated by one of the earliest promises to Abraham, near to Jacob's well and his ancestor Joseph's tomb, or under shadow of the two mountains, Ebal and Gerizim, where so solemn a transaction had taken place after his people entered the land. He asks for nothing of the kind, but for a spot on one of the highland hills of Ephraim, a place so obscure that no trace of it remains. It is described in Judg. ii. 9 as " Timnath-heres, in the hill country of Ephraim, on the north of the mountain of Gaash." The north side of the mountain does not indicate a spot remarkable either for amenity or fertility. In the days of Jerome, his friend Paula is said to have expressed surprise that the distributer of the whole country reserved so wild and mountainous a district for himself.

Could it have been that it was a farm rejected by every one else? that the head of the nation was content with what no one else would have? If it was so, how must this have exalted Joshua in the eyes of his countrymen, and how well fitted it is to exalt him in ours! Whether it was a portion that every one else had despised or not, it undoubtedly was comparatively a poor and far-off inheritance. His choice of it was a splendid rebuke to the grumbling of his tribe, to the pride and selfishness of the "great people" who would not be content with a single lot, and wished an additional one to be assigned to them. "Up with you to the mountain" was Joshua's spirited reply; "cut down the wood, and drive out the Canaanites!"

And Joshua was not the man to give a prescription to others that he was not prepared to take to himself. Up to the mountain he certainly did go; and as he was now too old to fight, he quite probably spent his last years in clearing his lot, cutting down timber, and laboriously preparing the soil for crops. In any case, he set a splendid example of disinterested humility. He showed himself the worthy successor of Moses, who had never hinted at any distinction for his family or any possession in the country beyond what might be given to an ordinary Levite. How nobly both contrasted with men like Napoleon, who used his influence so greedily for the enrichment and aggrandisement of every member of his family! Joshua came very near to the spirit of our blessed Lord, who "though He was in the form of God, and thought it no robbery to be equal with God, made Himself of no reputation, and took on Him the form of a servant, and was made in the likeness of man." As we see the Old Testament Jesus retiring in His old age, not to a paradise in some fertile and flowery vale, but to a bleak and rocky farm on the north side of the mountain of Gaash, or to a shaggy forest, still held by the wolf and the bear, we are reminded of the Joshua of the New Testament: "Foxes have holes, and the birds of the air have nests; but the Son of man hath not where to lay his head."

CHAPTER XXVII.

THE CITIES OF REFUGE.

JOSHUA XX.

CITIES of refuge had a very prominent place assigned to them in the records of the Mosaic legislation. First, in that which all allow to be the earliest legislation (Exod. xx.—xxiii.) intimation is given of God's intention to institute such cities (Exod. xxi. 13); then in Numbers (xxxv. 9-34) the plan of these places is given in full, and all the regulations applicable to them; again in Deuteronomy (xix. 1-13) the law on the subject is rehearsed; and finally, in this chapter, we read how the cities were actually instituted, three on either side of Jordan. This frequent introduction of the subject shows that it was regarded as one of great importance, and leads us to expect that we shall find principles underlying it of great value in their bearing even on modern life.[1]

Little needs to be said on the particular cities selected, except that they were conveniently dispersed

---

[1] These frequent references do not prevent modern critics from affirming that the cities of refuge were no part of the Mosaic legislation. They found this view upon the absence throughout the history of all reference to them as being in actual use. They were not instituted, it is said, till after the Exile. But the very test that rejects them from the early legislation fails here. There is no reference to them as actually occupied in the post-exilian books, amounting, as these

over the country. Kedesh in Galilee in the northern part, Shechem in the central, and Hebron in the south, were all accessible to the people in these regions respectively; as were also, on the other side the river, Bezer in the tribes of Reuben, Ramoth in Gilead, and Golan in Bashan. Those who are fond of detecting the types of spiritual things in material, and who take a hint from Heb. vi. 18, connecting these cities with the sinner's refuge in Christ, naturally think in this connection of the nearness of the Saviour to all who seek Him, and the certainty of protection and deliverance when they put their trust in Him.

1. The first thought that naturally occurs to us when we read of these cities concerns the sanctity of human life; or, if we take the material symbol, the preciousness of human blood. God wished to impress on His people that to put an end to a man's life under any circumstances, was a serious thing. Man was something higher than the beasts that perish. To end a human career, to efface by one dread act all the joys of a man's life, all his dreams and hopes of coming good; to snap all the threads that bound him to his fellows, perhaps to bring want into the homes and desolation into the hearts of all who loved him or leant on him—this, even if done unintentionally, was a very serious thing. To mark this in a very emphatic way was the purpose of these cities of refuge. Though in certain respects (as we shall see) the practice of

---

are said to do, to half the Old Testament. Their occupation, it is said, with the other Levitical cities, was postponed to the time of Messiah. The shifts to which the critics are put in connection with this institution do not merely indicate a weak point in their theory; they show also how precarious is the position that when you do not *hear* of an institution as in actual operation you may conclude that it was of later date.

avenging blood by the next-of-kin indicated a relic of barbarism, yet, as a testimony to the sacredness of human life, it was characteristic of civilization. It is natural for us to have a feeling, when through carelessness but quite unintentionally one has killed another; when a young man, for example, believing a gun to be unloaded, has discharged its contents into the heart of his sister or his mother, and when the author of this deed gets off scot-free,—we may have a feeling that something is wanting to vindicate the sanctity of human life, and bear witness to the terribleness of the act that extinguished it. And yet it cannot be denied that in our day life is invested with pre-eminent sanctity. Never, probably, was its value higher, or the act of destroying it wilfully, or even carelessly, treated as more serious. Perhaps, too, as things are with us, it is better in cases of unintentional killing to leave the unhappy perpetrator to the punishment of his own feelings, rather than subject him to any legal process, which, while ending with a declaration of his innocence, might needlessly aggravate a most excruciating pain.

It is not a very pleasing feature of the Hebrew economy that this regard to the sanctity of human life was limited to members of the Hebrew nation. All outside the Hebrew circle were treated as little better than the beasts that perish. For Canaanites there was nothing but indiscriminate slaughter. Even in the times of King David we find a barbarity in the treatment of enemies that seems to shut out all sense of brotherhood, and to smother all claim to compassion. We have here a point in which even the Hebrew race were still far behind. They had not come under the influence of that blessed Teacher who taught us to love our enemies. They had no sense of the obligation arising from the great truth that "God hath made of one blood all the nations of men for to dwell on all the face of the earth." This is one of the points at which we are enabled to see the vast change that was effected by the spirit of Jesus Christ. The very psalms in some places reflect the old spirit, for the writers had not learned to pray as He did—" Father, forgive them; for they know not what they do."

2. Even as apportioned to the Hebrew people, there was still an uncivilized element in the arrangements connected with these cities of refuge. This lay in the practice of making the go-el, or nearest of kin, the avenger of blood. The moment a man's blood was shed, the nearest relative became responsible for avenging it. He felt himself possessed by a spirit of retribution, which demanded, with irrepressible urgency, the blood of the man who had killed his relation. It was an unreasoning, restless spirit, making no allowance for the circumstances in which the blood was shed, seeing nothing and knowing nothing save that his relative had been slain, and that it was his duty, at the earliest possible moment, to have blood for blood. Had the law been perfect, it would have simply handed over the killer to the magistrate, whose duty would have been calmly to investigate the case, and either punish or acquit, according as he should find that the man had committed a crime or had caused a misfortune. But, as we have seen, it was characteristic of the Hebrew legislation that it adapted itself to the condition of things which it found, and not to an ideal perfection which the people were not capable of at once realizing. In the office of the go-el there was much that was of wholesome tendency. The feeling was deeply rooted in the Hebrew mind that the nearest of kin was the

guardian of his brother's life, and for this reason he was bound to avenge his death; and instead of crossing this feeling, or seeking wholly to uproot it, the object of Moses was to place it under salutary checks, which should prevent it from inflicting gross injustice where no crime had really been committed. There was something both sacred and salutary in the relation of the go-el to his nearest of kin. When poverty obliged a man to dispose of his property, it was the go-el that was bound to intervene and "redeem" the property. The law served as a check to the cold spirit that is so ready to ask, in reference to one broken down, "Am I my brother's keeper?" It maintained a friendly relation between members of families that might otherwise have been entirely severed from each other. The avenging of blood was regarded as one of the duties resulting from this relation, and had this part of the duty been rudely or summarily superseded, the whole relationship, with all the friendly offices which it involved, might have suffered shipwreck.

3. The course to be followed by the involuntary manslayer was very minutely prescribed. He was to hurry with all speed to the nearest city of refuge, and stand at the entering of the gate till the elders assembled, and then to declare his cause in their ears. If he failed to establish his innocence, he got no protection; but if he made out his case he was free from the avenger of blood, so long as he remained within the city or its precincts. If, however, he wandered out, he was at the mercy of the avenger. Further, he was to remain in the city till the death of the high priest. Some have sought a mystical meaning in this last regulation, as if the high priest figured the Redeemer, and the death of the high priest the completion of

redemption by the death of Christ. But this is too far-fetched to be of weight. The death of the high priest was probably fixed on as a convenient time for releasing the manslayer, it being probable that by that time all keen feeling in reference to his deed would have subsided, and no one would then think that justice had been defrauded when a man with blood on his hands was allowed to go at large.

4. As it was, the involuntary manslayer had thus to undergo a considerable penalty. Having to reside in the city of refuge, he could no longer cultivate his farm or follow his ordinary avocations; he must have found the means of living in some new employment as best he could. His friendships, his whole associations in life, were changed; perhaps he was even separated from his family. To us all this appears a harder line than justice would have prescribed. But, on the one hand, it was a necessary testimony to the strong, though somewhat unreasonable feeling respecting the awfulness, through whatever cause, of shedding innocent blood. A man had to accept of this quietly, just as many a man has to accept the consequences— the social outlawry, it may be, and other penalties—of having had a father of bad character, or of having been present in the company of wicked men when some evil deed was done by them. Then, on the other hand, the fact that the involuntary destruction of life was sure, even at the best, to be followed by such consequences, was fitted to make men very careful. They would naturally endeavour to the utmost to guard against an act that might land them in such a situation; and thus the ordinary operations of daily life would be rendered more secure. And perhaps it was in this way that the whole appointment secured

its end. Some laws are never broken. And here may be the explanation of the fact that the cities of refuge were not much used. In all Bible history we do not meet with a single instance; but this might indicate, not the non-existence of the institution, but the indirect success of the provision, which, though framed to cure, operated by preventing. It made men careful, and thus in silence checked the evil more effectually than if it had often been put in execution.

The desire for vengeance is a very strong feeling of human nature. Nor is it a feeling that soon dies out; it has been known to live, and to live keenly and earnestly, even for centuries. We talk of ancient barbarism; but even in comparatively modern times the story of its deeds is appalling. Witness its operation in the island of Corsica. The historian Filippini says that in thirty years of his own time 28,000 Corsicans had been murdered out of revenge. Another historian calculates that the number of the victims of the Vendetta from 1359 to 1729 was 330,000.[1] If an equal number be allowed for the wounded, we have 666,000 Corsicans victims of revenge. And Corsica was but one part of Italy where the same passion raged. In former ages Florence, Bologna, Verona, Padua, and Milan were conspicuous for the same wild spirit. And, however raised, even by trifling causes, the spirit of vengeance is uncontrollable. The causes, indeed, are often in ludicrous disproportion to the effects. "In Ireland, for instance, it is not so long since one of these blood-feuds in the county of Tipperary had acquired such formidable proportions that the authorities of the Roman Catholic Church there were compelled

---

[1] Gregorovius, "Wanderings in Corsica."

to resort to a mission in order to put an end to it. A man had been killed nearly a century before in an affray which commenced about the age of a colt. His relatives felt bound to avenge the murder, and their vengeance was again deemed to require fresh vengeance, until faction fights between the 'Three Year Olds' and the 'Four Year Olds' had grown almost into petty wars."[1] When we find the spirit of revenge so blindly fierce even in comparatively modern times, we can the better appreciate the necessity of such a check on its exercise as the cities of refuge supplied. The mere fact that blood had been shed was enough to rouse the legal avenger to the pitch of frenzy; in his blind passion he could think of nothing but blood for blood; and if, in the first excitement of the news, the involuntary manslayer had crossed his path, nothing could have restrained him from falling on him and crimsoning the ground with his blood.

In New Testament times the practice that committed the avenging of blood to the nearest of kin seems to have fallen into abeyance. No such keen desire for revenge was prevalent then. Such cases as those now provided for were doubtless dealt with by the ordinary magistrate. And thus our Lord could grapple directly with the spirit of revenge and retaliation in all its manifestations. "Ye have heard that it was said of old time, An eye for an eye, and a tooth for a tooth; but I say unto you, Resist not him that is evil; but whosoever smiteth thee on thy right cheek, turn to him the other also" (R.V.). The old practice was hurtful, because, even in cases where punishment was deserved, it made vengeance or retribution so much a matter of personal

---

[1] "Pulpit Comment.," *in loco*.

feeling. It stimulated to the utmost pitch what was fiercest in human temper. It is a far better system that commits the dealing with crime to the hands of magistrates, who ought to be, and who are presumed to be, exempt from all personal feeling in the matter. And now, for those whose personal feelings are roused, whether in a case of premeditated or of unintended manslaughter, or of any lesser injury done to themselves, the Christian rule is that those personal feelings are to be overcome; the law of love is to be called into exercise, and retribution is to be left in the hands of the great Judge:—"Vengeance is Mine; I will recompense, saith the Lord."

The attempt to find in the cities of refuge a typical representation of the great salvation fails at every point but one. The safety that was found in the refuge corresponds to the safety that is found in Christ. But even in this point of view the city of refuge rather affords an illustration than constitutes a type. The benefit of the refuge was only for unintentional offences; the salvation of Christ is for all. What Christ saves from is not our misfortune but our guilt. The protection of the city was needed only till the death of the high priest; the protection of Christ is needed till the great public acquittal. All that the manslayer received in the city was safety; but from Christ there is a constant flow of higher and holier blessings. His name is called Jesus because He saves His people from their sins. Not merely from the penalty, but from the sins themselves. It is His high office not only to atone for sin, but to destroy it. "If the Son makes you free, ye shall be free indeed." The virtue that goes out of Him comes into contact with the lust itself and transforms it. The final benefit of Christ is the blessing of transformation. It is the acquisition of the Christlike spirit. " Moreover whom He did foreknow, them He also did predestinate to be conformed to the image of His Son, that He might be the firstborn of many brethren."

In turning an incident like this to account, as bearing on our modern life, we are led to think how much harm we are liable to do to others without intending harm, and how deeply we ought to be affected by this consideration, when we discover what we have really done. We may be helped here by thinking of the case of St. Paul. What harm he did in the unconverted period of his life, without intending to do harm, cannot be calculated. But when he came to the light, nothing could have exceeded the depth of his contrition, and, to his last hour, he could not think of the past without horror. It was his great joy to know that his Lord had pardoned him, and that he had been able to find one good use of the very enormity of his conduct—to show the exceeding riches of His pardoning love. But, all his life long, the Apostle was animated by an overwhelming desire to neutralise, as far as he could, the mischief of his early life, and very much of the self-denial and contempt of ease that continued to characterise him was due to this vehement feeling. For though Paul felt that he had done harm in ignorance, and for this cause had obtained mercy, he did not consider that his ignorance excused him altogether. It was an ignorance that proceeded from culpable causes, and that involved effects from which a rightly ordered heart could not but recoil.

In the case of His own murderers our blessed Lord, in His beautiful prayer, recognised a double condition,—they were ignorant, yet they were guilty,

"Father, forgive them; for they know not what they do." They were ignorant of what they were doing, and yet they were doing what needed forgiveness, because it involved guilt. And what we admire in Paul is, that he did not make his ignorance a self-justifying plea, but in the deepest humility owned the inexcusableness of his conduct. To have done harm to our fellow-creatures under any circumstances is a distressing thing, even when we meant the best; but to have down harm to their moral life owing to something wrong in our own, is not only distressing, but humiliating. It is something which we dare not lightly dismiss from our minds, under the plea that we meant the best, but unfortunately we were mistaken. Had we been more careful, had our eye been more single, we should have been full of light, and we should have known that we were not taking the right way to do the best. Errors in moral life always resolve themselves into disorder of our moral nature, and, if traced to their source, will bring to light some fault of indolence, or selfishness, or pride, or carelessness, which was the real cause of our mistaken act.

And where is the man—parent, teacher, pastor, or friend—that does not become conscious, at some time or other, of having influenced for harm those committed to his care? We taught them, perhaps, to despise some good man whose true worth we have afterwards been led to see. We repressed their zeal when we thought it misdirected, with a force which chilled their enthusiasm and carnalised their hearts. We failed to stimulate them to decision for Christ, and allowed the golden opportunity to pass which might have settled their relation to God all the rest of their life. The great realities of the spiritual life were not brought home to them with the earnestness, the fidelity, the affection that was fitting. "Who can understand his errors?" Who among us but, as he turns some new corner in the path of life, as he reaches some new view-point, as he sees a new flash from heaven reflected on the past,—who among us but feels profoundly that all his life has been marred by unsuspected flaws, and almost wishes that he had never been born? Is there no city of refuge for us to fly to, and to escape the condemnation of our hearts?

It is here that the blessed Lord presents Himself to us in a most blessed light. "Come unto Me, all ye that labour and are heavy laden, and I will give you rest." Do we not labour indeed, are we not in truth very heavy laden, when we feel the burden of unintentional evil, when we feel that unconsciously we have been doing hurt to others, and incurring the curse of him who causeth the blind to stumble? Are we not heavy laden indeed when we cannot be sure that even yet we are thoroughly on the right track—when we feel that peradventure we are still unconsciously continuing the mischief in some other form? Yet is not the promise true?—"I will give you rest." I will give you pardon for the past, and guidance for the future. I will deliver you from the feeling that you have been all your life sowing seeds of mischief, sure to spring up and pervert those whom you love most dearly. I will give you comfort in the thought that as I have guided you, I will guide them, and you shall have a vision of the future, that may no doubt include some of the terrible features of the shipwreck of St. Paul, but of which the end will be the same—"and so it came to pass that they escaped all safe to land."

And let us learn a lesson of charity. Let us learn

to be very considerate of mischief done by others either unintentionally or in ignorance. What more inexcusable than the excitement of parents over their children or of masters over their servants, when, most undesignedly and not through sheer carelessness, an article of some value is broken or damaged? Have you never done such a thing yourself? And if a like torrent fell on you then from *your* parent or master, did you not feel bitterly that it was unjust? And do you not even now have the same feeling when your temper cools? How bitter the thought of having done injustice to those dependent on you, and of having created in their bosoms a sullen sense of wrong! Let them have their city of refuge for undesigned offences, and never again pursue them or fall on them in the excited spirit of the avenger of blood!

So also with regard to opinions. Many who differ from us in religious opinion differ through ignorance. They have inherited their opinions from their parents or their other ancestors. Their views are shared by nearly all whom they love and with whom they associate; they are contained in their familiar books; they are woven into the web of their daily life. If they were better instructed, if their minds were more free from prejudice, they might agree with us more. Let us make for them the allowance of ignorance, and let us make it not bitterly but respectfully. They are doing much mischief, it may be. They are retarding the progress of beneficent truth; they are thwarting your endeavours to spread Divine light. But they are doing it ignorantly. If you are not called to provide for them a city of refuge, cover them at least with the mantle of charity. Believe that their intentions are better than their acts. Live in the hope of a day

" when perfect light shall pour its rays," when all the mists of prejudice shall be scattered, and you shall perhaps find that in all that is vital in Christian truth and for the Christian life, you and your brethren were not so far separate after all.

CHAPTER XXVIII.

THE INHERITANCE OF THE LEVITES.

JOSHUA xxi. 1—42.

ONCE and again we have found reference made to the fact that Levites received no territorial inheritance among their brethren (xiii. 14, 33, xiv. 3, 4). They had a higher privilege: the Lord was their inheritance. In the present chapter we have an elaborate account of the arrangements for their settlement; it will therefore be suitable here to rehearse their history, and ascertain the relation they now stood in to the rest of the tribes.

In the days of the patriarchs and during the sojourn in Egypt there were no official priests. Each head of a house discharged the duties of the priesthood in patriarchal times, and a similar arrangement prevailed during the residence in Egypt. The whole nation was holy; in this sense it was a nation of priests; all were set apart for the service of God. By-and-by it pleased God to select a portion of the nation specially for His service, to establish, as it were, a holy of holies within the consecrated nation. The first intimation of this was given on that awful occasion when the firstborn of the Egyptians was slain. In token of His mercy in sparing Israel on that night, all the firstborn of Israel, both of man and beast, were specially consecrated to the Lord. The animals were to be offered in sacrifice, except in the case of some, such as the ass, not suited for sacrifice; these were to be redeemed by the sacrifice of another animal. Afterwards a similar arrangement was made with reference to the firstborn of men, the tribe of Levi being substituted for them (see Numb. iii. 12). But this arrangement was not made till after the tribe of Levi had shown, by a special act of service, that they were fitted for this honour.

Certainly we should not have thought beforehand that the descendants of Levi would be the specially sacred tribe. Levi himself comes before us in the patriarchal history in no attractive light. He and Simeon were associated together in that massacre of the Shechemites, which we can never read of without horror (Gen. xxxiv. 25). Levi was likewise an accomplice with his brethren in the lamentable tragedy of Joseph. And as nothing better is recorded of him, we are apt to think of him as through life the same. But this were hardly fair. Why should not Levi have shared in that softening influence which undoubtedly came on the other brethren? Why may he not have become a true man of God, and transmitted to his tribe the memory and the example of a holy character? Certain it is that we find among his descendants in Egypt some very noble specimens of godliness. The mother of Moses, a daughter of the house of Levi, is a woman of incomparable faith. Moses, her son, is emphatically "the man of God." Aaron, his brother, moved by a Divine influence, goes to the wilderness to find him when the very crisis of oppression seems to indicate that God's time for the deliverance of Israel is drawing nigh. Miriam, his sister, though far from faultless, piously watched his bulrush-cradle, and afterwards led the choir whose praises rose to God in a great volume of thanksgiving after crossing the sea.

The first honour conferred on Levi in connection with religious service was the appointment of Aaron and his sons to the special service of the priesthood (Exod. xxviii. ; Numb. xviii. 1). This did not necessarily involve any spiritual distinction for the whole tribe of which Aaron was a member, nor was that distinction conferred at that time. It was after the affair of the golden calf that the tribe of Levi received this honour. For when Moses, in his holy zeal against that scandal, called upon all who were on the Lord's side to come to him, "all the sons of Levi gathered themselves unto him" (Exod. xxxii. 26). This seems to imply that that tribe alone held itself aloof from the atrocious idolatry into which even Aaron had been drawn. And apparently it was in connection with this high act of service that Levi was selected as the sacred tribe, and in due time formally substituted for the firstborn in every family (Numb. iii. 12, *sqq*., viii. 6 *sqq*., xviii. 2 *sqq*.). From this time the tribe of Levi stood to God in a relation of peculiar honour and sacredness, and had duties assigned to them in harmony with this eminent position.

The tribe of Levi consisted of three main branches, corresponding to Levi's three sons—Kohath, Gershon, and Merari. The Kohathites, though apparently not the oldest (see Numb. iii. 17) were the most distinguished, Moses and Aaron being of that branch. As Levites, the Kohathites had charge of the ark and its sacred furniture, guarding it at all times, and carrying it from place to place during the journeys of the wilderness. The Gershonites had charge of the tabernacle, with its cords, curtains, and coverings. The sons of Merari had charge of the more solid parts of the tabernacle, "its boards and bars, its pillars and its pins, and all the vessels thereof." Korah, the leader of the rebellion against Moses and Aaron, was, like them, of the family of Kohath, and the object of his rebellion was to punish what he considered the presumption of the two brothers in giving to Aaron the special honours of a priesthood which, in former days, had belonged alike to all the congregation (Numb. xvi. 3). We are accustomed to think that the supernatural proofs of the Divine commission to Moses were so overwhelming that it would have been out of the question for any man to challenge them. But many things show that, though we might have thought opposition to Moses impossible, it prevailed to a great extent. The making of the golden calf, the report of the spies and the commotion that followed, the rebellion of Korah, and many other things, prove that the prevalent spirit was usually that of unbelief and rebellion, and that it was only after many signal miracles and signal judgments that Moses was enabled at last to exercise an unchallenged authority. The rationalist idea, that it was enthusiasm for Moses that led the people to follow him out of Egypt, and endure all the hardships of the wilderness, and that there is nothing more in the Exodus than the story of an Eastern nation leaving one country under a trusted leader to settle in another, is one to which the whole tenor of the history offers unqualified contradiction. And not the least valid ground of opposition is the bitter, deadly spirit in which attempts to frustrate Moses were so often made.

Many of the duties of the Levites as detailed in the Pentateuch were duties for the wilderness. After the settlement in Canaan, and the establishment of the tabernacle at Shiloh, these duties would undergo a change. The Levites were not all needed to be about the tabernacle. The Gibeonites indeed had been retained as "hewers of wood and drawers of water for the congregation and for the altar of the Lord," so that the more laborious part of the work at Shiloh would be done by them. If the Levites had clustered like a swarm of bees around the sacred establishment, loss would have been sustained alike by themselves and by the people. It was desirable, in accordance with the great law of distribution already referred to, that they should be dispersed over the whole country. The men that stood nearest to God, and who were a standing testimony to the superiority of the spiritual over the secular, who were Divine witnesses, indeed, to the higher part of man's nature, as well as to God's pre-eminent claims, must have failed egregiously of their mission had they been confined to a single city or to the territory of a single tribe. Jacob had foretold both of Simeon and Levi that they would be "divided in Jacob and scattered in Israel." In the case of Levi, the scattering was overruled for good. Designed to point God-wards and heavenwards, the mission of Levi was to remind the people over the whole country that they were not mere earth-worms, created to grub and burrow in the ground, but beings with a nobler destiny, whose highest honour it was to be in communion with God.

The functions of the Levites throughout the country seem to have differed somewhat in successive periods of their history. Here, as in other matters, there was doubtless some development, according as new wants appeared in the spiritual condition of the people, and consequently new obligations for the Levites to fulfil.

When the people fell under special temptations to idolatry, it would naturally fall to the Levites, in connection with the priesthood, to warn them against these temptations, and strive to keep them faithful to their God. But it does not appear that even the Levites could be trusted to continue faithful. It is a sad and singular fact that a grandson of Moses was one of the first to go astray. The Authorized Version, indeed, says that the young man who became a priest to the Danites when they set up a graven image in the city of Dan, was Jonathan, the son of Gershom, the son of Manasseh (Judg. xviii. 30). But the Revised Version, not without authority, calls him Jonathan, the son of Gershom, the son of Moses. Here we have a glimpse of two remarkable facts: in the first place, that a grandson of Moses, a Levite, was located in so confined a place that he had to leave it in search of another, "to sojourn where he could find a place"—so entirely had Moses abstained from steps to secure superior provision for his own family; and, in the second place, that even with his remarkable advantages and relations, this Jonathan, in defiance of the law, was tempted to assume an office of priesthood, and to discharge that office at the shrine of a graven image. We are far indeed from the truth when we suppose that the whole nation of Israel submitted to the law of Moses from the beginning with absolute loyalty, or when we accept the prevalent practice among them at any one period as undoubted evidence of what was then the law.

But let us now turn our attention to the distribution of the Levites as it was planned. We say deliberately "as it was planned," because there is every reason to believe that the plan was not effectually carried out. In no case does there seem to have been such a failure of official arrangements as in the case of Levi. And the reason is not difficult to find. Few of the cities allotted to them were free of Canaanites at the time. To get actual possession of the cities they must have dispossessed the remaining Canaanites. But, scattered as they were, this was peculiarly difficult. And the other tribes seem to have been in no humour to help them. Hence it is that in the early period of the Judges we find Levites wandering here and there seeking for a settlement, and glad of any occupation they could find (Judg. xviii. 7, xix. 1).

The provision made by Joshua for the Levites was that out of all the other tribes, forty-eight cities with their suburbs, including the six cities of refuge, were allotted to them. It is necessary for us here to call to mind how much Canaan, like other Eastern countries and some countries not Eastern, was a land of towns and villages. Cottages and country-houses standing by themselves were hardly known. A house in its own grounds—"a lodge in a garden of cucumbers"—might shelter a man for a time, but could not be his permanent home. The country was too liable to hostile raids for its inhabitants to dwell thus unprotected. Most of the people had their homes in the towns and villages with which their fields were connected. In consequence of this each town had a circuit of land around it, which always fell to the conquerors when the town was taken. And it is this fact that sometimes makes the boundaries of the tribes so difficult to follow, because these boundaries had to embrace all the lands connected with the cities which they embraced. If it be asked, Did the Levites receive as part of their inheritance all the lands adjacent to their cities, the answer is, No. For in that case the only difference between them and the other tribes would have been that the Levites had forty-eight little territories instead of one large possession, and there would have been no ground for the distinction so emphatically made that "the Lord was their inheritance," or "the sacrifices of the Lord made by fire."

The cities given to the Levites, even when cleared of Canaanites, were not possessed by Levites alone. We may gather the normal state of affairs from what is said regarding Hebron and Caleb. Hebron was a Levitical city, a city of the priests, a city of refuge; they gave to the Kohathites the city, with the suburbs thereof roundabout; "but the fields of the city, and the villages thereof, gave they to Caleb the son of Jephunneh for his possession" (vv. 11, 12). What are called "suburbs," or, as some prefer to render, "cattle-drives," extended for two thousand cubits round about the city on every side (Numb. xxxv. 5), and were used only for pasture. It behoved the Levites to have cattle of some kind to supply them with their food, the main part of which, besides fruit, was milk and its produce. But, beyond this, the Levites were not entangled with the business of husbandry. They were left free for more spiritual service. It was their part to raise the souls of the people above the level of earth, and, like the angel in the "Pilgrim's Progress," call on those who might otherwise have worshipped the mud-rake to lift up their eyes to the crown of glory, and accept the heavenly gift.

In fact, the whole function of the Levites, ideally at least, was as Moses sung :—

"And of Levi he said,
Let thy Urim and thy Thummim be with thy godly one,
Whom thou didst prove at Massah,

> With whom thou didst strive at the waters of Meribah;
> Who said of his father, and of his mother, I have not seen him;
> Neither did he acknowledge his brethren,
> Nor knew his own children:
> For they have observed Thy word,
> And kept Thy covenant.
> *They shall teach Jacob Thy judgments,*
> *And Israel Thy law:*
> They shall put incense before Thee,
> And whole burnt offering upon Thine **altar.**
> Bless, Lord, his substance,
> And accept the work of his hands:
> Smite through the loins of them that rise up against **him,**
> And of them that hate him, that they rise not again."
> Deut. xxxiii. 8-11 (R.V.).

But to come now to the division itself. The Kohathites, or leading family, had no fewer than thirteen cities in the tribes of Judah, Benjamin, and Simeon, and ten more in Ephraim, Dan, and Manasseh. The thirteen in Judah, Benjamin, and Simeon were for the priests; the other ten were for the other branches of the Kohathites. At first the priests, strictly so called, could not occupy them all. But, as the history advances, the priests become more and more prominent, while the Levites as such seem to hold a less and less conspicuous place. In the Psalms, for example, we sometimes find the house of Levi left out when all classes of worshippers are called on to praise the Lord. In the 135th Psalm all are included:—

> "O house of Israel, bless ye the Lord:
> O house of Aaron, bless ye the Lord:
> O house of Levi, bless ye the Lord:
> Ye that fear the Lord, bless ye the Lord."

But in the 115th the Levites are left out:—

> "O Israel, trust thou in the Lord:
> He is their help and their shield.
> O house of Aaron, trust ye in the Lord:
> He is their help and their shield.

> Ye that fear the Lord, trust in the Lord;
> He is their help and their shield."

And in the 118th:—

> "Let Israel now say
> That His mercy endureth for ever.
> Let the house of Aaron now say
> That His mercy endureth for ever.
> Let them now that fear the Lord say
> That His mercy endureth for ever."

There is this to be said for the region where the priests, the house of Aaron, had their cities, viz., the tribe of Judah, that it maintained its integrity longest of any; nor did it thoroughly succumb to idolatry till the dark days of Manasseh, one of its later kings. But, on the other hand, in New Testament times, Judæa was the most bigoted part of the country, and the most bitterly opposed to our Lord. And the explanation is, that the true spirit of Divine service had utterly evaporated from among the priesthood, and the miserable spirit of formalism had come in. The living sap of the institution had been turned into stone, and the plant of renown of early days had become a stony fossil. So true is it that the best institutions, when perverted from their true end, become the sources of greatest evil, and the highest gifts of heaven, when seized by the devil and turned to his purposes, become the most efficient instruments of hell.

The other portions of the family of Kohath were distributed in ten cities over the central part of Western Palestine. Some of them were important centres of influence, such as Bethhoron, Shechem, and Taanach. But the influence of the Levites for good seems to have been feeble in this region, for it was here that Jeroboam reigned, and here that Ahab and Jezebel all but obliterated the worship of Jehovah.

It is commonly believed that Samuel was a member of the tribe of Levi, although there is some confusion in the genealogy as given in 1 Chron. vi. 28, 34; yet Ramathaim Zophim, his father's place of abode, was not one of the Levitical cities. And Samuel's influence was exerted more on the southern than the central district; for, after the destruction of Shiloh, Mizpeh appears to have been his ordinary residence (1 Sam. vii. 6), and afterwards Ramah[1] (vii. 17). It would indeed be a pleasant thought that the inefficiency of the Kohathites as a whole was in some measure redeemed by the incomparable service of Samuel. If Samuel was a Levite, he was a noble instance of what may be done by one zealous and consecrated man, amid the all but universal defection of his official brethren.

The Gershonites were placed in cities in eastern Manasseh, Issachar, Asher, and Naphtali; while the Merarites were in Zebulun, and in the transjordanic tribes of Gad and Reuben. They thus garrisoned the northern and eastern districts. Those placed in the north ought to have been barriers against the gross idolatry of Tyre and Sidon, and those in the east, besides resisting the idolatry of the desert tribes, should have held back that of Damascus and Syria. But there is very little to show that the Levites as a whole rose to the dignity of their mission in these regions, or that they formed a very efficient barrier against the idolatry and corruption which they were designed to meet. No doubt they did much to train the people to the outward observance of the law. They would call them to the celebration of the great annual festivals, and

---

[1] Ramathaim and Ramah are used interchangeably (1 Sam. i. 1 and 19, ii. 11)

of the new moons and other observances that had to be locally celebrated. They would look after cases of ceremonial defilement, and no doubt they would be careful to enjoin payment of the tithes to which they had a claim. They would do their best to maintain the external distinctions in religion, by which the nation was separated from its neighbours. But, except in rare cases, they do not appear to have been spiritually earnest, nor to have done much of that service which Samuel did in the southern part of the country. Externalism and formalism seem to have been their most frequent characteristics; and externalism and formalism are poor weapons when the enemy cometh in like a flood.

And, whatever may have been the usual life and work of the Levites over the country, they never seem to have realized the glory of the distinction divinely accorded to them—"The Lord is their inheritance." Few, indeed, in any age or country have come to know what is meant by having God for their portion. Unbelief can never grasp that there is a life in God— a real life, so full of enjoyment that all other happiness may be dispensed with; a real property, so rich in every blessing, that the goods and chattels of this world are mere shadows in comparison. Yet that there have been men profoundly impressed by these convictions, in all ages and in many lands, amid prevailing ungodliness, cannot be denied. How otherwise is such a life as that of St. Bernard or that of St. Francis to be accounted for? Or that of St. Columba and the missionaries of Iona? Or, to go farther back, that of St. Paul? There is a magic virtue, or rather a Divine power, in real consecration. "Them that honour Me, I will honour." It is the want of such men that makes our churches feeble. It is our mixing up our own interests with the interests of God's kingdom and refusing to leave self out of view while we profess to give ourselves wholly to God, that explains the slowness of our progress. If the Levites had all been consecrated men, idolatry and its great brood of corruptions would never have spread over the land of Israel. If all Christian ministers were like their Master, Christianity would spread like wildfire, and in a very little time the light of salvation would brighten the globe.

NOTE.—In this chapter we have accepted the statements of the Pentateuch regarding the Levites as they stand. We readily own that there are difficulties not a few connected with the received view. The modern critical theory that maintains that the Levitical order was a much later institution would no doubt remove many of these difficulties, but only by creating other difficulties far more serious. Besides, the hypothesis of Wellhausen that the tribe of Levi was destroyed with Simeon at the invasion of Canaan—having no foundation to rest on, except the assumption that the prophecy ascribed to Jacob was written at a later date—is ludicrously inadequate to sustain the structure made to rest on it. Nor is it conceivable that, after the captivity, the priests should have been able to make the people believe a totally different account of the history of one of the tribes from that which had previously been received. It is likewise incredible that the Levites should have been "annihilated" or "extinguished" in the days of Joshua, without a single allusion in the history to so terrible a fact. How inconsistent with the concern expressed when the tribe of Benjamin was in danger of extinction (Judg. xxi. 17). The loss of a tribe was like the loss of a limb; it would have marred essentially the symmetry of the nation.

CHAPTER XXIX.

NO FAILURE OF GOD'S PROMISE.

JOSHUA xxi. 43—45.

THE historian has reached a point where he may stand still and look back. One look is comparatively limited; another reaches very far. The immediate survey extends only over the last few years; the remote embraces centuries, and goes back to the time of Abraham.

The historian sees the venerable patriarch of the nation among his flocks and herds in Ur of the Chaldees; receiving there a Divine summons to remove to an unknown land; obeying the call, tarrying at Haran, then traversing the desert, and crossing the Jordan. At Shechem, at Bethel, at Mamre, and at Beersheba, he perceives him listening to the Divine voice that promises that, stranger and pilgrim though he was, the Lord would give his posterity all that land; that he would bless those that blessed him, and curse those that cursed him; and that in him and in his seed all the nations of the earth should be blessed.

For one hundred long years Abraham had wandered over the country without so much as a house or homestead in it. Isaac had come after him, living the same pilgrim life. Jacob, with a much more stirring and troubled life, had in his old age gone down to

Joseph in Egypt, leaving but one field in the country which he could call his own.

Then came the long centuries of Egyptian bondage. At last the Divine call is heard to leave Egypt, but after this, forty long years have still to be spent in the wilderness. Then Moses, the great leader of the people, dies—dies at the very time when he is apparently most needed, just at the very crisis of Israel's history.

But Joshua comes in Moses' room, and the Lord is with Joshua; He rewards his faith and gives him victory over all his enemies. And now at last comes the fulfilment of the promises to the fathers, hoary with age, and seemingly long forgotten. The bill has at last matured and fallen due. After so many generations, it might be thought that it would have been enough to discharge the main substance of the obligation or that some compromise might have been proposed reducing the claim. After having lain long out of their money, creditors are usually ready to accept a composition. But this was not God's method of settlement. During the whole period of Joshua's leadership, God had been doing nothing but discharging old obligations. Not one word of the original bill had been obliterated; not one item had been allowed to lapse through time. East and west and north and south He had been giving what He had promised to give. And now, as the transaction comes to an end, it is seen that nothing has been omitted or forgotten. "There failed not ought of any good thing which the Lord had spoken concerning Israel; all came to pass." He proved Himself, as Moses had said, "the faithful God, which keepeth covenant and mercy with them that love Him, and keep His commandments to a thousand generations."

Three gifts are specified which God bestowed on Israel: possessions, rest, and victory. First, He gave them the land which He had sworn to give unto their fathers, and they possessed it; next, He gave them rest round about, according to all that He had sworn to their fathers; and, lastly, He gave them victory over all their enemies. "He satisfied the longing soul, and filled the hungry soul with goodness." He brought His bride to her home, and surrounded her with comforts. And had the bride only been as faithful to her obligations as the Divine bridegroom, it might have been said that

"Time had run back, and fetched the age of gold."

But, it may perhaps be said,—this is only the historian's view of the matter, and it is hardly in accordance with facts. Are we not told that, at an early period, a colony of the tribe of Dan had to go elsewhere in search of land, because they were too hampered in the allotment they had received? And, in the beginning of Judges, are we not told that after the death of Joshua, Judah and Simeon had a desperate tussle with Canaanites and Perizzites who were still in their territories, and that in Bezek alone there were slain of them ten thousand men? And is not the whole of the first chapter of Judges a record of the relations of Israel in various places to the original inhabitants, from which it appears that very many of the Canaanites continued to dwell in the land? Surely this was not what God's promise to the fathers was fitted to convey. Had not God promised that He would "drive out" the seven nations, and give the seed of Abraham possession of the whole? How then could His word be said to be implemented when so many of the original inhabitants remained? And, in particular, how could the historian of Joshua say so explicitly that "there failed not ought of any good thing which the Lord had spoken unto the house of Israel."

In answer to this objection it is to be remarked that God had never promised to give the people full possession of the land *save through their own exertions made in dependence on Him.* Their possessions were not to fall into their hands as the manna fell in the wilderness or as the water gushed from the rock. The seven nations were not to rush from before them the moment they crossed the Jordan. God always meant that they were to be His instruments for clearing the country. Now, that clearance was evidently designed to be effected in two ways. First, under Joshua, a general encounter with the former possessors was to take place, their confederacies were to be shattered, their spirit was to be broken, and to a certain extent their lands were to be set free. But beyond this, there was to be a further process of clearing out. When each tribe was settled in its lot, it was to address itself, in detail, to the task of dispossessing such Canaanites as yet lingered there. It might not be expedient that all should be engaged in this task together, for this would necessarily interfere with the ordinary operations of agriculture. It was judged better that it should be done piecemeal, and therefore God was asked to say which of the tribes ought to begin it. Judah was named, and Judah aided by Simeon did his work well, and set a good example to the rest. But the other tribes did not act with Judah's spirit, and therefore they did not enjoy his reward. The testimony of the historian is, that nothing failed of any good thing which *the Lord had spoken* unto the house of Israel. The Lord faithfully performed every part of His obligation. He did not add Israel's obligations to His own, and discharge them too, when they were remiss concerning them. The ultimate result of the whole business was, that trouble befell Israel, inasmuch as he neglected his obligations, while the Lord faithfully performed every one of His. Time therefore did not run back and fetch the age of gold. Israel did not enjoy all the possessions that had been allotted to him. Canaanites remained in the country to torment him like thorns in his sides. But this was Israel's fault, not God's. Though you were to give a lazy farmer the finest farm in the country, you could not make him prosperous if he neglected his fields and idled away the time that should be spent in continuous labour. You cannot keep a man in health if he breathes unwholesome air or drinks water poisoned with putrid matter. No more could Israel be wholly prosperous if he allowed Canaanites to settle quietly at his side. If he had roused himself, and attacked them with courage and in faith, God would have made him to prevail. But, since he preferred ease and quiet to the painfulness of duty, God left him to reap as he had sowed, and suffer the consequences of his neglect. He had seldom long periods of prosperity, and often he had very bitter experiences of calamity and distress.

Certainly God had furnished His people with the materials for a happy and prosperous life, if only they had used them aright. There was first the element of possessions. They had comfortable homes and all the requisites of a comfortable life. It is most true that "a man's life consisteth not in the abundance of the things which he possesseth." But moderate possessions are one element, though not the chief or most essential of human prosperity. Possessions, however rich or manifold, in connection with a discontented temper, an ungodly spirit, or a selfish nature, can bring no genuine pleasure. In addition to possessions, the Lord had given Israel rest. Their enemies were not disposed to attack them even when dwelling by their side. True it is that the rest into which Joshua brought them was not the true, the ultimate rest. If Joshua had given them that rest, the Holy Spirit would not have spoken of a rest that was still to come (Heb. iv. 8). But external rest, like external possessions though not all, was one contribution towards prosperity. Moreover, none of their enemies had been able to stand before them; in every encounter that had yet taken place the Lord had delivered them into their hand.

This was a blessed presage for the future. Whatever encounters might yet remain, they might count on the same result, if they lifted up their eyes to God. Their life in the future would not be without toil, without anxiety, without danger. But if they looked to Him and made the requisite efforts, God was ready to bless their toil, He was able to overcome their anxieties, He was sure as in the past to subdue their enemies. The gifts that God had conferred on them, and the materials of enjoyment with which He had surrounded them, were not designed to make them independent, as if they could now do everything for themselves. God's purpose was the very reverse. He wished to keep up the sense of dependence on Him, and to encourage at every turn the habit that seeks unto God, and goes to Him for help.

For this, after all, is the great lesson for all human beings. The great thing for us all is to keep up a living connection with God, so that our whole nature shall be replenished out of His fulness, and purified and elevated by His Divine influence. Whatever draws us to God draws us to the fountain of all that is best and purest and noblest. God would have conferred but a poor blessing on Israel if He had just settled them in the land, and then left them to themselves, without any occasion or inducement to fellowship with Him. The inducements to resort to Him which they were to be continually under were by far the most valuable part of what God now conferred upon them. The certainty that all would go wrong, that their possessions would be invaded and their rest disturbed, and that their enemies would prove victorious unless they sought continually to their God, fostered the most precious of all habits—that drawing near to God which brings with it all spiritual blessing.

> "Nearer, my God, to Thee,
> Nearer to Thee!
> E'en though it be a cross
> That raiseth me,
> Still all my song would be
> Nearer, my God, to Thee,
> Nearer to Thee!"

There is no small amount of instruction to be drawn by all of us from this record of Israel's experience.

First, it is of supreme importance for us all to have our hearts firmly established in the conviction of the faithfulness of God. It should be our habit to regard this as an attribute on which we not only may, but must rely. To ascribe to God any laxity as to His word or promises were to cast a fearful imputation on His holy nature. "Heaven and earth shall pass away, but My word shall not pass away." "He is not a man that he should lie, or the son of man that he should repent." Nothing can be conceived that could make it better to God to break His word than to keep it. This is the root of all religion; it is the basis of faith, the true ground of trust. To train our minds to habitual reliance on all that God has said, is one of the most vital and blessed exercises of spiritual religion. It is alike honouring to God and beneficial to ourselves. To search out from the body of Scripture the promises of God; to fasten our attention on them one by one; and to exercise our minds on the thought that in Christ Jesus they are yea, and in Him Amen, is a most blessed help to spiritual stability and spiritual growth. And in our prayers there is nothing more fitted to give us confidence than to plead in this spirit the promises that God has made. No plea is more powerful than the Psalmist's—" Remember Thy word unto Thy servant, upon which Thou hast caused me to hope." How many sadly perplexed men have found rest from the words: " Commit thy way unto the Lord; trust also in Him, and He shall bring it to pass." " Faithful is He that calleth you, who also will do it."

But secondly, we may learn from this passage that, wherever the promises of God *seem* to fail, the fault is not His, but ours. On the one hand, we are taught clearly that delay is not failure, and on the other that where there does seem to be failure there is none really on the part of God. At least five-and-twenty long years elapsed between God's first promise to Abraham and the birth of Isaac. Four hundred years were to be spent by the chosen seed in bondage in Egypt. And even after the deliverance from Egypt there came the sojourn in the wilderness of other forty years. Yet God was faithful all the time. How often we need to recall the text, that one day is with the Lord as a thousand years, and a thousand years as one day! " Though the vision tarry," do not give it up in despair, but " wait for it " (Hab. ii. 3).

Perhaps it is in the matter of answers to prayer that we are most liable to the temptation that God forgets His promises. Have we not the most explicit and abundant promises that prayer will be answered ? Yet how many have prayed, and seemingly prayed in vain ! Nay, does not the very opposite of what we pray for often come ? We entreat God to spare a beloved life ; that life is taken away. We pray for victory over temptation ; the temptation seems to acquire a redoubled force. We pray for success in business ; the clouds seem to thicken the more. We ask, " Has God forgotten to be gracious ? Is His mercy clean gone for ever ? Does His promise fail for evermore ? " Nay, let us rally our faith. " Then I said, This is my infirmity: but I will remember the years of the right hand of the Most High " (Psalm lxxvii. 10). If my prayer was not answered, it was not God's fault. It may be that, like Israel, I failed in my part. I may have been laying the whole burden on God, and omitting something that it fell to me to do. I may have been asking for something that would not have been for my good or for God's glory. I may have failed in that spirit of affectionate trust which is a requisite of acceptable prayer. Let us remember that God knows what things we have need of before we ask Him. And God is infinitely kind and willing to bless us. What He longs for on our part is the spirit of filial trust. What He values prayer for is that it is the channel of this spirit. We can never say that God disregards prayer unless we can say that we approached Him, and spoke to Him like confiding children dealing with a loving father, and He cast us off. But how often do we go to the footstool half hoping, half doubting, instead of going in the full conviction,—" Our gracious Father is sure to hear us; and if He do not give us the precise thing we ask, He is sure to give us something better." Let prayer ever be the outcome of a profound belief in the infinite love of God, and His constant readiness to bless us in Christ; let it be the communing of a child with his father; and let it never be darkened by a shade of suspicion that the Hearer of prayer will not be faithful to His word.

It is the happy experience both of individuals and the Church to have occasional periods of fulfilment—it may be after long periods of expectation and trial. The patriarch Job had a terrible time of trial, when God seemed so untrue to His promises that he was sometimes on the very edge of blaspheming His name. But a time of fulfilment came at last, and through all the mystery of the past Job at length saw " the end of the Lord, that the Lord is very pitiful and of tender mercy " (James v. 11). The aged Simeon and the aged Anna in the temple had waited long, but the hour came at last when all that they had been looking for was accomplished, and with a feeling of perfect satisfaction they could sing their " Nunc dimittis." The souls under the altar of them that were slain for the word of God and for the testimony which they held, when they groaned out their sad " How long ? " had still to wait a little season; but the time came when, clothed in white robes and with palms in their hands, they attained complete satisfaction, crying with a loud voice, " Salvation to our God that sitteth on the throne, and to the Lamb " (Rev. vi. 10, vii. 10). And in more recent times there have been eras of fulfilment and corresponding rejoicing. When St. Augustine, after year upon year of restless tossing, at length found pardon and peace in Christ; when Columbus, after perils and privations innumerable, at length saw the dim coast which he had often prayed to behold; when Wilberforce heard the slave trade declared an illegal traffic, and Fowell Buxton saw the last fetter struck from the slave in the dominions of Great Britain; when Lord Shaftesbury found the ten hours factory bill turned into law; or when the friends of the slave learned that the President of the United States had signed the proclamation which set four millions at liberty—the old experience of Joshua's days seemed to be repeated, and gratitude to Him who had failed in no good thing was the one feeling that filled the heart. Sometimes the death-bed affords a retrospect that kindles the same emotion. The dying man looks along the way by which he has been led, and, with the walls of the New Jerusalem gleaming before him, he owns that he has been conducted by the right way to the city of habitation. The objects of earth and heaven are seen by him in a truer light. Valuations are made more accurately on the margin of eternity. The things that have been shaken and that have perished—of how little value are they seen to be, compared to the things that cannot be shaken! The loving purpose of Divine providence in shattering so many hopes, in defeating so many projects, in inflicting so much pain, is clearly apprehended. The heart is grieved that it was so near charging God foolishly when His purpose was really so merciful and so kind. The bright era of fulfilment is at hand; and even already, while the day is only dawning, the soul can give forth its testimony that "no good thing has failed of all that the Lord hath spoken."

And then at last will come the end of the mystery. The Lord shall send His angels with a great sound of a trumpet, and they shall gather together His elect from the four winds, from the one end of heaven to the other. On the sea of glass mingled with fire they take their stand, having the harps of God, and sing the song of Moses, the servant of God, and the song of the Lamb: "Great and marvellous are Thy works, Lord God Almighty; just and true are Thy ways, Thou King of saints." What a scene and what a sensation! What joy in entering on possession of the Promised Land, in experiencing the rest of the redeemed, and in the consciousness that not a single enemy survives to annoy! What delight in the harmonious working of the new nature, in the free and happy play of all its faculties and feelings, and in the conscious presence of a God and Saviour to whose image you have been thoroughly conformed! The last shadow that dimmed your vision on earth shall have fled away; the last vestige of complaint of your earthly lot shall have vanished. Whatever you may have thought once, no other feeling will now occupy your heart but gratitude to Him who has not only not failed to fulfil all His promises, but has done in you exceeding abundantly above all that ye could ask or think!

CHAPTER XXX.

THE ALTAR ED.

Joshua xxii.

THE two tribes and a half had behaved well. They had kept their word, remained with their brethren during all Joshua's campaign, and taken their part in all the perils and struggles through which the host had passed. And now they receive the merited reward of honourable conduct. They are complimented by their general; their services are rehearsed with approval; their threefold fidelity, to God, to Moses, and to Joshua, is commended; they are dismissed with honour, and they receive as their reward a substantial share of the spoil which had been taken from the enemy. "Return," said Joshua, "with much riches unto your tents, and with very much cattle, with silver and with gold, and with brass, and with iron, and with very much raiment; divide the spoil of your enemies with your brethren." It thus appeared that honour, like honesty, is the best policy. Had these two tribes and a half chosen the alternative of selfishness, refused to cross the Jordan to help their brethren, and devoted their whole energies at once to their fields and flocks, they would have fared worse in the end. No doubt as they recrossed the Jordan, bearing with them the treasure which had been acquired on the western side, their hearts would be full of that happy feeling which results from duty faithfully performed, and honourable conduct amply rewarded. They brought back "peace with honour," and prosperity to the bargain. After all, it is high principle that pays. It demands a time of patient working and of patient waiting, but its bills are fully implemented in the end.

In sending away the two tribes and a half Joshua pressed two counsels on them. One was that they were to divide the spoil with those of their brethren that had remained at home. Here, again, selfishness might possibly have found a footing. Why should the men that had incurred none of the labour and the peril enjoy any of the spoil? Would it not have been fair that those who had borne the burden and heat of the day should alone enjoy its rewards? But, in point of fact, there had been good reason why a portion should remain at home. To leave the women and children wholly undefended would have been recklessness itself. Some arrangement, too, had to be made for looking after the flocks and herds. And as the supply of manna had ceased, the production of food had to be provided for. The men at home had been doing the duty assigned to them as well as the men abroad. If they could not establish a claim in justice to a share of the spoil, the spirit of brotherhood and generosity pleaded on their behalf. The soldier-section of the two and a half tribes had done their part honourably and generously to the nine and a half; let them act in the same spirit to their own brethren. Let them share in the good things which they had brought home, so that a spirit of joy and satisfaction might be diffused throughout the community, and the welcome given to those who had been absent might be cordial and complete, without one trace of discontent or envy.

Occasions may occur still on which this counsel of Joshua may come in very suitably. It does not always happen that brothers or near relatives who have prospered abroad are very mindful of those whom they have left at home. They like to enjoy their abundance, and if the case of their poor relations comes across their minds, they dismiss it with the thought that men's lots must differ, and that they are not going to lose all the benefit of their success by supporting other families besides their own. Yet, how much good might accrue from a little generosity, though it were but an occasional gift, towards those who are straitened? And how much better it would be to kindle by this means a thankful and kindly feeling, than to have envy and jealousy rankling in their hearts!

The other counsel of Joshua bore upon that which was ever uppermost in his heart—loyalty to God. "Take diligent heed to do the commandment and the law, which Moses the servant of the Lord charged you, to love the Lord your God, and to walk in all His ways, and to keep all His commandments, and to cleave unto Him, and to serve Him with all your heart and with all your soul." It is evident that Joshua poured his whole heart into this counsel. He was evidently anxious as to the effect which their separation from their brethren would have on their religious condition. It was west of the Jordan that the sanctuary had been placed, and that the great central influence in support of the national worship would mainly operate. Would not these eastern tribes be in great danger of drifting away from the recognised worship of God, and becoming idolaters? Joshua knew well that as yet the nation was far from being weaned from idolatry (see xxiv. 14). He knew that among many there were strong propensities towards it. He had something of the feeling that an earnest Christian parent would have in sending off a son, not very decided in religion, to some colony where the public sentiment was loose, and where the temptations to worldliness and religious indifference were strong. He was therefore all the more earnest in his exhortations to them, for he felt that all their prosperity, all their happiness, their very life itself, depended on their being faithful to their God.

We cannot tell how long time had elapsed when word was brought to the western side that the two and a half tribes had built a great altar on the edge of Jordan, apparently as a rival to the ecclesiastical establishment at Shiloh. That this was their intention seems to have been taken for granted, for we find the congregation or general assembly of Israel assembled at Shiloh to prepare for war with the schismatical tribes. War had evidently become a familiar idea with them, and at first no other course suggested itself for arresting the proposal. It was one of the many occasions of unreasoning impetuosity which the history of Israel presents.

No mention is made of Joshua in the narrative of this transaction ; he had retired from active life, and perhaps what is here recorded did not take place for a considerable time after the return of the two and a half tribes. It may be that we have here an instance of the method so often pursued in Hebrew annals, of recording together certain incidents pertaining to the same transaction, or to the same people, though these incidents were separated from each other by a considerable interval of time.

It was well that the congregation assembled at Shiloh. They would be reminded by the very place that great national movements were not to be undertaken rashly, since God was the supreme ruler of the nation. We are not told whether the usual method of asking counsel of God was resorted to, but certainly the course followed was more reasonable than rushing into war. It was resolved to begin by remonstrating with the two and a half tribes. The idea that their proposal was schismatical, nay, even idolatrous, was not given up, but it was thought that if a solemn remonstrance and warning were addressed to them, they might be induced to abandon their project.

A deputation was sent over, consisting of Phinehas, the son of Eleazar the priest, as representing the religious interest, and ten princes, representing the ten tribes, to have an interview with the heads of the two and a half tribes. When they met, the deputation opened very fiercely on their brethren. They charged them with unheard-of wickedness. What they had done was a daring act of rebellion. It was worthy to be classed with the iniquity of Peor—one of the vilest deeds that ever disgraced the nation. It was fitted to bring down God's judgments on the whole nation, and would certainly do so. If the secret act of Achan involved the congregation in wrath, what calamity to the whole people would not result from this daring and open deed of rebellion? They were not safe for a single day. The vials of the Divine wrath could not but be ready, and in twenty-four hours the whole congregation of Israel might be overwhelmed by the tokens of His displeasure.

One should have said that if anything was fitted to have a bad effect on the two and a half tribes, it was this mode of dealing. It is not wise to assume that your brother is a villain. And scolding, as has been well said, does not make men sorry for their sins. But one thing was said by the deputation that was fitted to have a different effect. " Notwithstanding, if the land of your possession be unclean, then pass ye over unto the land of the possession of the Lord, wherein the Lord's tabernacle dwelleth, and take possession among us : but rebel not against the Lord, nor rebel against us, in building you an altar beside the altar of the Lord our God."

Here was a generous, a self-denying proposal ; the ten tribes were some of them in straits themselves, finding the room available for them far too narrow; nevertheless they were prepared to divide what they had with their brethren, if their real feeling was that the east side of the Jordan was outside the hallowed and hallowing influence of the presence of the Lord.

Instead, therefore, of firing up at the fierce reproof of their brethren, the two and a half tribes were softened by this really kind proposal and returned a reassuring answer. They solemnly repudiated all idea of a rival establishment. They knew that there was but one place where the tabernacle and the ark of the covenant could be, and they had not the remotest intention of interfering with the spot that had been chosen for that purpose. They had never entertained the thought of offering burnt offerings, or meat offerings, or peace offerings on their altar. They solemnly abjured all intention to show disrespect to the Lord, or to His law. The altar which they had built had a very different purpose. It was occasioned by the physical structure of the country, and the effect which that might have on their children in years to come. " In time to come your children might speak unto our children, saying, What have ye to do with the Lord

God of Israel? For the Lord hath made Jordan a border between us and you, ye children of Reuben and children of Gad; ye have no part in the Lord: so shall your children make our children cease from fearing the Lord. Therefore we said, Let us now prepare to build us an altar, not for burnt offering, nor for sacrifice; but that it may be a witness between us, and you, and our generations after us." It was not a rival, but a witness, a pattern; a reminder to the two and a half tribes that the true altar, the Divine sanctuary, hallowed by the token of God's presence was elsewhere, and that there, and only there, were the public sacrifices to be offered.

The acquaintance with the physical structure of Palestine which we have obtained in recent years enables us to appreciate the feeling of the two and a half tribes better than could have been done before. The mere fact that a river separated the east from the west of Palestine would not have been enough to account for the sense of isolation and the fear thence arising which had taken hold of the heads of the two and a half tribes. It is the peculiar structure of the valley in which the river runs that explains the story. The Jordan valley, as has already been mentioned, is depressed below the level of the Mediterranean Sea, the depression increasing gradually as the river flows towards the Dead Sea, where it amounts to 1300 feet. In addition to this, the mountainous plateau on each side of the Jordan valley rises to the height of 2000 or 2500 feet above the sea, so that the entire depression, counting from the top of the plateau to the edge of the river, is between three and four thousand feet. On each side the approach to the Jordan is difficult, while, during the warm season, the great heat increases the fatigue of travelling and discourages the attempt. All these things make the separation between the two parts of the country caused by the river and its valley much more complete than in ordinary cases of river boundaries. There can be no doubt now that the heads of the two and a half tribes had considerable ground for their apprehensions. There was some risk that they should cease to be regarded as part of the nation; and their explanation of the altar seems to have been an honest one. It was designed simply as a memorial, not for sacrifices. We see what a happy thing it was for the whole nation that the deputation was sent across before resorting to arms. A new light was thrown on what had seemed a daring sin; it was but an innocent arrangement; and the terrible forebodings which it awakened are at once scattered to the winds.

But who can estimate all the misery that has come in almost every age, in circles both public and private, from hasty suspicions of evil, which a little patience, a little inquiry, a little opportunity of explanation, might have at once averted? History, tradition, fiction, alike furnish us with instances. We recall the story of Llewellyn and his dog Gelert, stabbed by his master, who thought the stains upon his mouth were the blood of his beloved child; while, on raising the cradle which had been turned over, he found his child asleep and well, and a huge wolf dead, from whose fangs the dog had delivered him. We remember the tragedy of Othello and Desdemona; we see how the fondest love may be poisoned by hasty suspicion, and the dearest of wives murdered, when a little patience would have shown her innocent—shown her all too pure to come in contact with even a vestige of the evil thing. We think of the many stories of crusaders and others leaving their homes with their love pledged to another, detained in distant lands without means of communication, hearing a rumour that their beloved one had turned false, and doing some rash and irrevocable deed, while a little further waiting would have realized all their hopes. But perhaps it is in less tragic circumstances that the spirit of suspicion and unjust accusation is most commonly manifested. A rumour unfavourable to your character gets into circulation; you suspect some one of being the author, and deal fiercely with him accordingly; it turns out that he is wholly innocent. A friend has apparently written a letter against you which has made you furious; you pour a torrent of reproaches upon him; it turns out that the letter was written by some one else with a similar name. But indeed there is no end to the mischief that is bred by impatience, and by want of inquiry, or of waiting for explanations that would put a quite different complexion on our matters of complaint. True charity "thinketh no evil," for it "rejoiceth not in iniquity, but rejoiceth in truth. It beareth all things, believeth all things, hopeth all things, endureth all things." If its gentle voice were more regarded, what a multitude of offences would vanish, and how much wider would be the reign of peace!

The explanation that had been offered by Reuben, Gad, and Manasseh proved satisfactory to Phinehas and the princes of the congregation, and likewise to the people of the west generally, when the deputation reported their proceedings. The remark of Phinehas before he left his eastern brethren was a striking one: "This day do we perceive that the Lord is among us, because ye have not committed this trespass against the Lord; now ye have delivered the children of Israel out of the hand of the Lord." There was a great difference between the Lord being among them, and their being in the hand of the Lord. If the Lord were among them they were under all manner of gracious influence; if they were in the hand of the Lord they were exposed to the utmost visitations of His wrath. It was the joy of Phinehas to find not only that no provocation had been given to God's righteous jealousy, but that proof had been afforded that He was graciously blessing them. If God often departs from us without our suspecting it, He is sometimes graciously present with us when we have been fearing that He was gone. So it was now. Phinehas in imagination had seen the gathering of a terrible storm, as if the very enemy of man had been stirring up his countrymen to rebellion and contempt of God; but in place of that, he sees that they have been consulting for God's honour, for the permanence of His institutions, and for the preservation of unity between the two sections of the nation; and in this he finds a proof that God has been graciously working among them. For God is the God of peace, not of strife, and the Spirit is the Spirit of order, and not of confusion. And when two sections of a community are led to desire the advancement of His service and the honour of His name, even by methods which are not in all respects alike, it is a proof that He is among them, drawing their hearts to Himself and to one another.

Perhaps the common adage might have been applied to the case—that there were faults on both sides. If the ten tribes were too hasty in preparing for war, the two and a half tribes had been too hasty in deciding on the erection of their altar, without communication with the priests and the civil heads of the nation. In a matter so sacred, no such step should have been taken without full consultation and a clear view of duty. The goodness of their motive did not excuse them for not taking all available methods to carry out their plan in a way wholly unexceptional. As it was, they ran a great risk of kindling a fire which might have at once destroyed themselves and weakened the rest of the nation through all time. In their effort to promote unity, they had almost occasioned a fatal schism. Thus both sections of the nation had been on the edge of a fearful catastrophe.

But now it appeared that the section that had seemed to be so highly offending were animated by a quite loyal sentiment. Phinehas gladly seized on the fact as a proof that God was among them. A less godly man would not have thought of this as of much importance. He would hardly have believed in it as anything that could exist except in a fanatical imagination. But the more one knows of God the more real does the privilege seem, and the more blessed. Nay, it comes to be felt as that which makes the greatest conceivable difference between one individual or one community and another. The great curse of sin is that it has severed us from God. The glory of the grace of God in Christ is that we are brought together. Man without God is like the earth without the sun, or the body without the soul. Man in fellowship with God is man replenished with all Divine blessings and holy influences. A church in which God does not dwell is a hold of unclean spirits and a cage of every unclean and hateful bird. A church inhabited by God, like the bride in the Song of Solomon, "looketh forth as the morning, fair as the moon, clear as the sun, and terrible as an army with banners."

CHAPTER XXXI.

JEHOVAH THE CHAMPION OF ISRAEL.

JOSHUA xxiii.

THE last two chapters of Joshua are very like each other. Each professes to be a report of the aged leader's farewell meeting with the heads of the people. No place of meeting is specified in the one; Shechem is the place named in the other. The address reported in the twenty-third chapter is in somewhat general terms; in the twenty-fourth, we have more of detail. The question arises, Were there two meetings, or have we in these chapters different reports of the same? The question is of no great importance in itself; but it bears on the structure of the book. In our judgment, both reports bear on the same occasion; and if so, all that needs to be said as to their origin is, that the author of the book, having obtained two reports from trustworthy sources, did not adopt the plan of weaving them into one, but gave them separately, just as he had received them. The circumstance is a proof of the trustworthiness of the narrative; had the writer put on record merely what Joshua might be *supposed* to have said, he would not have adopted this twofold form of narrative.

Joshua had been a close follower of Moses in many things, and now he follows him by calling the people together to hear his closing words. On the edge of the future life, on the eve of giving in his own account, in the crisis when men are most disposed to utter the truth, the whole truth, and nothing but the truth, he calls his children around him to hear his parting words. He knows, as Moses also knew, the impulsive, fitful temper of the people. All the more did he regard it as desirable not to omit such an opportunity of impression. "All pathetic occasions," it has been well said, "should be treasured in the memory; the last interview, the last sermon, the last prayer, the last fond, lingering look; all these things may be frivolously treated as sentimental; but he who treats them so is a fool in his heart. Whatever can subdue the spirit, chasten the character, and enlarge the charity of the soul, should be encouraged as a ministry from God."[1]

What was the burden of Joshua's address? What was alike the keynote, and the central note, and the closing note—the beginning, and the middle, and the end? You have it in the words—"The Lord your God is He that fighteth for you"; therefore "cleave unto the Lord your God." You owe everything to the Lord; therefore render to Him all His due. Let Him receive from you in the proportion in which He has given to you; let Him be honoured by you in the ratio in which you have been blessed by Him; and see that none of you ever, to the last day of your lives, give the faintest countenance to the idolatry of your neighbours, or consent to any entangling connection that would furnish a temptation to join in their wickedness.

This starting-point of Joshua's address—" The Lord

---

[1] "The People's Bible," by Joseph Parker.

your God is He that fighteth for you "—is a serious one, and demands careful investigation. God is expressly set forth as the champion of Israel, fighting for him against the Canaanites, and driving them out. He is here the God of battles; and the terrible desolation that followed the track of Israel is here ascribed to the championship of the Most High.

There are some expositors who explain these sayings in a general sense. There are great laws of conquest, they say, roughly sanctioned by Providence, whereby one race advances upon another. Nations enervated through luxury and idleness are usually supplanted by more vigorous races. The Goths and Vandals overcame the Romans; the Anglo-Saxons subdued the Britons, to be in time conquered by the Normans; Dutch rule has prevailed over the negro, English over the Hindu, American over the native Indian. In the treatment of the conquered races by the conquerors, there has often been much that is gross and objectionable. Even when a civilized and cultured race has had to deal with a barbarous one, instead of the sweetness and light of culture you have often had the devices of injustice and oppression. We cannot vindicate all the rule of the British in India; greed, insolence, and lust have left behind them many a stain. Still, the result on the whole has been for good. The English have a higher conception of human life than the Hindus. They have a higher sense of order, of justice, of family life, of national well-being. There is a vigour about them that will not tolerate the policy of drifting; that cannot stand still or lie still and see everything going wrong; that strives to remedy injustice, to reform abuse, to correct what is vicious and disorderly, and foster organization and progress. In these respects British rule has been a benefit to India. There may have been deeds of oppression and wrong that curdle the blood, or habits of self-indulgence may have been practised at the expense of the natives that shock our sense of humanity, as if the inferior race could have no rights against the superior; but these are but the eddies or by-play of a great beneficent current, and in the summing up of the long account they hold but an insignificant place. In themselves, they are to be detested and denounced; but when you are estimating great national forces, when you are trying the question whether on the whole these forces have been beneficent or evil, whether they have been of heaven or of the devil, these episodes of wrong are not to be allowed to determine the whole question. You are constrained to take a wider view. And when you survey the grand result; when you see a great continent like India peaceable and orderly that used to be distracted on every side by domestic warfare; when you see justice carefully administered, life and property protected, education and civilization advanced, to say nothing of the spirit of Christianity introduced, you are unable to resist the conclusion that the influence of its new masters has been a gain to India, and therefore that the British rule has had the sanction of heaven.

We say there are some expositors who hold that it is only in a way parallel to this that the conquest of Canaan by the Israelites enjoyed the sanction of God. Without making a great deal of the wickedness of the Canaanite tribes, they dwell on their weakness, their poor ideas of life, their feeble aims, their want of developing power, their inability to rise. Into the heart of these tribes there comes a race that somehow possesses extraordinary capabilities and force. History has shown it to be one of the great dominant races of the world. The new people apply themselves with extraordinary energy to acquire the country of the other. Dispossession of one race by another was the common practice of the times, and in a moral point of view was little thought of. The times were rude and wild, property had not become sacred, human life was cheap, pain and suffering got small consideration. Having spent some centuries in Egypt, the new race brought with it a share of Egyptian culture and accomplishment; but its great strength lay in its religious ardour, and in the habits of order and self-control which its religion fostered. The memory of their ancestors, who had dwelt as pilgrims in that country, but under the strongest promises on the part of God that He would give it as an inheritance to their descendants, increased the ardour of the invasion and the confidence of the invaders. With all the enthusiasm of a heaven-guided race, they dashed against the old inhabitants, who staggered under the blow. To a large extent the former occupants fell under the usual violence of invaders—the sword of battle and the massacre after victory. The process was accompanied by many wild deeds, which in these days of ours would excite horror. Had it been completely successful it would have utterly annihilated the native races; but the courage and perseverance of the invaders were not equal to this result; many of the original inhabitants remained, and were finally amalgamated with their conquerors.

Now, in this case, as in the conquest of India by Britain, a process went on which was a great benefit on a large scale. It was not designed to be of benefit to the original inhabitants, as was the British occupation of India, for they were a doomed race, as we shall immediately see. But the settlement of the people of Israel in Canaan was designed and was fitted to be a great benefit to the world. Explain it as we may, Israel had higher ideas of life than the other nations, richer gifts of head and heart, more capacity of governing, and a far purer religious sentiment. Wherever Israel might be planted, if he remained in purity, mankind must be benefited. A people so gifted, with such intellectual capacity, with such moral and spiritual power, with such high ideals, and producing from time to time men of such remarkable character and influence, could not but help to elevate other races. That such a people should prevail over tribes emasculated by vice, degraded by idolatrous superstition, and enfeebled and stunted through mutual strife, was only in accordance with the nature of things. On the principle that a race like this must necessarily prevail over such tribes as had occupied Palestine before, the conquest of Joshua might well be said to have Divine approval. God might truly be said to go forth with the armies of Israel, and to scatter their enemies as smoke is scattered by the wind.

But this was not all. There was already a judicial sentence against the seven nations of which Israel was appointed to be the executioner. Even in Abraham's time we have abundant proof that they were far gone in corruption, and the destruction of Sodom and Gomorrah was but an early stroke of that holy sword which was to come down over a far wider area when the iniquity of the Amorites should become full. We have no elaborate account of the moral and religious condition of the people in Joshua's time, but we have certain glimpses which tell much. In the story of Baal-peor we have an awful picture of the idolatrous debauchery of the Moabites; and the Moabites were not so sunk in vice as the Canaanites. The first Canaanite house that any of the Israelites entered was that of an immoral woman, who, however, was saved by her faith, as any and every Canaanite would have been had he believed. The most revolting picture we have of Canaanite vice is connected with the burning of children alive in sacrifice to the gods. What a hideous practice it was! Who can estimate its effect on the blithe nature of children, or tell how the very thought of it and the possibility of suffering from it must have weighed like a nightmare on many a child, converting the season of merry childhood into a time of dreadful foreboding, if not for themselves, at least for some of their companions. Loathsome vice consecrated by the seal of religion; unnatural lust, turning human beings into worse than beasts; natural affection converted into an instrument of the most horrid cruelty—could any practices show more powerfully the hopeless degradation of these nations in a moral and religious sense, or their ripeness for judgment? Israel was the appointed executioner of God's justice against them, and in order that Israel might fulfil that function, God went before him in his battles and delivered his enemies into his hands. And what Israel did in this way was done under a solemn sense that he was inflicting Divine retribution. That the process was carried out with something of the solemnity of an execution appears, as we have already seen, from the injunction at Jericho, which forbade all on pain of death to touch an atom of the spoil. And this lesson was burnt into their inmost souls by the terrible fate of Achan. Afterwards, it is true, they were allowed to appropriate the spoil, but not till after they had been taught most impressively at Jericho that the spoil was God's, so that, even when it became theirs, it was as if they had received it from His hand.

We cannot suppose that the people uniformly acted with the moderation and self-restraint becoming God's executioners. No doubt there were many instances of unwarrantable and inhuman violence. Such excesses are unavoidable when human beings are employed as the executioners of God. To charge these on God is not fair. They were the spots and stains that ever indicate the hand of man, even when doing the work of God. It is not necessary to approve of these while we vindicate the law which doomed the Canaanites to extermination, and made the Israelites their executioners. It is not necessary to vindicate all that the English have done in India, while we hold that their presence and influence there have been in accordance with a Divine and beneficent purpose. Where God and man are in partnership, we may expect a chequered product, but never let us ascribe the flaws of one to the influence of the other.

If it be said that the language of the historian seems sometime to ascribe to God what really arose from the passions of the people, it is to be observed that we are not told in what form the Lord communicated His commands. No doubt the Hebrews were disposed to claim Divine authority for what they did to the very fullest extent. There may have been times when they imagined that they were fulfilling the requirements of God, when they were only giving effect to feelings of their own. And generally they may have been prone to suppose that modes of slaughter that seemed to them quite proper were well pleasing in the sight of God. They may have believed that God participated in what was in reality but the spirit of the age. Thus they may have been led to think, and through them the impression may have come to us, that God had a more active hand, so to speak, in many of the details of warfare than we ought to ascribe to Him. For God often accomplishes His holy purposes by leaving His instruments to act in their own way.

But we have wandered from Joshua, and the assembly of Israel. What we have been trying is to show the soundness of Joshua's fundamental position—that God fought for Israel. The same thing might be shown by a negative process. If God had not been actively and supernaturally with Israel, Israel could never have become what he was. What made Israel so remarkable and powerful a nation? If you appeal to heredity and go back to his forefather, you find the whole career of Abraham determined by what he undoubtedly regarded as a supernatural promise, that in him and his seed all the families of the earth should be blessed. If you speak of Moses as the founder of the nation, you find a man who was utterly defeated and humiliated when he acted on his own resources, and successful only when he came in contact with supernatural might. If you inquire into the cause of the military superiority of Israel, you cannot find it in their slave condition in Egypt, nor in their wandering, pastoral life in the desert. You are baffled in trying to account for the warlike energy and skill that swept the Canaanites with all their resources before their invincible might. That an Alexander the Great, or a Cæsar, or a Napoleon, with their long experience, their trained legions, their splendid prestige and unrivalled resources, should have swept the board of their enemies we do not wonder. But Moses and his bevy of slaves, Joshua and his army of shepherds—what could have made such soldiers of these men if the Lord had not fought on their side?

The getting possession of Canaan, as Joshua reminded the people, was a threefold process: God fighting for them had subdued their enemies; Joshua had divided the land; and now God was prepared to expel the remaining people, but only through their instrumentality. Emphasis is laid on "expelling" and "driving out" (ver. 5), from which we gather that further massacre was not to take place, but that the remainder of the Canaanites must seek settlements elsewhere. A sufficient retribution had fallen on them for their sins, in the virtual destruction of their people and the loss of their country; the miserable remnant might have a chance of escape, in some ill-filled country where they would never rise to influence and where terror would restrain them from their former wickedness.

Joshua was very emphatic in forbidding intermarriage and friendly social intercourse with Canaanites. He saw much need for the prayer, "Lead us not into temptation." He understood the meaning of enchanted ground. He knew that between the realm of holiness and the realm of sin there is a kind of neutral territory, which belongs strictly to neither, but which slopes towards the realm of sin, and in point of fact most commonly furnishes recruits not a few to the army of evil. Alas, how true is this still! Marriages between believers and unbelievers; friendly social fellowship, on equal terms, between the Church and the world; partnership in business between the godly and the ungodly—who does not know the usual result? In a few solitary cases, it may be, the child of the world is brought into the kingdom; but in how many instances do we find the buds of Christian promise nipped, and lukewarmness and backsliding, if not apostasy, coming in their room! There is no better help for the Christian life, no greater encouragement to fellowship with God, than congenial fellowship with other Christians, especially in the home, as there is no greater hindrance to these things than an alien spirit there. And if men and women would remember that of all that concerns them in this life their relation to God is infinitely the most momentous, and that whatever brings that relation into peril is the evil of all others most to be dreaded, we should not find them so ready for entangling connections which may be a gain for the things of this world, but for the things of eternity are commonly a grievous loss.

It is a very vivid picture that Joshua draws of the effects of that sinful compromise with their Canaanite neighbours against which he had warned them. "If ye do in any wise go back, and cleave unto the remnant of these nations, even these that remain among you, and shall make marriages with them, and go in unto them, and they to you: know for a certainty that the Lord your God will no more drive out any of these nations from before you; but they shall be snares and traps unto you, and scourges in your sides, and thorns in your eyes, until ye perish from off this good land which the Lord your God hath given you."

The Garden of Eden was not the only paradise that sin ruined. Here was something like a new paradise for the children of Israel; and yet there was a possibility—more than a possibility—of its being ruined by sin. The history of the future showed that Joshua was right. The Canaanites remaining in the land were scourges and thorns to the people of Israel, and the compliance of Israel with their idolatrous ways led first to invasion and oppression, then to captivity and exile, and finally to dispersion over the face of the earth. However sin may deceive at the beginning, in the end it always proves true to its real character—"the wages of sin is death." The trouble is that men will not believe what they do not like to believe. Sin has many a pleasure; and as long as the pleasure is not gross, but wears an air of refinement, there seems no harm in it, and it is freely enjoyed. But, unseen, it works like dry-rot, pulverising the soul, destroying all traces of spiritual relish or enjoyment of Divine things, and attaching the heart more strongly to mere material good. And sometimes when death comes in sight and it is felt that God has to be reckoned with, and the effort is honestly made to prepare for that solemn meeting by looking to the Divine Redeemer, the bent of the heart is found to be entirely the other way. Faith and repentance will not come; turning Godwards is an uncongenial, an impossible attitude; the heart has its roots too much in the world to be thus withdrawn from it. They allowed themselves to be drawn away from their early hope by the influence of worldly fellowship, to find that it profits a man nothing to gain the whole world if he lose his own soul.

How awful are the words of St. James: "Ye adulterers and adulteresses, know ye not that the friendship of the world is enmity with God? Whosoever, therefore, will be a friend of the world is the enemy of God."

CHAPTER XXXII.

JOSHUA'S LAST APPEAL.

JOSHUA xxiv.

IT was at Shechem that Joshua's last meeting with the people took place. The Septuagint makes it Shiloh in one verse (ver. 1), but Shechem in another (ver. 25); but there is no sufficient reason for rejecting the common reading. Joshua might feel that a meeting which was not connected with the ordinary business of the sanctuary, but which was more for a personal purpose, a solemn leave-taking on his part from the people, might be held better at Shechem. There was much to recommend that place. It lay a few miles to the north-west of Shiloh, and was not only distinguished (as we have already said) as Abraham's first resting-place in the country, and the scene of the earliest of the promises given in it to him; but likewise as the place where, between Mounts Ebal and Gerizim, the blessings and curses of the law had been read out soon after Joshua entered the land, and the solemn assent of the people given to them. And whereas it is said (ver. 26) that the great stone set up as a witness was "by the sanctuary of the Lord," this stone may have been placed at Shiloh after the meeting, because there it would be more fully in the observation of the people as they came up to the annual festivals (see 1 Sam. i. 7, 9). Shechem was therefore the scene of Joshua's farewell address. Possibly it was delivered close to the well of Jacob and the tomb of Joseph; at the very place where, many centuries later, the New Testament Joshua sat wearied with His journey, and unfolded the riches of Divine grace to the woman of Samaria.

1. In the record of Joshua's speech contained in the twenty-fourth chapter, he begins by rehearsing the history of the nation. He has an excellent reason for beginning with the revered name of Abraham, because Abraham had been conspicuous for that very grace, loyalty to Jehovah, which he is bent on impressing on them. Abraham had made a solemn choice in religion. He had deliberately broken with one kind of worship, and accepted another. His fathers had been idolaters, and he had been brought up an idolater. But Abraham renounced idolatry for ever. He did this at a great sacrifice, and what Joshua entreated of the people was, that they would be as thorough and as firm as he was in their repudiation of idolatry. The rehearsal of the history is given in the words of God to remind them that the whole history of Israel had been planned and ordered by Him. He had been among them from first to last; He had been with them through all the lives of the patriarchs; it was He that had delivered them from Egypt by Moses and Aaron, that had buried the Egyptians under the waters of the sea, that had driven the Amorites out of the eastern provinces, had turned the curse of Balaam into a blessing, had dispossessed the seven nations, and had settled the Israelites in their pleasant and peaceful abodes.

We mark in this rehearsal the well-known features of the national history, as they were always represented; the frank recognition of the supernatural, with no indication of myth or legend, with nothing of the mist or glamour in which the legend is commonly enveloped. And, seeing that God had done all this for them, the inference was that He was entitled to their heartiest loyalty and obedience. "Now therefore fear the Lord, and serve Him in sincerity and in truth : and put away the gods which your fathers served on the other side of the flood, and in Egypt; and serve ye the Lord." It seems strange that at that very time the people needed to be called to put away other gods. But this only shows how destitute of foundation the common impression is, that from and after the departure from Egypt the whole host of Israel were inclined to the law as it had been given by Moses. There was still a great amount of idolatry among them, and a strong tendency towards it. They were not a wholly reformed or converted people. This Joshua knew right well; he knew that there was a suppressed fire among them liable to burst into a conflagration; hence his aggressive attitude, and his effort to foster an aggressive spirit in them; he must bind them over by every consideration to renounce wholly all recognition of other gods, and to make Jehovah the one only object of their worship. Never was a good man more in earnest, or more thoroughly persuaded that all that made for a nation's welfare was involved in the course which he pressed upon them.

2. But Joshua did not urge this merely on the strength of his own conviction. He must enlist their reason on his side; and for this cause he now called on them deliberately to weigh the claims of other gods and the advantages of other modes of worship, and choose that which must be pronounced the best. There were four claimants to be considered: (1) Jehovah; (2) the Chaldæan gods worshipped by their ancestors;

(3) the gods of the Egyptians ; and (4) the gods of the Amorites among whom they dwelt. Make your choice between these, said Joshua, if you are dissatisfied with Jehovah. But could there be any reasonable choice between these gods and Jehovah ? It is often useful, when we hesitate as to a course, to set down the various reasons for and against,—it may be the reasons of our judgment against the reasons of our feelings; for often this course enables us to see how utterly the one outweighs the other. May it not be useful for us to do as Joshua urged Israel to do ?

If we set down the reasons for making God, God in Christ, the supreme object of our worship, against those in favour of the world, how infinitely will the one scale outweigh the other ! In the choice of a master, it is reasonable for a servant to consider which has the greatest claim upon him ; which is intrinsically the most worthy to be served ; which will bring him the greatest advantages ; which will give him most inward satisfaction and peace ; which will exercise the best influence on his character, and which comes recommended most by old servants whose testimony ought to weigh with him. If these are the grounds of a reasonable choice in the case of a servant engaging with a master, how much more in reference to the Master of our spirits ! Nothing can be plainer than that the Israelites in Joshua's time had every conceivable reason for choosing their fathers' God as the supreme object of their worship, and that any other course would have been alike the guiltiest and the silliest that could have been taken. Are the reasons a whit less powerful why every one of us should devote heart and life and mind and soul to the service of Him who gave Himself for us, and has loved us with an everlasting love ?

3. But Joshua is fully prepared to add example to precept. Whatever you do in this matter, my mind is made up, my course is clear—"as for me and my house, we will serve Jehovah." He reminds us of a general exhorting his troops to mount the deadly breach and dash into the enemy's citadel. Strong and urgent are his appeals; but stronger and more telling is his act when, facing the danger right in front, he rushes on, determined that, whatever others may do, he will not flinch from his duty. It is the old Joshua back again, the Joshua that alone with Caleb stood faithful amid the treachery of the spies, that has been loyal to God all his life, and now in the decrepitude of old age is still prepared to stand alone rather than dishonour the living God. "As for me and my house, we will serve the Lord." He was happy in being able to associate his house with himself as sharing his convictions and his purpose. He owed this, in all likelihood, to his own firm and intrepid attitude throughout his life. His house saw how consistently and constantly he recognised the supreme claims of Jehovah. Not less clearly did they see how constantly he experienced the blessedness of his choice.

4. Convinced by his arguments, moved by his eloquence, and carried along by the magnetism of his example, the people respond with enthusiasm, deprecate the very thought of forsaking Jehovah to serve other gods, and recognise most cordially the claims he has placed them under, by delivering them from Egypt, preserving them in the wilderness, and driving out the Amorites from their land. After this an ordinary leader would have felt quite at ease, and would have thanked God that his appeal had met with such a response, and that such demonstration had been given

of the loyalty of the people. But Joshua knew something of their fickle temper. He may have called to mind the extraordinary enthusiasm of their fathers when the tabernacle was in preparation; the singular readiness with which they had contributed their most valued treasures, and the grievous change they underwent after the return of the spies. Even an enthusiastic burst like this is not to be trusted. He must go deeper; he must try to induce them to think more earnestly of the matter, and not trust to the feeling of the moment.

5. Hence he draws a somewhat dark picture of Jehovah's character. He dwells on those attributes which are least agreeable to the natural man, His holiness, His jealousy, and His inexorable opposition to sin. When he says, "He will not forgive your transgressions nor your sins," he cannot mean that God is not a God of forgiveness. He cannot wish to contradict the first part of that gracious memorial which God gave to Moses: "The Lord, the Lord God merciful and gracious, longsuffering and abundant in goodness and truth, forgiving iniquity and transgression and sin." His object is to emphasize the clause, "and that will by no means clear the guilty." Evidently he means that the sin of idolatry is one that God cannot pass over, cannot fail to punish, until, probably through terrible judgments, the authors of it are brought to contrition, and humble themselves in the dust before him. "Ye cannot serve the Lord," said Joshua; "take care how you undertake what is beyond your strength!" Perhaps he wished to impress on them the need of Divine strength for so difficult a duty. Certainly he did not change their purpose, but only drew from them a more resolute expression. "Nay; but we will serve the Lord.

And Joshua said unto the people, Ye are witnesses against yourselves that ye have chosen the Lord to serve Him. And they said, We are witnesses."

6. And now Joshua comes to a point which had doubtless been in his mind all the time, but which he had been waiting for a favourable opportunity to bring forward. He had pledged the people to an absolute and unreserved service of God, and now he demands a practical proof of their sincerity. He knows quite well that they have "strange gods" among them. Teraphim, images, or ornaments having a reference to the pagan gods, he knows that they possess. And he does not speak as if this were a rare thing, confined to a very few. He speaks as if it were a common practice, generally prevalent. Again we see how far from the mark we are when we think of the whole nation as cordially following the religion of Moses, in the sense of renouncing all other gods. Minor forms of idolatry, minor recognitions of the gods of the Chaldæans and the Egyptians and the Amorites, were prevalent even yet. Probably Joshua called to mind the scene that had occurred at that very place hundreds of years before, when Jacob, rebuked by God, and obliged to remove from Shechem, called on his household : " Put away the strange gods that are among you, and be clean, and change your garments. . . . And they gave unto Jacob all the strange gods which were in the land, and all the ear-rings which were in their ears ; and Jacob hid them under the oak which was by Shechem." Alas ! that, centuries later, it was necessary for Joshua in the same place to issue the same order,—Put away the gods which are among you, and serve ye the Lord. What a weed sin is, and how it is for ever reappearing ! And reappearing among ourselves too, in a different variety, but

essentially the same. For what honest and earnest heart does not feel that there are idols and images among ourselves that interfere with God's claims and God's glory as much as the teraphim and the ear-rings of the Israelites did? The images of the Israelites were little images, and it was probably at by-times and in retirement that they made use of them; and so, it may not be on the leading occasions or in the outstanding work of our lives that we are wont to dishonour God. But who that knows himself but must think with humiliation of the numberless occasions on which he indulges little whims or inclinations without thinking of the will of God; the many little acts of his daily life on which conscience is not brought to bear; the disengaged state of his mind from that supreme controlling influence which would bear on it if God were constantly recognised as his Master? And who does not find that, despite his endeavour from time to time to be more conscientious, the old habit, like a weed whose roots have only been cut over, is ever showing itself alive?

7. And now comes the closing and clinching transaction of this meeting at Shechem. Joshua enters into a formal covenant with the people; he records their words in the book of the law of the Lord; he takes a great stone and sets it up under an oak that was by the sanctuary of the Lord; and he constitutes the stone a witness, as if it had heard all that had been spoken by the Lord to them and by them to the Lord. The covenant was a transaction invested with special solemnity among all Eastern peoples, and especially among the Israelites. Many instances had occurred in their history, of covenants with God, and of other covenants, like that of Abraham with Abimelech, or

that of Jacob with Laban. The wanton violation of a covenant was held an act of gross impiety, deserving the reprobation alike of God and man. When Joshua got the people bound by a transaction of this sort, he seemed to obtain a new guarantee for their fidelity; a new barrier was erected against their lapsing into idolatry. It was natural for him to expect that some good would come of it, and no doubt it contributed to the happy result; "for Israel served the Lord all the days of Joshua, and all the days of the elders which overlived Joshua, and which had known all the works of the Lord that He had done for Israel." And yet it was but a temporary barrier against a flood which seemed ever to be gathering strength unseen, and preparing for another fierce discharge of its disastrous waters.

At the least, this meeting secured for Joshua a peaceful sunset, and enabled him to sing his "Nunc dimittis." The evil which he dreaded most was not at work as the current of life ebbed away from him; it was his great privilege to look round him and see his people faithful to their God. It does not appear that Joshua had any very comprehensive or far-reaching aims with reference to the moral training and development of the people. His idea of religion seems to have been, a very simple loyalty to Jehovah, in opposition to the perversions of idolatry. It is not even very plain whether or not he was much impressed by the capacity of true religion to pervade all the relations and engagements of men, and brighten and purify the whole life. We are too prone to ascribe all the virtues to the good men of the Old Testament, forgetting that of many virtues there was only a progressive development, and that it is not reasonable to look for excellence beyond the measure of the age. Joshua was a soldier, a soldier of the Old Testament, a splendid man for his day, but not beyond his day. As a soldier, his business was to conquer his enemies, and to be loyal to his heavenly Master. It did not lie to him to enforce the number-less bearings which the spirit of trust in God might have on all the interests of life—on the family, on books, on agriculture and commerce, or on the development of the humanities, and the courtesies of society. Other men were raised up from time to time, many other men, with commission from God to devote their energies to such matters.

It is quite possible that, under Joshua, religion did not appear in very close relation to many things that are lovely and of good report. A celebrated English writer (Matthew Arnold) has asked whether, if Virgil or Shakespeare had sailed in the *Mayflower* with the puritan fathers, they would have found themselves in congenial society. The question is not a fair one, for it supposes that men whose destiny was to fight as for very life, and for what was dearer than life, were of the same mould with others who could devote themselves in peaceful leisure to the amenities of literature. Joshua had doubtless much of the ruggedness of the early soldier, and it is not fair to blame him for want of sweetness and light. Very probably it was from him that Deborah drew somewhat of her scorn, and Jael, the wife of Heber, of her rugged courage. The whole Book of Judges is penetrated by his spirit. He was not the apostle of charity or gentleness. He had one virtue, but it was the supreme virtue—he honoured God. Wherever God's claims were involved, he could see nothing, listen to nothing, care for nothing, but that He should obtain His due. Wherever God's claims were acknowledged and fulfilled, things were essentially right, and other interests would come right. For his absolute and supreme loyalty to his Lord he is entitled to our highest reverence. This loyalty is a rare virtue, in the sublime proportions in which it appeared in him. When a man honours God in this way, he has something of the appearance of a supernatural being, rising high above the fears and the feebleness of poor humanity. He fills his fellows with a sort of awe.

Among the reformers, the puritans, and the covenanters such men were often found. The best of them, indeed, were men of this type, and very genuine men they were. They were not men whom the world loved; they were too jealous of God's claims for that, and too severe on those who refused them. And we have still the type of the fighting Christian. But alas! it is a type subject to fearful degeneration. Loyalty to human tradition is often substituted, unconsciously no doubt, for loyalty to God. The sublime purity and nobility of the one passes into the obstinacy, the self-righteousness, the self-assertion of the other. When a man of the genuine type does appear, men are arrested, astonished, as if by a supernatural apparition. The very rareness, the eccentricity of the character, secures a respectful homage. And yet, who can deny that it is the true representation of what every man should be who says, "I believe in God, the Father Almighty, Maker of heaven and earth"?

After a life of a hundred and ten years the hour comes when Joshua must die. We have no record of the inner workings of his spirit, no indication of his feelings in view of his sins, no hint as to the source of his trust for forgiveness and acceptance. But we readily think of him as the heir of the faith of his father Abraham, the heir of the righteousness that is by faith, and as passing calmly into the presence of his Judge, because, like Jacob, he has waited for His salvation. He was well entitled to the highest honours that the nation could bestow on his memory; for all owed to him their homes and their rest. His name must ever be coupled with that of the greatest hero of the nation: Moses led them out of the house of bondage; Joshua led them into the house of rest. Sometimes, as we have already said, it has been attempted to draw a sharp antithesis between Moses and Joshua, the one as representing the law, and the other as representing the gospel. The antithesis is more in word than in deed. Moses represented both gospel and law, for he brought the people out of the bondage of Egypt; he brought them to their marriage altar, and he unfolded to the bride the law of her Divine husband's house. Joshua conducted the bride to her home, and to the rest which she was to enjoy there; but he was not less emphatic than Moses in insisting that she must be an obedient wife, following the law of her husband. It were difficult to say which of them was the more instructive type of Christ, both in feeling and in act. The love of each for his people was most intense, most self-denying; and neither of them, had he been called on, would have hesitated to surrender his life for their sake.

It is probably a mere incidental arrangement that the book concludes with a record of the burial of Joseph, and of the death and burial of Eleazar, the son of Aaron. In point of time, we can hardly suppose that the burial of Joseph in the field of his father Jacob in Shechem was delayed till after the death of Joshua. It would be a most suitable transaction after the division of the country, and especially after the territory that contained the field had been assigned to Ephraim, Joseph's son. It would be like a great doxology—a Te Deum celebration of the fulfilment of the promise in which, so many centuries before, Joseph had so nobly shown his trust.

But why did not Joseph's bones find their resting-place in the time-honoured cave of Macpelah? Why was he not laid side by side with his father, who would doubtless have liked right well that his beloved son should be laid at his side? We can only say in regard to Joseph as in regard to Rachel, that the right of burial in that tomb seems to have been limited to the wife who was recognised by law, and to the son who inherited the Messianic promise. The other members of the family must have their resting-place elsewhere; moreover, there was this benefit in Joseph having his burial-place at Shechem, that it was in the very centre of the country, and near the spot where the tribes were to assemble for the great annual festivals. For many a generation the tomb of Joseph would be a memorable witness to the people; by it the patriarch, though dead, would continue to testify to the faithfulness of God; while he would point the hopes of the godly people still onward to the future, when the last clause of the promise to Abraham would be emphatically fulfilled, and that Seed would come forth among them in whom all the families of the earth would be blessed.

Was there a reason for recording the death of Eleazar? Certainly there was a fitness in placing together the record of the death of Joshua and the death of Eleazar. For Joshua was the successor of

Moses, and Eleazar was the successor of Aaron. The simultaneous mention of the death of both is a significant indication that the generation to which they belonged had now passed away. A second age after the departure from Egypt had now slipped into the silent past. It was a token that the duties and responsibilities of life had now come to a new generation, and a silent warning to them to remember how

> "Time like an ever-rolling stream
> Bears all its sons away;
> They fly forgotten, as a dream
> Dies at the opening day."

How short the life of a generation seems when we look back to these distant days! How short the life of the individual when he realizes that his journey is practically ended! How vain the expectation once cherished of an indefinite future, when there would be ample time to make up for all the neglects of earlier years! God give us all to know the true meaning of that word, "the time is short," and "so teach us to number our days, that we may apply our hearts unto wisdom!"

CHAPTER XXXIII.

JOSHUA'S WORK FOR ISRAEL.

IT now only remains for us to take a retrospective view of the work of Joshua, and indicate what he did for Israel and the mark he left on the national history.

1. Joshua was a soldier—a believing soldier. He was the first of a type that has furnished many remarkable specimens. Abraham had fought, but he had fought as a quaker might be induced to fight, for he was essentially a man of peace. Moses had superintended military campaigns, but Moses was essentially a priest and a prophet. Joshua was neither quaker, nor priest, nor prophet, but simply a soldier. There were fighting men in abundance, no doubt, before the flood, but so far as we know, not believing men. Joshua was the first of an order that seems to many a moral paradox—a devoted servant of God, yet an enthusiastic fighter. His mind ran naturally in the groove of military work. To plan expeditions, to devise methods of attacking, scattering, or annihilating opponents, came naturally to him. A military genius, he entered *con amore* into his work.

Yet along with this the fear of God continually controlled and guided him. He would do nothing deliberately unless he was convinced that it was the will of

God. In all his work of slaughter, he believed himself to be fulfilling the righteous purposes of Jehovah. His life was habitually guided by regard to the unseen. He had no ambition but to serve his God and to serve his country. He would have been content with the plainest conditions of life, for his habits were simple and his tastes natural. He believed that God was behind him, and the belief made him fearless. His career of almost unbroken success justified his faith.

There have been soldiers who were religious in spite of their being soldiers—some of them in their secret hearts regretting the distressing fortune that made the sword their weapon; but there have also been men whose energy in religion and in fighting have supported and strengthened each other. Such men, however, are usually found only in times of great moral and spiritual struggle, when the brute force of the world has been mustered in overwhelming mass to crush some religious movement. They have an intense conviction that the movement is of God, and as to the use of the sword, they cannot help themselves; they have no choice, for the instinct of self-defence compels them to draw it. Such are the warriors of the Apocalypse, the soldiers of Armageddon; for though their battle is essentially spiritual, it is presented to us in that military book under the symbols of material warfare. Such were the Ziskas and Procopses of the Bohemian reformation; the Gustavus Adolphuses of the Thirty Years' War; the Cromwells of the Commonwealth, and the General Leslies of the Covenant. Ruled supremely by the fear of God, and convinced of a Divine call to their work, they have communed about it with Him as closely and as truly as the missionary about his preaching or his translating, or the philanthropist about his homes or his rescue agencies. To God's great goodness it has ever been their habit to ascribe their successes; and when an enterprise has failed, the causes of failure have been sought for in the Divine displeasure. Nor in their intercourse with their families and friends have they been usually wanting in gentler graces, in affection, in generosity, or in pity. All this must be freely admitted, even by those to whom war is most obnoxious. It is quite consistent with the conviction that a large proportion of wars has been utterly unjustifiable, and that in ordinary circumstances the sword is no more to be regarded as the right and proper weapon for settling the quarrels of nations than the duel for settling the quarrels of individuals. And the best of soldiers cannot but feel that fighting is at best a cruel necessity, and that it will be a happy day for the world when men shall beat their swords into ploughshares and their spears into pruning-hooks.

2. Being a soldier, Joshua confined himself in the main to the work of a soldier. That work was to conquer the enemy and to divide the land. To these two departments he limited himself, in subordination, however, to his deep conviction that they were only means to an end, and that that end would be utterly missed unless the people were pervaded by loyalty to God and devotion to the mode of worship which He had prescribed. No opportunity of impressing that consideration on their minds was neglected. It lay at the root of all their prosperity; and if Joshua had not pressed it on them by every available means, all his work would have been like pouring water on sand or sowing seed upon the rocks of the seashore.

Joshua was not called to ecclesiastical work, certainly not in the sense of carrying out ecclesiastical details

That department belonged to the high priest and his brethren. While Moses lived, it had been under him, because Moses was head of all departments. Neither did Joshua take in hand the arrangement in detail of the civil department of the commonwealth. That was mainly work for the elders and officers appointed to regulate it. It is from the circumstance that Joshua personally confined himself to his two great duties, that the book which bears his name travels so little beyond these. Reading Joshua alone, we might have the impression that very little attention was paid to the ritual enacted in the books of Moses. We might suppose that but little was done to carry out the provisions of the Torah, as the law came to be called. But the inference would not be warranted, for the plain reason that such things did not come within the sphere of Joshua or the scope of the book which bears his name. We may make what we can of incidental allusions, but we need not expect elaborate descriptions. There are many things that it would have been highly interesting for us to know regarding this period of the history of Israel; but the book limits itself as Joshua limited himself. It is not a full history of the times. It is not a chapter of universal national annals. It is a history of the settlement, and of Joshua's share in the settlement.

And the fact that it has this character is a testimony to its authenticity. Had it been a work of much later date, it is not likely that it would have been confined within such narrow limits. It would in all likelihood have presented a much larger view of the state and progress of the nation than the existing book does. The fact that it is made to revolve so closely round Joshua seems to indicate that Joshua's personality was still a great power; the remembrance of him was bright and vivid when the book was written. Moreover, the lists of names, many of which seem to have been the old Canaanite names, and to have dropped out of the Hebrew history because the cities were not actually taken from the Canaanites, and did not become Hebrew cities, is another testimony to the contemporary date of the book, or of the documents on which it is founded.

3. If we examine carefully Joshua's character as a soldier, or rather as a strategist, we shall probably find that he had one defect. He does not appear to have succeeded in making his conquests permanent. What he gained one day was often won back by the enemy after a little time. To read the account of what happened after the victory of Gibeon and Bethhoron, one would infer that all the region south of Gibeon fell completely into his hands. Yet by-and-by we find Hebron and Jerusalem in possession of the enemy, while a hitherto unheard-of king has come into view, Adonibezek, of Bezek, of whose people there were slain, after the death of Joshua, ten thousand men (Judg. i. 4). With regard to Hebron we read first that Joshua "fought against it and took it, and smote it with the edge of the sword, and the king thereof, and all the cities thereof, and all the souls that were therein; he left none remaining, but destroyed it utterly, and all the souls that were therein" (Josh. x. 37). Yet not long after, when Caleb requested Hebron for his inheritance, it was (as we have seen) on the very ground that it was strongly held by the enemy: "if so be the Lord will be with me, then I shall be able to drive them out, as the Lord said" (xiv. 12). Again, in the campaign against Jabin, King of Hazor, while it is said that Hazor was utterly destroyed, it is also said that Joshua

did not destroy "the cities that stood on their mounds" (xi. 13, R.V.); accordingly we find that some time after, another Jabin was at the head of a restored Hazor, and it was against him that the expedition to which Barak was stimulated by the prophetess Deborah was undertaken (Judg. iv. 2). Whether Joshua miscalculated the number and resources of the Canaanites in the country; or whether he was unable to divide his own forces so as to prevent the re-occupation and restoration of places that had once been destroyed; or whether he over-estimated the effects of his first victories and did not allow enough for the determination of a conquered people to fight for their homes and their altars to the last, we cannot determine; but certainly the result was, that after being defeated and scattered at the first, they rallied and gathered together, and presented a most formidable problem to the tribes in their various settlements. There is no reason for resorting to the explanation of our modern critics that we have here traces of two writers, of whom the policy of the one was to represent that Joshua was wholly victorious, and of the other that he was very far from successful. The true view is, that his first invasion, or run-over, as it may be called, was a complete success, but that, through the rallying of his opponents, much of the ground which he gained at the beginning was afterwards lost.

4. The great service of Joshua to his people (as we have already remarked) was, that he gave them a settlement. He gave them—Rest. Some, indeed, may be disposed to question whether that which Joshua did give them was worthy of the name of rest. If the Canaanites were still among them, disputing the possession of the country; if savage Adonibezeks were

still at large, whose victims bore in their mutilated bodies the marks of their cruelty and barbarity; if the power of the Philistines in the south, the Sidonians in the north, and the Geshurites in the north-east was still unbroken, how could they be said to have obtained rest?

The objection proceeds from inability to estimate the force of the comparative degree. Joshua gave them rest in the sense that he gave them homes of their own. There was no more need for the wandering life which they had led in the wilderness. They had more compact and comfortable habitations than the tents of the desert with their slim coverings that could effectually shut out neither the cold of winter, nor the heat of summer, nor the drenching rains. They had brighter objects to look out on than the scanty and monotonous vegetation of the wilderness. No doubt they had to defend their new homes, and in order to do so they had to expel the Canaanites who were still hovering about them. But still they were real homes; they were not homes which they merely expected or hoped to get, but homes which they had actually gotten. They were homes with the manifold attractions of country life—the field, the well, the garden, the orchard, stocked with vine, fig, and pomegranate; the olive grove, the rocky crag, and the quiet glen. The sheep and the oxen might be seen browsing in picturesque groups on the pasture grounds, as if they were part of the family. It was an interest to watch the progress of vegetation, to mark how the vine budded, and the lily sprang into beauty, to pluck the first rose, or to divide the first ripe pomegranate. Life had a new interest when on a bright spring morning the young man could thus invite his bride :—

> "Rise up my love, my fair one, and come away.
> For, lo, the winter is past,
> The rain is over and gone;
> The flowers appear on the earth;
> The time of the singing of birds is come,
> And the voice of the turtle is heard in our land;
> The fig tree putteth forth her green figs,
> And the vines with the tender grape give a good smell.'

This, as it were, was Joshua's gift to Israel, or rather God's gift through Joshua. It was well fitted to kindle their gratitude, and though not yet complete or perfectly secure, it was entitled to be called " rest." For if there was still need of fighting to complete the conquest, it was fighting under easy conditions. If they went out under the influence of that faith of which Joshua had set them so memorable an example, they were sure of protection and of victory. Past experience had shown to demonstration that none of their enemies could stand before them, and the future would be as the past had been. God was still among them; if they called on Him, He would arise, their enemies would be scattered, and they that hated Him would flee before Him. Fidelity to Him would secure all the blessings that had been read out at Mount Gerizim, and to which they had enthusiastically shouted, Amen. The picture drawn by Moses before his death would be realized in its brightest colours : " Blessed shalt thou be in the city, and blessed shalt thou be in the field. Blessed shall be the fruit of thy body, and the fruit of thy ground, and the fruit of thy cattle, the increase of thy kine, and the flocks of thy sheep. Blessed shall be thy basket and thy store. Blessed shalt thou be when thou comest in, and blessed when thou goest out."

But here a very serious objection may be interposed. Is it conceivable, it may be asked, that this serene satisfaction was enjoyed by the Israelites when they had got their new homes only by dispossessing the former owners ; when all around them was stained by the blood of the slain, and the shrieks and groans of their predecessors were yet sounding in their ears ? If these homes were not haunted by the ghosts of their former owners, must not the hearts and consciences of the new occupants have been haunted by recollections of the scenes of horror which had been enacted there ? is it possible that they should have been in that tranquil and happy frame in which they would really enjoy the sweetness of their new abodes ?

The question is certainly a disturbing one, and any answer that may be given to it must seem imperfect, just because we are incapable of placing ourselves wholly in the circumstances of the children of Israel.

We are incapable of entering into the callousness of the Oriental heart in reference to the sufferings or the death of enemies. Exceptions there no doubt were ; but, as a rule, indifference to the condition of enemies, whether in life or in death, was the prevalent feeling.

Two parts of their nature were liable to be affected by the change which put the Israelites in possession of the houses and fields of the destroyed Canaanites— their consciences and their hearts.

With regard to their consciences the case was clear : " The earth is the Lord's, and the fulness thereof ; the world, and they that dwell therein." God, as owner of the land of Canaan, had given it, some six hundred years before, to Abraham and his seed. That gift had been ratified by many solemnities, and belief in it had been kept alive in the hearts of Abraham's descendants from generation to generation. There had been no secret about it, and the Canaanites must have been familiar with the tradition. Consequently, during all these centuries, they had been but tenants at will. When, under the guidance of Jehovah, Israel crossed the Red Sea and the army of Pharaoh was drowned, a pang must have shot through the breasts of the Canaanites, and the news must have come to them as a notice to quit. The echoes of the Song of Moses reverberated through the whole region :—

" The peoples have heard, they tremble:
Pangs have taken hold of the inhabitants of Philistia.
Then were the dukes of Edom amazed ;
The mighty men of Moab, trembling taketh hold of them;
All the inhabitants of Canaan are melted away.
Terror and dread falleth upon them ;
By the greatness of Thine arm they are as still as a stone;
Till Thy people pass over, O Lord,
Till the people pass over which Thou hast purchased.
Thou shalt bring them in, and plant them in the mountain of Thine inheritance
The place, O Lord, which Thou hast made for Thee to dwell in,
The sanctuary, O Lord, which Thy hands have established.
The Lord shall reign for ever and ever."

It was well known, therefore, that, so far as Divine right went, the children of Israel were entitled to the land. But even after that, the Canaanites had a respite and enjoyed possession for forty years. Besides, they had been judicially condemned on account of their sins ; and, moreover, when they first came into the country, they had dispossessed the former inhabitants. At last, after long delay, the hour of destiny arrived. When the Israelites took possession they felt that they were only regaining their own. It was not they, but the Canaanites, that were the intruders, and any feeling on the question of right in the minds of the Israelites would rather be that of indignation at having been kept out so long of what had been promised to Abraham, than of squeamishness at dispossessing the Canaanites of property which was not their own.

Still, one might suppose there remained scope for natural pity. But this was not very active. We may gather something of the prevalent feeling from the song of Deborah and the action of Jael. It was not an age of humanity. The whole period of the Judges was indeed an "iron age." Gideon, Jephthah, Samson, were men of the roughest fibre. Even David's treatment of his Ammonite prisoners was revolting. All that can be said for Israel is, that their treatment of enemies did not reach that infamous pre-eminence of cruelty for which the Assyrians and the Babylonians were notorious. But they had enough of the prevailing callousness to enable them to enter without much discomfort on the homes and possessions of their dispossessed foes. They had no such sentimental reserve as to interfere with a lively gratitude to Joshua as the man who had given them rest.

Probably, in looking back on those times, we fail to realize the marvellous influence in the direction of all that is humane and loving that came into our world, and began to operate in full force, with the advent of our Lord and Saviour Jesus Christ. We forget how much darker a world it *must* have been before the true light entered, that lighteth every man coming into the world. We forget what a gift God gave to the world when Jesus entered it, bringing with Him the light and love, the joy and peace, the hope and the holiness of heaven. We forget that the coming of Jesus was the rising of the Sun of Righteousness with healing in His wings. Coming among us as the incarnation of Divine love, it was natural that He should correct the prevailing practice in the treatment of enemies, and infuse a new spirit of humanity. Even the Apostle who afterwards became the Apostle of Love could manifest all the bitterness of the old spirit when he suggested the calling down of fire from heaven to burn up the Samaritan village that would not receive them. "Ye know not what manner of spirit ye are of, for the Son of man came not to destroy men's lives, but to save them." Who does not feel the humane spirit of Christianity to be one of its brightest gems, and one of its chief contrasts with the imperfect economy that preceded it? It is when we mark the inveteracy of the old spirit of hatred that we see how great a change Christ has introduced. If it was the great distinction of Christ's love that "while we were yet enemies, Christ died for us," His precept to us to love our enemies ought to meet with our readiest obedience. Not without profound prophetic insight did the angel who announced the birth of Jesus proclaim, "Glory to God in the highest, on earth peace, good-will to men."

Alas! it is with much humiliation we must own that in practising this humane spirit of her Lord the progress of the Church has been slow and small. It seemed to be implied in the prophecies that Christianity would end war; yet one of the most outstanding phenomena of the world is, the so-called Christian nations of Europe armed to the teeth, expending millions of treasure year by year on destructive armaments, and withdrawing millions of soldiers from those pursuits which increase wealth and comfort, to be supported by taxes wrung from the sinews of the industrious, and to be ready, when called on, to scatter destruction and death among the ranks of their enemies. Surely it is a shame to the diplomacy of Europe that so little is done to arrest this crying evil ; that nation after nation goes on increasing its armaments, and that the only credit a good statesman can gain is that of retarding a collision, which, when it does occur, will be the widest in its dimensions, and the vastest and most hideous in the destruction it deals, that the world has ever seen ! All honour to the few earnest men who have tried to make arbitration a substitute for war.

And surely it is no credit to the Christian Church that, when its members are divided in opinion, there should be so much bitterness in the spirit of its controversies. Grant that what excites men so keenly is the fear that the truth of God being at stake, that which they deem most sacred in itself, and most vital in its influence for good is liable to suffer ; hence they regard it a duty to rebuke sharply all who are apparently prepared to betray it or compromise it. Is it not apparent that if love is not mingled with the controversies of Christians, it is vain to expect violence and war to cease among the nations ? More than this, if love is not more apparent among Christians than has been common, we may well tremble for the cause itself. One of the leaders of German unbelief is said to have remarked that he did not think Christianity could be Divine, because he did not find the people called Christians paying more heed than others to the command of Jesus to love their enemies.

5. One other service of Joshua to the nation of Israel remains to be noticed : he sought with all his heart that they should be a God-governed people, a people that in every department of life should be ruled by the endeavour to do God's will. He pressed this on them with such earnestness, he commended it by his own example with such sincerity, he brought his whole

authority and influence to bear on it with such momentum, that to a large extent he succeeded, though the impression hardly survived himself. " The people served the Lord all the days of Joshua, and all the days of the elders that outlived Joshua, who had seen all the great work of the Lord that He had wrought for Israel." Joshua seemed always to be contending with an idolatrous virus which poisoned the blood of the people, and could not be eradicated. The only thing that seemed capable of crushing it was the outstretched arm of Jehovah, showing itself in some terrible form. While the effect of that display lasted the tendency to idolatry was subdued, but not extirpated ; and as soon as the impression of it was spent, the evil broke out anew. It was hard to instil into them ruling principles of conduct that would guide them in spite of outward influences. As a rule, they were not like Abraham, Isaac, and Jacob, or like Moses who "endured as seeing Him who is invisible." Individuals there were among them, like Caleb and Joshua himself, who walked by faith ; but the great mass of the nation were carnal, and they exemplified the drift or tendency of that spirit—" The carnal mind is enmity against God."

Still Joshua laboured to press the lesson—the great lesson of the theocracy—Let God rule you ; follow invariably His will. It is a rule for nations, for churches, for individuals. The Hebrew theocracy has passed away ; but there is a sense in which every Christian nation should be a modified theocracy. So far as God has given abiding rules for the conduct of nations, every nation ought to regard them. If it be a Divine principle that righteousness exalteth a nation ; if it be a Divine command to remember the Sabbath day to keep it holy ; if it be a Divine instruction to rulers to deliver the needy when he crieth, the poor also and him that hath no helper, in these and in all such matters nations ought to be divinely ruled. It is blasphemous to set up rules of expediency above these eternal emanations of the Divine will.

So, too, churches should be divinely ruled. There is but one Lord in the Christian Church, He that is King of kings, and Lord of lords. There may be many details in Church life which are left to the discretion of its rulers, acting in accordance with the spirit of Scripture; but no church should accept of any ruler whose will may set aside the will of her Lord, nor allow any human authority to supersede what He has ordained.

And for individuals the universal rule is: "Whatsoever ye do in word or deed, do all in the name of the Lord Jesus, giving thanks unto God and the Father by Him." Each true Christian heart is a theocracy—a Christ-governed soul. Not ruled by external appliances nor by mechanical rules, nor by the mere effort to follow a prescribed example; but by the indwelling of Christ's Spirit, by a vital force communicated from Himself. The spring of the Christian life is here—"Not I, but Christ liveth in me." This is the source of all the beautiful and fruitful Christian lives that ever have been, of all that are, and of all that ever shall be.

THE END.

John Eadie Titles

Solid Ground is delighted to announce that we have republished several volumes by John Eadie, gifted Scottish minister. The following are in print:

Commentary on the Greek Text of Paul's Letter to the Galatians
Part of the classic five-volume set that brought world-wide renown to this humble man, Eadie expounds this letter with passion and precision. In the words of Spurgeon, "This is a most careful attempt to ascertain the meaning of the Apostle by painstaking analysis of his words."

Commentary on the Greek Text of Paul's Letter to the Ephesians
Spurgeon said, "This book is one of prodigious learning and research. The author seems to have read all, in every language, that has been written on the Epistle. It is also a work of independent criticism, and casts much new light upon many passages."

Commentary on the Greek Text of Paul's Letter to the Philippians
Robert Paul Martin wrote, "Everything that John Eadie wrote is pure gold. He was simply the best exegete of his generation. His commentaries on Paul's epistles are valued highly by careful expositors. Solid Ground Christian Books has done a great service by bringing Eadie's works back into print."

Commentary on the Greek Text of Paul's Letter to the Colossians
According to the New Schaff-Herzog Encyclopedia of Religious Knowledge, "These commentaries of John Eadie are marked by candor and clearness as well as by an evangelical unction not common in works of the kind." Spurgeon said, "Very full and reliable. A work of utmost value."

Commentary on the Greek Text of Paul's Letters to the Thessalonians
Published posthumously, this volume completes the series that has been highly acclaimed for more than a century. Invaluable.

Paul the Preacher: A Popular and Practical Exposition of His Discourses and Speeches as Recorded in the Acts of the Apostles
Very rare volume intended for a more popular audience, this volume begins with Saul's conversion and ends with Paul preaching the Gospel of the Kingdom in Rome. It perfectly fills in the gaps in the commentaries. Outstanding work!

DIVINE LOVE: A Series of Doctrinal, Practical and Experimental Discourses
Buried over a hundred years, this volume consists of a dozen complete sermons from Eadie's the pastoral ministry. "John Eadie, the respected nineteenth-century Scottish Secession minister-theologian, takes the reader on an edifying journey through this vital biblical theme." - Ligon Duncan

Lectures on the Bible to the Young for Their Instruction and Excitement
"Though written for the rising generation, these plain addresses are not meant for mere children. Simplicity has, indeed, been aimed at in their style and arrangement, in order to adapt them to a class of young readers whose minds have already enjoyed some previous training and discipline." – Author's Preface

Other Solid Ground Titles

THE COMMUNICANT'S COMPANION by *Matthew Henry*
THE SECRET OF COMMUNION WITH GOD by *Matthew Henry*
THE MOTHER AT HOME by *John S.C. Abbott*
LECTURES ON THE ACTS OF THE APOSTLES *by John Dick*
THE FORGOTTEN HEROES OF LIBERTY by *J.T. Headley*
LET THE CANNON BLAZE AWAY by *Joseph P. Thompson*
THE STILL HOUR: *Communion with God in Prayer* by *Austin Phelps*
COLLECTED WORKS of James Henley Thornwell (4 vols.)
CALVINISM IN HISTORY *by Nathaniel S. McFetridge*
OPENING SCRIPTURE: *Hermeneutical Manual by Patrick Fairbairn*
THE ASSURANCE OF FAITH *by Louis Berkhof*
THE PASTOR IN THE SICK ROOM *by John D. Wells*
THE BUNYAN OF BROOKLYN: *Life & Sermons of I.S. Spencer*
THE NATIONAL PREACHER: *Sermons from 2nd Great Awakening*
FIRST THINGS: *First Lessons God Taught Mankind Gardiner Spring*
BIBLICAL & THEOLOGICAL STUDIES *by 1912 Faculty of Princeton*
THE POWER OF GOD UNTO SALVATION *by B.B. Warfield*
THE LORD OF GLORY *by B.B. Warfield*
A GENTLEMAN & A SCHOLAR: *Memoir of J.P. Boyce* by *J. Broadus*
SERMONS TO THE NATURAL MAN *by W.G.T. Shedd*
SERMONS TO THE SPIRITUAL MAN *by W.G.T. Shedd*
HOMILETICS AND PASTORAL THEOLOGY *by W.G.T. Shedd*
A PASTOR'S SKETCHES 1 & 2 *by Ichabod S. Spencer*
THE PREACHER AND HIS MODELS *by James Stalker*
IMAGO CHRISTI: *The Example of Jesus Christ by James Stalker*
LECTURES ON THE HISTORY OF PREACHING *by J. A. Broadus*
THE SHORTER CATECHISM ILLUSTRATED *by John Whitecross*
THE CHURCH MEMBER'S GUIDE *by John Angell James*
THE SUNDAY SCHOOL TEACHER'S GUIDE *by John A. James*
CHRIST IN SONG: *Hymns of Immanuel from All Ages* by *Philip Schaff*
DEVOTIONAL LIFE OF THE S.S. TEACHER *by J.R. Miller*

Call us Toll Free at 1-877-666-9469
Send us an e-mail at sgcb@charter.net
Visit us on line at solid-ground-books.com
Uncovering Buried Treasure to the Glory of God

www.ingramcontent.com/pod-product-compliance
Lightning Source LLC
Chambersburg PA
CBHW021827220426
43663CB00005B/152